Chronic Health Conditions and Work

OCCUPATIONAL HEALTH PSYCHOLOGY: CURRENT DIRECTIONS IN WORKER HEALTH, SAFETY, AND WELL-BEING

Titles in the series

Chronic Health Conditions and Work: Proactive Strategies for Supporting Employees and Doing Well by Doing Good
Alyssa K. McGonagle

Chronic Health Conditions and Work

Proactive Strategies for Supporting Employees and Doing Well by Doing Good

Alyssa K. McGonagle

OXFORD
UNIVERSITY PRESS

Oxford University Press is a department of the University of Oxford.
It furthers the University's objective of excellence in research, scholarship,
and education by publishing worldwide. Oxford is a registered trade mark of
Oxford University Press in the UK and in certain other countries.

Published in the United States of America by Oxford University Press
198 Madison Avenue, New York, NY 10016, United States of America.

© Alyssa K. McGonagle 2025

All rights reserved. No part of this publication may be reproduced, stored in a retrieval system, transmitted, used for text and data mining, or used for training artificial intelligence, in any form or by any means, without the prior permission in writing of Oxford University Press, or as expressly permitted by law, by license or under terms agreed with the appropriate reprographics rights organization. Inquiries concerning reproduction outside the scope of the above should be sent to the Rights Department, Oxford University Press, at the address above.

You must not circulate this work in any other form
and you must impose this same condition on any acquirer.

Library of Congress Cataloging-in-Publication Data
Names: McGonagle, Alyssa K., author.
Title: Chronic health conditions and work / Alyssa K. McGonagle.
Description: New York, NY : Oxford University Press, [2025] | Series: Occupational health psychology:
current directions in worker health, safety, and well-being |
Includes bibliographical references and index.
Identifiers: LCCN 2024060765 (print) | LCCN 2024060766 (ebook) |
ISBN 9780197660638 (hardback) | ISBN 9780197660652 (epub) |
ISBN 9780197660669 (online)
Subjects: LCSH: Chronically ill—Employment. | Occupational health services. |
Employees—Medical care. | Medicine, Industrial.
Classification: LCC RC963 .M3954 2025 (print) | LCC RC963 (ebook) |
DDC 362.16—dc23/eng/20250228
LC record available at https://lccn.loc.gov/2024060765
LC ebook record available at https://lccn.loc.gov/2024060766

DOI: 10.1093/9780197660669.001.0001

Printed by Integrated Books International, United States of America

To Sean, who was there for every step of this journey.

Contents

Preface   xi
Acknowledgments   xiv

Introduction   1

PART I. BACKGROUND

1. Overview, Prevalence, and Burden   7
  1.1 Definition and Overview   7
  1.2 Work–Health Challenges   9
  1.3 Prevalence   11
    1.3.1 Age   11
    1.3.2 Sex and Gender   12
    1.3.3 Race and Ethnicity   13
    1.3.4 Socioeconomic Status   13
    1.3.5 Multiple CHCs   13
    1.3.6 Chronic Pain   14
    1.3.7 Long COVID   15
  1.4 Costs   15
    1.4.1 Direct Financial Costs   16
    1.4.2 Indirect Financial Costs   16
    1.4.3 Financial Burdens to Individuals   17
    1.4.4 Psychosocial Costs   18
  1.5 Takeaways   20

2. Disability and the Legal Landscape   21
  2.1 Understanding Disabilities   21
    2.1.1 Medical Model   22
    2.1.2 Social Model   23
    2.1.3 Defining Disability   24
    2.1.4 Chronic Health Conditions as Disabilities   26
  2.2 US Law   27
    2.2.1 Preventing Disability Discrimination: ADA and ADAAA   28
    2.2.2 Other ADA Provisions   30
    2.2.3 Rehabilitation Act of 1973 and Sections 501, 503, 504, and 508   35
    2.2.4 Family and Medical Leave Act   35
    2.2.5 Health Insurance Portability and Accountability Act   37
  2.3 Takeaways and Recommendations   37

viii Contents

3. Intervention Framework and Typical Approaches 42
   3.1 Primary, Secondary, and Tertiary Intervention Framework 42
      3.1.1 Primary Prevention Strategies 43
         3.1.1.1 Workplace Wellness Programs 45
      3.1.2 Secondary Prevention Strategies 47
      3.1.3 Tertiary Prevention Strategies 49
   3.2 Return-to-Work (RTW) Programs as Tertiary Prevention 50
      3.2.1 Components of RTW Programs 52
      3.2.2 Effectiveness of RTW Programs 53
      3.2.3 Additional Factors That Affect Successful RTW 54
   3.3 A Case for More Proactive Approaches 55
   3.4 Takeaways and Recommendations 56

PART II. CHALLENGES

4. Work–Health Challenges for Workers and Practical Tips for Managers 59
   4.1 Organizing Frameworks 59
      4.1.1 The Job Demands–Resources Model and Work Ability 59
      4.1.2 Spoon Theory 63
   4.2 Work–Health Challenges 64
      4.2.1 Work–Health Management Interference 64
      4.2.2 Maintaining Work Ability Despite Symptoms 66
      4.2.3 Stigma and Discrimination 67
      4.2.4 Disclosure and Identity Management 73
      4.2.5 Career and Work Identity Implications 77
   4.3 Final Points 78
   4.4 Takeaways and Recommendations 79

5. Organizational Challenges and Hindrances to Supporting Workers 81
   5.1 Operational and Other Practical Management-Related Challenges 82
   5.2 Lack of Understanding and Compassion, Stigma, and Discrimination 84
   5.3 Employees Not Disclosing CHCs 86
   5.4 Lack of Knowledge and Skills to Handle CHC-Related Issues 88
   5.5 Unsupportive Organizational Culture 90
   5.6 Lack of Communication and Cooperation between Various Stakeholders 92
   5.7 Takeaways and Recommendations 94

PART III. STRATEGIES

6. Organization-Focused Strategies 99
   6.1 Benefits 100
      6.1.1 Healthcare Coverage 100
      6.1.2 Life Insurance and Long-Term Care Insurance 103

6.1.3 Time Off Benefits and Policies	104
6.1.4 Disability Benefits	105
6.1.5 Employee Assistance Programs	106
6.1.6 Wellness Programs	106
6.2 Universal Design	107
6.3 Organizational Culture	108
6.3.1 Values of Worker Well-Being and DEIA	109
6.3.2 Culture Strategies	110
6.3.3 Examples of Culture-Related Strategies	114
6.3.3.1 Employee Resource Groups	115
6.3.3.2 Trainings	116
6.3.3.3 Summary of Recommendations: Culture	117

7. Work- and Management-Focused Strategies — 119

7.1 Work Design Strategies: Autonomy and Flexibility	119
7.1.1 Job Control	120
7.1.2 Flexible Work Arrangements	122
7.1.2.1 Best Practices for Flexible Work Arrangements	124
7.2 Management Strategies: Supervisor Support	126
7.2.1 Types of Support	127
7.2.2 Support Pitfalls	129
7.2.3 Supportive Responses to a Health Disclosure	131
7.2.4 Supervisor Training	134
7.3 Examples of Work Design and Management Interventions	134
7.3.1 STAR Intervention to Increase Flexibility and Supervisor Support	134
7.3.2 Interventions to Increase Support for Worker Mental Health	136
7.4 Secondary Work-Focused Strategies	137
7.4.1 Job Modifications/Accommodations	137
7.4.2 Reduced-Load Work	139
7.5 Summary of Recommendations: Work-Focused Strategies	141

8. Individual Worker-Focused Strategies — 143

8.1 Individualized Programs	144
8.1.1 Coaching	145
8.1.2 Mentoring Programs	151
8.1.3 Vocational Counseling Programs	153
8.2 Online Programs	154
8.2.1 Pain at Work Toolkit (PAW)	154
8.2.2 Job Demands and Accommodation Planning Tool (JDAPT)	155
8.3 Group Programs	155
8.3.1 Manage at Work Program	156
8.3.2 Chronic Disease Self-Management Program	157
8.3.3 Other Group Programs	159
8.4 Summary and Recommendations	160
8.5 Takeaways and Recommendations	162

9. Implementing and Evaluating an Integrated Approach — **164**
   9.1 Making a Business Case — 164
   9.2 An Integrated Approach — 167
   9.3 Assessing Return on Investment and Value of Investment — 173
   9.4 Conclusion — 176
   9.5 Takeaways and Recommendations — 176

Glossary — 178
References — 181
Index — 205

Preface

I begin with a personal story. Twenty-two years ago, I was sitting at my desk at my internship. I had recently moved to a new state to start a master's degree program, and since moving I had been experiencing some odd symptoms—burning pain and numbness in my leg and sensations that felt like electricity down my spine. I attributed these to disc issues in my spine, since this is what my doctors repeatedly told me over the past three years. The phone rang; it was my new primary care doctor, with my spinal MRI results. I was expecting him to tell me about my disc issues, and I was ready to ask him questions about treatment. Instead, he said, "I think you have multiple sclerosis (MS)." I was in shock and disbelief. I didn't know anything about MS, and after he told me I would need another MRI to confirm, I remember asking, "What will we do for my disc issues, when we rule out MS?"

The next few months involved more MRIs, other tests, and appointments with two neurologists, one of whom proclaimed it was probably *not* MS, since I was able to hold down my 20-hour-a-week internship, plus another part-time job, plus a full-time graduate courseload. But the evidence was clear: I had MS. I was only 25 years old and had barely started my career, but my future place in the workforce was suddenly questionable at best.

I attempted to reclaim some control over my future by resolving to do everything in my power to ensure I could work as long as possible. In addition to medically managing my MS as best I could, this included a change of career plans—instead of ending my education with my master's degree and pursuing an applied career in human resources or organizational development, I would continue my education, attain a PhD, and pursue an academic career. Multiple mentors advised me not to tell anyone about the MS, as it would surely prevent me from career opportunities—so I kept it to myself. My former manager's words replayed in my head, reminding me of the importance of this: she had joked that an employee with MS just "smoked too much weed" and didn't really need time off during a flare-up. I admit I did not think much of this comment at the time (prediagnosis). After my diagnosis, its memory hit hard.

For the next several years, I devoted nearly all my available energy to pursuing an academic career path. Given my constant medical appointments and complex medical treatment that involved self-injections and intermittent infusions—both of which came with severe side effects—I imagined the only job I would be able to maintain was a flexible one that allowed me to work where and when I physically could.

During my PhD studies I focused on occupational health psychology, studying factors that affect worker health, safety, and well-being. Early in my coursework, I noticed there was nothing in the textbooks or research articles I read, and nothing in the courses I took about disabilities or chronic health conditions in the workplace. As someone living with a serious chronic health condition that affected almost every aspect of life in profound ways (and who, similarly, had family members with disabilities and chronic health conditions), this was an obvious omission, and one that I decided to address in my dissertation research.

Starting with my dissertation, and for the next 15 years, I conducted several research studies on various topics related to working with chronic health conditions, including stigma and discrimination, concealment of illness, conflicts between work and health management, effects of chronic pain at work, work factors affecting disease self-management, trainings to mitigate disability bias, and coaching to improve work ability and alleviate burnout in workers with chronic health conditions. In doing so, I have surveyed and interviewed thousands of workers with chronic health conditions. I have also interviewed managers and human resource professionals to get their perspectives on challenges related to managing workers with chronic health conditions, along with viable solutions. This book includes insights from all these studies, as well as studies by other researchers, on these and other related topics. Importantly, I have also managed several employees with CHCs in my career.

I have shared this personal information with you for the sake of transparency because it has, of course, informed my perspectives on the topics in this book. I have not only studied these topics; I have lived them as an employee with a CHC, a manager of employees with CHCs, and as a researcher who studies CHCs in the workplace. I am fortunate that my health is now stable, and my overall ability to work is strong. I am privileged in many ways that allowed me to pursue a PhD and mold a career that worked with my health needs and limitations. I also recognize that I have benefitted enormously from the dramatic advances in MS treatments that have occurred in the last 20 years. Yet many others are not so fortunate. Working with a serious chronic health condition can be very difficult, and workers need and deserve destigmatization, support, accessibility, and inclusion in organizations.

In presenting my research to and talking with applied audiences over the years, I have found that company leaders and others are hesitant to engage with the topic. It understandably can be an uncomfortable topic to discuss, and leaders may be wary of legal issues. However, the scope of chronic health conditions is already too big to ignore. Over half of US adults have at least one chronic health condition, and COVID-19 will likely cause this estimate to increase. In addition, cultural trends are shifting around this issue, with workers increasingly expecting support from their organizations for what were once considered problems for them to shoulder alone. Progressive companies will get ahead by supporting their workers with chronic health conditions and viewing it as an investment —retaining talent and being seen as a supportive place to work are competitive advantages.

This book is a research translation for leaders, managers, human resource professionals, consultants, coaches, DEI professionals, and other practitioners in organizations who want to learn how to better support the large percentage of employees with chronic health conditions in their organizations. It contains research-based practical solutions and steps to help leaders and frontline managers, such as yourself, better support employees, and to help organizations gain a competitive advantage through attracting and retaining valued employees. Not only are these strategies good for business—they also are the right thing to do.

Acknowledgments

Thank you to my friends and family who have supported me in immeasurable ways during this time—especially Alexia, Bibi, Craig, Erika, Erin, Katie, and Maeghan. Your love and support mean everything to me.

Thank you to my PhD advisor, Janet Barnes-Farrell, who supported my pursuit of this research area over 15 years ago, when it was unconventional and lacked precedent in my field. Janet, you helped me have confidence to take this path.

Thank you to my book editors, Hayley Singer and Russell Matthews. Russell, your encouragement and unwavering support—for both this topic and my contribution to it—will never be forgotten.

Thank you to my colleagues who have helped shape my thinking on this topic through our discussions over the years, especially Bill Shaw, Rosalind Joffe, Joy Beatty, and Brent Reed.

Finally, thank you to the many research study participants who have so generously shared their stories, perspectives, and experiences with me over the last 15 years. Your perspectives matter, and I have done my very best to portray them accurately and thoroughly in this book.

Introduction

Kudos to you for picking up this book—you are one of a small but growing group of forward-thinkers engaging with the underrecognized topic of chronic health conditions in the workplace. In my 15 years of researching chronic health conditions in US workplaces, I have noticed a pattern where organizations, and those who run and make decisions in them, are hesitant to engage with this topic. Case in point: even with assured confidentiality for participants and generous incentives, it is difficult to find industry leaders willing to partner with researchers to evaluate interventions to support workers with chronic health conditions. In short, as you may have noticed, this topic is generally not one that people discuss in the context of work, perhaps unless they or a loved one experiences a serious chronic health issue and the profound associated challenges that may arise.

Why is this the case? There are likely many reasons. In talking with folks I have heard about, for instance, fear of legal implications, uncertainty around how to discuss these issues, and being stretched too thin—all of which surely contribute to ambivalence about this topic and reluctance to engage with it. Cultural norms in the US have also historically dictated that personal issues, such as chronic health conditions, are to be handled individually and are not to be openly addressed at work or supported by employers. Notably, cultural norms in many other countries, including Canada and some European nations, are more open to discussing this topic, and the US lags them in terms of research and best practices.

In any cany case, I predict that this ambivalence and reluctance *will* change—it must, for organizations to thrive. Even before the COVID-19 pandemic, *more than half* of all working age US adults had one or more chronic health conditions; numbers of affected workers are skyrocketing now, in part due to long-COVID and COVID-19 causing other chronic health conditions. And organizations are likely already feeling the squeeze. A common question during the pandemic was "Why does no one want to work anymore?" While the reasons for this labor market trend are complex and include low pay and poor working conditions, another important but overlooked question is, "Why is it that so many people are *unable to work in these jobs*?"

Further, there is an ongoing cultural shift in terms of the supports employees expect from their employers. What were once deemed "personal" issues, such as work–family or work–life balance, have now become "workplace" issues, and this shift will occur with chronic health conditions as well. If this is difficult for you to imagine, think about the evolution in our culture's thinking about work–family issues over the last few decades. Thirty years ago, work–family issues were marginalized—organizations and those who ran them implicitly assumed these were personal issues that were up to the worker to figure out. Now, "work–life balance" is a mainstream term. There are several thousands of research studies on work–family and work–life topics, a growing host of well-known organizational interventions to help improve work–family and work–life balance, and several research centers to help promote work–family topics. Further, the most progressive organizations have generous benefits to promote the effective management of work and one's personal life (e.g., schedule flexibility, remote work, maternity and paternity leave, and financial support for family planning (e.g., adoption, egg freezing). Organizations shifted to maintain a competitive advantage; focusing on work–life benefits and work–family balance allows them to recruit and retain top talent. This shift has also helped increase the percentage of women in the workforce, who often bear a greater load of childcare than men.

Soon we will realize as a society that we need a similar reckoning around chronic health issues in the workplace. Just as addressing work–family issues is important to representation of women in the workforce, addressing work–health issues is important to representation of people with disabilities in the workforce. Ignoring work–health issues not only leads to the loss of needed talent, but also fails to recognize and support an important diversity category in organizations. Thus, supporting employees with chronic health conditions is both a business imperative and a social responsibility.

You may be thinking that we have already seen a cultural shift to focus on employee health. For example, most large organizations provide wellness program benefits to their employees. Yet wellness programs, which tend to focus on lifestyle factors such as promoting exercise and disease prevention (e.g., health screening), are inadequate to support the large percentage of employees with existing chronic health conditions who are facing complex work–health challenges. Employees facing stigma related to their health condition, difficult decisions around disclosure of their health condition, and declining work ability due their health condition need more than wellness programs—they need changes to organizational culture, increasing levels of supervisor support, changes to their jobs to be more flexible and autonomous, and perhaps even a trusted confidant to help them problem-solve. More recently, a growing number of organizations are paying more attention to worker mental health and are implementing mental health benefits and leadership training to better support employees. It is not a stretch to imagine this extending to all health conditions—mental and physical.

Notably, supporting employees with chronic health conditions involves attending to not only employee health and well-being but also *inclusion*, and in this book I describe issues with and solutions related to both. Disability is an often-overlooked diversity category in organizations, and chronic health conditions are a subset of disabilities with shared characteristics that set them apart from other disabilities. For example, chronic health conditions require ongoing management, they are often nonapparent or invisible to others, and their impacts on work functioning change over time, sometimes unpredictably. Full inclusion of employees with chronic health conditions therefore requires stigma reduction, acknowledgment of their unique challenges, and support and accessibility to allow employees to perform to their best capabilities.

As a reader of this book, you likely already have bought in to the need for increased attention on this topic. This book will help expand your understanding of the ways chronic health conditions interact with work to create challenges and provide you with skills and tools to help you make an impact in your workplace to positively affect your employees with chronic health conditions and your organization. In other words, this book is intended to have a transformative effect on leaders such as yourself who likely already care about these critical issues. As you may have surmised by this point, this book does not focus on medical management of chronic health conditions, nor is it intended to help your company with healthcare savings. Instead, it focuses on intervening to proactively support workers with chronic health conditions and their managers with organization-focused, job-focused, management-focused, and individual-focused strategies. As you read the suggested strategies, I encourage you to imagine which of these may be possible to implement in your organization.

The book has three parts. Part I provides background information on chronic health conditions and their effects on individual workers, managers, organizations, and society (Chapter 1); on chronic health conditions as disabilities, and associated legal rights and responsibilities for individuals and organizations (Chapter 2); and on ways organizations have traditionally supported workers with chronic health-related issues through wellness programs and return-to-work programs (Chapter 3). Part II provides a deep dive into challenges chronic health conditions pose to workers (Chapter 4), along with managers, human resource professionals, and leaders in organizations

(Chapter 5). Taking a forward-thinking perspective, Part III provides strategies for supporting workers with chronic health conditions, including those that are organization-focused (Chapter 6), job- and management-focused (Chapter 7), and individual-focused (Chapter 8), as well as how to implement an integrated approach that includes strategies across levels (Chapter 9). Throughout the book, quotes from employees with chronic health conditions and managers, leaders, and human resource professionals are included to illustrate points. Exercises help make the material more concrete and personal to the reader. For all chapters, key terms are defined both in the text and in the glossary at the end of this book. Finally, each chapter closes with key takeaways and recommendations.

As a final note, at the time this book is in its production phase (early 2025), there is much uncertainty in the US around policies and practices related to diversity, equity, and inclusion (DEI). There has been backlash against DEI policies in the workplace across various states in the US, and the Trump administration has issued executive orders for federal agencies, contractors, and recipients of federal funding to halt DEI policies and practices. Like many people, you are likely wondering how this might affect you or your organization, and how it applies to chronic health conditions and disabilities. First, it is important to know that the executive order does not directly apply to the private sector. Second, it is helpful to keep in mind that federal laws remain unchanged. In other words, it is still the case that companies are prohibited from discriminating based on protected characteristics in all personnel functions, including disability status. Third, employers have a responsibility to maintain psychological safety for all employees. Those with identities being targeted by these executive orders may feel like they are under attack or unsafe, and it is important to keep that in mind while working to help promote the well-being of all your employees. This book will provide some helpful strategies for doing so.

PART I
BACKGROUND

Chapter 1
Overview, Prevalence, and Burden

> It's really easy to feel that you are at the mercy of your illness, and while to some extent it's true, it doesn't need to be the only truth. We need to continue to fight to stay employed in some way. We can't give up. The chronically ill are smart, passionate, and valuable people—but far too often we aren't able to find employment situations that will accept our illness as well as our talents. We need understanding, flexibility and opportunity to give our best. I'm hopeful for a future of living with chronic illness that allows me to work and fulfill my potential. I'm not ready to give up yet!
>
> —communication specialist with Sjogren's syndrome and fibromyalgia, age 39

As this quote from a research study participant illustrates, chronic health conditions (subsequently referred to as CHCs) can and do create challenges for workers who want to remain employed—and there is good reason to help address those challenges and be supportive of workers. This chapter begins with an overview of CHCs: what they are, what common characteristics they share, and how those characteristics can create work-related challenges. I then provide details on CHC prevalence by different demographics, including age, sex and gender, race and ethnicity, and socioeconomic status. Finally, I provide information on CHC-associated costs, including financial and psychosocial costs. I conclude with a recap on key takeaways from this chapter.

1.1 Definition and Overview

CHCs are diseases, illness, or other health issues that are ongoing—lasting at least one year, though most are lifelong—and require ongoing management and/or restrict an individual's activities.[1] For this book, CHCs include all long-term, ongoing physical and mental health conditions, illnesses, diseases, and symptoms, such as chronic pain or fatigue, that require ongoing management and/or limit activities.[2] Examples of some of the most prevalent and deadliest CHCs include cardiovascular diseases, diabetes, respiratory diseases, cancers, and mood disorders.[3,4] At the time of writing this book, long COVID is an increasingly prevalent CHC that affects millions of people in the US and worldwide.[5]

If it seems to you that CHCs are becoming more common, it is because they are. *More than half of US adults* have at least one CHC, with large anticipated increases in prevalence over time.[1,6,7] Projected increases are attributed in part to an aging population and medical advances that prolong life and delay disability.[8] Organizational leaders such as yourself should therefore expect that a sizeable proportion of their workforces have one or more CHCs, and that this proportion will only increase in coming years.

Not only are CHCs prevalent, but they have enormous associated costs. CHCs account for 90% of an annual $4.1 trillion in healthcare spending in the US,[9] and work-related productivity losses from CHCs due to absenteeism and sickness at work are even costlier than healthcare expenditures.[10] For example, productivity loss due to hypertension and diabetes alone costs more than $2 billion annually.[11] CHCs are also a main cause of work disability claims, with musculoskeletal conditions and mental health conditions being among the top disabling conditions.[12] Of course, costs are not solely financial; CHCs have significant ramifications for the psychological, social, and work-related well-being for those affected.

You would likely agree with the notion that CHCs present complex challenges for both workers and their employing organizations. In 2018 I surveyed 292 full-time US workers, including managers (55%), human resource professionals (12%), and employees (33%)—64% of whom had at least one CHC. Of those surveyed, 98% agreed that CHCs pose major challenges for affected workers. Many of these work-related challenges are common across different types of CHCs and are unique to people with CHCs. I refer to these throughout this book as *work–health challenges,* and detail them in Chapter 4. Work–health challenges contribute to declines in worker productivity, well-being, and work ability, which is workers' assessments of their ability to continue working in their current job.[13] Of course, as detailed in Chapter 5, challenges are not solely faced by affected employees—indeed, in the aforementioned survey, 93% of managers and 89% of human resource professionals agreed that CHCs pose major problems for organizations.

Work–health challenges are underrecognized, and further, they are *not proactively addressed by typical workplace programs and supports.* Currently, targeted programs to promote work ability and solve work–health challenges are almost solely relegated to return-to-work programs, which are reactive in nature and only provide support once disability occurs, or wellness programs, which are mainly focused on prevention of disease rather than inclusion and promotion of work-related well-being and work ability for those with existing CHCs. *More proactive strategies to support workers with CHCs are needed.*

As detailed in Chapter 9, proactive approaches to support inclusion and promotion of work ability and well-being in workers with CHCs have great *potential to return value on organizations' investments*, not only by reducing organizational costs due to disability claims, but also through promoting worker productivity and performance, and reducing turnover. Other potential benefits include reduced disability discrimination claims and grievances, and enhanced ability to recruit and retain top talent through demonstrated values of worker well-being and corporate social responsibility.

To address the underrecognized needs of this large and growing segment of the working population, this book integrates and translates research findings and theory from organizational science, occupational health psychology, disability studies, economics, human resource management, and public health to *illuminate challenges and recommend proactive strategies to promote inclusion, work ability, and work-related well-being for workers with CHCs*. Notably, in doing so this book does *not* substantially address CHC prevention or general health management efforts in the workplace—these topics have already amassed a considerable body of research and practice, with the majority of firms in the US currently offering workplace health promotion/wellness programs.[14]

To be clear, I am not arguing that workplace health prevention and management efforts are unimportant. On the contrary, research demonstrates that workplace health promotion and wellness efforts are quite valuable, particularly when implemented alongside systemic improvements to the work environment, job structure, and supervision.[15] Yet I agree with thought leaders who argue that a narrow-minded focus solely on prevention and treatment serves to perpetuate stigma and inequalities for people with disabilities, and that additional focus on maximizing health and inclusion of people with disabilities is critical.[16] I argue that organizations should move beyond a singular focus on CHC prevention and treatment to also place attention on inclusion, accessibility, and support for workers with CHCs to help promote quality of working life and prevent premature workforce departure of affected workers.

1.2 Work-Health Challenges

You may be wondering why I am not writing about disabilities more generally in this book. Why focus solely on CHCs? First, as I discuss in more detail in Chapter 2, many workers with CHCs have recognized disabilities under US law, yet not all those workers identify with having disabilities.

Additionally, workplace experiences of those with different types of disabilities (e.g., intellectual disabilities, sensory impairments, health impairments) differ substantially, and lumping them together can lead to overgeneralization and the risk of missing important implications for practice in organizations.[17]

I argue that CHCs are worthy of attention in their own right—not only do they affect more than half of the workforce and create substantial costs, but they also share unique, yet *common characteristics*, many of which set them apart from other disabilities and create associated work–health challenges. Certainly, CHCs differ in several dimensions, including their etiology, symptomatology, and course/progression, yet I focus on *common challenges and associated solutions* in this book. This means that the challenges discussed and the recommendations for supportive strategies will be widely applicable across many *different types of CHCs*. Focusing on common challenges can help organizations maximize the value of their investments in supportive interventions, as well as maximize the value of your time investment in learning about these issues as a busy leader.

Common characteristics of CHCs that often create work-related challenges are listed below. It is important for organizational leaders such as yourself to understand these challenges so that you may better support workers experiencing them and empower workers to take steps to address them. These challenges are elaborated in Chapter 4 of this book, and strategies for addressing them are in Chapters 6, 7, and 8. You may be familiar with some of these, as a person living with a CHC or with a loved one who has a CHC.

1. *CHCs require ongoing management*, including lifestyle changes, treatments, medical appointments, and sometimes hospitalizations, which often conflict with work role requirements.[20]
2. *CHC symptoms and/or disease activity are often not static, but intermittent, recurrent, or fluctuating.* As a result, work limitations also fluctuate—arising when disease course and symptoms flare, and subsequently remit. For this reason, CHCs are often referred to as "episodic disabilities."[18,19] As an added challenge, many times fluctuations are unpredictable, necessitating quick changes to accommodations or other supports.
3. *Maintaining work ability* can be challenging in the face of ongoing, progressing, or fluctuating symptoms and the need for ongoing management, particularly as they interact with job tasks and the work environment.[13]
4. *CHCs with more progressive courses* may lead to increasing work ability challenges and the need to create career contingency plans considering health limitations.[21]

5. *Many CHCs are stigmatized*, leading to fears of and experiences of discrimination at work, including accommodation denials, missed promotion opportunities, and worse.[22]
6. *Most CHCs are nonapparent to others (i.e., invisible to others or concealable with effort)*, which can further stigma due to others not believing accommodations are needed and create dilemmas around disclosure of a CHC at work.[18,23]
7. *CHC-related issues can be difficult to communicate with supervisors* and others; yet in many cases effective self-advocacy and clear, judicious communication is essential to attaining needed support and accommodations to help ensure continued productivity.[25]
8. *CHCs can create identity issues*; CHCs can be difficult to accept and integrate with one's work identity so that appropriate supports can be identified and used to assist with productivity and performance.[24]

1.3 Prevalence

As noted, CHCs are prevalent in the US and around the world. The most prevalent CHCs in the US include heart disease, cancer, stroke, chronic lung disease, Alzheimer's disease, diabetes, and kidney disease.[1,8] Currently, an estimated *60% of adults in the US have at least one CHC*, and *40% have two or more CHCs*.[1] These percentages will continue to rise. For example, autoimmune disease rates are increasing at alarming rates—with markers of autoimmunity increasing over 50% in less than 30 years—leading some physicians and researchers to refer to autoimmunity as a global epidemic.[26]

The following sections detail prevalence and impact of CHCs by age, sex and gender, race and ethnicity, and socioeconomic status. They also detail prevalence of chronic pain, which is very common and a leading cause of work disability, and long COVID, a relatively new CHC. Box 1.1 contains some quick facts about chronic health conditions from this section.

1.3.1 Age

Who ends up diagnosed with a CHC? It may not be who you think. While it is probably not surprising that increasing *age* is a well-known risk factor for CHCs,[7] *the average age of onset for many CHCs is well below typical retirement ages*.[3,27] As of 2019, 53.8% of US adults age 18–34 had at least one CHC, and 22.3% had more than one CHC.[28] Further, a third of millennials—aged 34–36 in 2017—reported having CHCs that *reduced their quality of life and life expectancy* in 2019, most commonly major depression, substance use disorders, hypertension, AD/HD, psychotic conditions, Crohn's disease or ulcerative colitis, high cholesterol, and type 2 diabetes.[29] Further, data suggest that onset age of many CHCs appears to be trending younger.[30–32] For instance, a recent study uncovered a sharp increase in the prevalence of antibodies associated with autoimmune disease in US teens aged 12–19.[33] In sum, organizational leaders and practitioners should be aware that much of their workforces, including relatively younger workers, are affected by CHCs, and the numbers of younger workers affected will likely continue to increase.

1.3.2 Sex and Gender

Evidence is mixed and inconclusive as to whether *sex* and *gender* affect risk of developing a CHC, and risk depends on the type of CHC. For example, evidence consistently shows that women are diagnosed with autoimmune diseases, such as type 1 diabetes, lupus, rheumatoid arthritis, and multiple sclerosis, at higher rates than men.[34] Yet men tend to experience greater severity of autoimmune diseases such as lupus and multiple sclerosis.[35] What about other types of CHCs? In one study, women had statistically higher prevalence of 10 of 18 CHCs examined than men (headache, chronic pain, arthritis, bronchitis, lung problems, asthma, hypertension, reproductive cancer, vision problems, and depression)—yet men were more likely to be hospitalized and die from CHCs related to smoking (cardiovascular disease, emphysema, and other lung disorders).[36] These gender differences in fatalities are attributed to differences in smoking behavior, as men have higher lifetime rates of smoking than women.[36] More recently, researchers have begun to separate *biological sex* from *socially constructed gender* when examining CHC prevalence. Emerging findings suggest that female biological sex is associated with greater somatic symptom prevalence and severity, but not a greater prevalence of diagnosed CHCs.[37]

Further, gender-based stereotypes are known to result in medical bias and discrimination for women. Studies show that women often wait longer for a diagnosis than men for chronic illnesses, including some cancers.[38,39] Women are often initially misdiagnosed with somatic or medically unexplained conditions, only to later be diagnosed with an organic chronic disease.[38] A review of 77 published studies found men presenting with pain symptoms to be commonly referred to as "stoic" and "autonomous," while women were presenting with pain symptoms were commonly referred to as (more) "sensitive" to pain than men and "hysterical."[40] This review also found that women's pain was also more often classified as medically unexplained, which was, unfortunately, associated with provider mistrust and neglect.[40,41] Perhaps not surprisingly, women also tend to be undertreated for pain compared to men.[42]

1.3.3 Race and Ethnicity

When considering *race and ethnicity*, most agree that there are wide health disparities in general health, and in many CHCs, with racial and ethnic minorities facing worse health outcomes. For example, diabetes is twice as prevalent in Hispanic and non-Hispanic Black Americans than non-Hispanic White Americans, and Hispanic and non-Hispanic Black Americans with diabetes are also more likely to have comorbid (co-occurring) cardiovascular disease.[43] Yet this does not hold across all CHCs—cancer and chronic lung diseases are relatively more prevalent for non-Hispanic White Americans, for example.[43] Across all ages, life expectancy for Black Americans is lower (age 70.8) than for White (age 76.4) Americans,[44] which may be partially attributable to Black Americans being diagnosed with CHCs such as heart failure and hypertension at *younger ages* than White Americans.[45] Many factors contribute to these racial disparities in health and life expectancy, including lower socioeconomic status among many racial and ethnic minority groups, along with higher levels of experienced stress and discrimination.[46,47]

1.3.4 Socioeconomic Status

Socioeconomic status is also a contributor to health discrepancies across all racial and ethnic groups. Lower-income Americans' risk factors, including lower access to healthcare, less access to fresh food, and higher rates of substance abuse lead to worse health and earlier death compared to higher-income Americans.[48]

1.3.5 Multiple CHCs

Current estimates suggest that worldwide, one in three adults have multiple CHCs,[49] and in the US 42% of adults have multiple CHCs, including 13% with two, 9% with three, 7% with four, and 12% with five or more CHCs.[1,3] Not surprisingly, people with CHCs, and particularly multiple CHCs account for more healthcare spending, and those with more CHCs have higher levels of pain, work limitations and disability.[3,50] Those with multiple CHCs tend to be older in age, and more women than men have multiple CHCs.[3] Having multiple CHCs may mean experiencing more symptoms and complex health management protocols, compounding work–health challenges for affected workers.

1.3.6 Chronic Pain

Chronic pain is prevalent, costly, and comorbid with many other CHCs. Between 18.4%—20.5% of US adults, or 40–50.2 million people in the U.S experience chronic pain.[51,52] To break this down further, an estimated 25.3 million people in the US experience *daily* chronic pain, 14 million experience pain *most days*, and 86.6 million experience pain *some days*. Further, of those who experience chronic pain, an estimated 23.4 million have *severe* and 14.4 million have *very severe* pain.[50] The most commonly reported areas of pain include the hip, knee, foot, and back.[52]

Increasing age is a risk factor for experiencing chronic pain. Also, in the US, non-Hispanic White individuals have a documented higher prevalence of pain than other ethnic or racial groups, yet this could be due to underreporting in ethnic and racial minority groups from less access to healthcare.[3] Women are more likely to experience chronic pain than men in general, yet this trend disappears when considering "high-impact chronic pain," which is pain experienced every day in the last three months that limits at least one life activity.[51]

Chronic pain is a common precursor to disability and unemployment— one study found that nearly 49% of those with chronic pain reported work limitations, and another study found that nearly 37% of those with severe pain are unable to work.[50] Chronic pain does not only affect workers' abilities to perform physical activities and tasks—it also commonly affects people's abilities to engage socially.[52] As detailed in Chapter 4, social issues may arise for workers with chronic pain due to the pain being invisible to others, and physical exhaustion and other limitations from pain can make communication and social engagement difficult. As one research study participant stated,

> Living with a chronic illness is very difficult. It is difficult not only in the physical aspect, but the social aspect as well. Generally, people don't understand chronic disease much less Ankylosing Spondylitis. I have some really bad days and other days are not so bad. Some of the issues that I have at work with my chronic illness: I have a difficult time walking around the building and a difficult time sitting in lengthy meetings. I usually end up with more pain after doing these activities.

People in other departments will give me strange looks when they see me with my cane one day and then not the next, or if I park in the handicap space at work. I had to drop out of a group called staff council. . . . I physically could not help with set-up, clean-up as well as helping during the actual events. . . . I never have issues with depression, anxiety or despair; however my pain and lack of ability to participate in many events have caused me to withdraw from others and not necessarily by choice.

—registered nurse with ankylosing spondylitis, age 41

1.3.7 Long COVID

Long COVID affects 200 million individuals globally, or 43% of those who have had COVID-19 worldwide. In the US, prevalence is estimated at 31% of those who have had COVID-19,[53] or 25 million people. Further, 9.6 million people in the US have three or more symptoms of long COVID.[54] Risk factors for long COVID include hospitalization for acute COVID infection, pre-existing asthma, and being female.[53] The most common symptoms include fatigue, memory problems, breathing problems, sleep problems, joint pain, cognitive problems/brain fog.[53] At the time I am writing this book, the scope and impact of long COVID is still in flux, yet some expect a "tsunami of disability" as a result.[55]

Box 1.1 CHC Prevalence: Fast Facts

- 60% of US adults have at least one CHC.
- 40% of US adults have two or more CHCs.
- Almost 54% of young adults aged 18–34 have at least one CHC.
- Women, ethnic and racial minorities, and those of low socioeconomic status are at greater risk of CHCs.
- Nearly one in five people in the US lives with chronic pain.
- 31% of those who had COVID-19 in the US experience long COVID.

1.4 Costs

CHCs have many associated costs to individuals, organizations, and society. Costs are not only financial (direct and indirect), but also psychosocial.

1.4.1 Direct Financial Costs

Direct healthcare costs include prescriptions, therapies, medical appointments and procedures, hospitalizations, and other health-related products and services to manage or treat CHCs. As noted in Section 1.1, CHCs account for 90% of an annual $4.1 trillion in healthcare spending in the US.[9] The Milken Institute estimated direct healthcare costs for 24 common CHCs in the US to total $1.1 trillion in 2016, with the most spending on cardiovascular conditions ($294.3 billion) and diabetes ($189.6 billion).[10] Healthcare spending is expected to increase over time, for example, reaching $748.7 billion for cardiovascular diseases by 2035.[56] All of these direct cost estimates exclude long COVID, which were conservatively estimated at $528 billion in 2023.[54,57]

1.4.2 Indirect Financial Costs

CHCs are also associated with *productivity losses*, which are estimated to be costlier than healthcare spending on CHCs. These include work absenteeism, *presenteeism* (attending work when feeling impaired; see Box 1.2), reduced hours, and workforce departure due to CHCs. The aforementioned Milken Institute report estimated $2.57 trillion in combined productivity-related costs of 24 common CHCs in the US in 2016, which is over 70% of total indirect and direct costs due to CHCs.[10] Productivity declines associated with chronic pain alone are estimated to cost between $299 and $335 billion annually in the US.[58] Absenteeism due to obesity, smoking, physical inactivity, hypertension, and diabetes is estimated to cost between $17,000 and $28,500 per year for a single large US employer.[11] Costs of presenteeism are thought to be even greater than costs of absenteeism—as much as 80% of lost productivity costs overall may be attributed to presenteeism.[59] I provide steps to estimate absenteeism and presenteeism costs for your organization in Chapter 9, and strategies to support workers and thereby help minimize productivity losses in Chapters 6–9.

Box 1.2 Presenteeism

Presenteeism refers to attending work when feeling impaired—for example, from illness, stress, or work–family conflict, and often results in lowered productivity.[59,60] Despite its association with illness, workers with CHCs do not always experience presenteeism; only when they feel debilitated or impaired from one of these or other factors.[60] Despite being linked to lower productivity, presenteeism can be functional in some cases, allowing an employee to sustain work ability while experiencing ill health.[61,62] One study participant reported intentionally slowing their pace of work in an effort to allow them to continue working in their job,

> I was always in a vicious circle with pushing myself nonstop but feeling very worn out, not having energy to complete tasks, not recognizing how I am feeling and how that might affect my work ability, etc. . . . it has been a struggle for me acknowledge that I have limitations and to slow down when I need to. This was probably the one thing that was most difficult for me and most of the issues I had revolved around pushing myself too hard and expecting too much from myself. I have made some major life changes so that I can slow down, heal and do the things I want to do while continuing to do my job.
> —research assistant with undifferentiated spondyloarthropathy, age 39

1.4.3 Financial Burdens to Individuals

In addition to these more macro-level costs of CHCs to organizations and society, it is important to remember that many individuals face financial burden from CHCs due to healthcare costs and impacts to their ability to work. People with CHCs in the US are currently able purchase health insurance (which was often denied due to pre-existing conditions before the Affordable Care Act was passed in the US in 2010). Yet as I describe in Chapter 6, many plans have high deductibles and coinsurance rates, making care expensive and even unaffordable to some working individuals. For example, diabetes medications cost up to $720 per month per prescription, and many people need multiple medications for CHCs such as diabetes.[63] Healthcare costs for individuals also, not surprisingly, increase with the number of CHCs they have. Healthcare costs for a person in the US with five or more CHCs are 18 times the costs for someone with no CHCs.[3] For low-wage workers in the US, healthcare costs are often a significant percentage of overall income.

Individuals' earnings are also affected by CHCs. As a case in point, an estimated 1.1 million US workers are not working due to long COVID,[64] which translates to $50 billion in lost income annually.[57] Individual earnings are reduced by 12% when someone is diagnosed with a CHC (attributed mostly to reduced working hours), and 18% over all working years (attributed mostly to early labor force withdrawal).[27] Those with CHCs are more likely to retire early due to ill health, and are less likely to gain *bridge employment*, or paid work after retiring from one's career before exiting the workforce.[65] People whose CHCs require them to leave the labor force may receive benefits from social safety nets, but nevertheless usually take a significant financial hit from leaving work. For example, one study estimated that individuals aged 45–64 who retired early due to depression had 73% lower income than their employed counterparts.[66] Further, those who retire for health-related reasons generally have poorer psychological well-being than those who retire voluntarily for other reasons.[65] In sum, it is financially advantageous for workers with CHCs to remain employed, and leaders such as yourself can help empower vulnerable workers to address work–health challenges and remain employed by using some of the recommendations in this book.

1.4.4 Psychosocial Costs

Of course, not all costs of CHCs are economic in nature; there is an enormous toll of CHCs on the well-being of affected individuals and their families. To start, people with CHCs generally have lower *quality of life* (perception of their well-being and position in life relative to their expectations and goals) than those without CHCs, and many CHCs carry risk of comorbid mental health issues. For example, people with all types of CHCs are more likely than the general population to experience depression.[67] Depression can also in turn worsen some physical CHCs through physiological mechanisms of inflammation and nervous system dysfunction,[68] as well as behavioral impacts, including difficulties adhering to treatment, eating well, and getting regular exercise and sleep.[69] Younger workers are at increased risk of mental health impacts from being diagnosed with CHCs than older workers, as being diagnosed at a young age may cause identity conflicts and struggles.[70] Younger people with CHCs may also find themselves at odds with societal expectations of health. For example, as one research study participant shared,

> On a day-to-day level, I feel very conscious of the space I take up. People "tut" at me in supermarkets for moving slowly and getting in the way, because I look young and fine, I think.
>
> —administrative assistant with fibromyalgia, age 30

Some CHCs, including heart disease, stroke, and cancer, are associated with increased risk of anxiety disorders.[67] For those with CHCs fears related to illness progression, treatment side effects, recurrence, and becoming a burden to family or others often lead to psychological distress.[71] Functional limitations may also lead to changed social and family roles for people with CHCs. One study of workers with back injuries and pain found that participants reported hindrances to their abilities to help with household chores, raising children, and participating in leisure activities with their spouses, which put a strain on family relationships.[72]

Living and working with a CHC can be thought of as a process of constant adjustment—for example, to diagnosis, physical and mental limitations, progression or recurrence, symptom flares, lost social connections, work limitations, stigma and discrimination, and financial issues. As one research study participant said,

> I could not work in a traditional law firm or corporation due to the time I need to spend on myself, and the way I have to work to be productive at my job . . . I was a full partner there when I left . . . . due to the attitudes of people against me. I tried to work it out and prove myself for 3 years. I nearly had a nervous breakdown. I left and started my own office for survival. It has worked well. I could be more successful, but I have adjusted my perception of success—happy people don't necessarily have everything, they just make the most of what they have. This gets me by. I worry if I get worse or if the legal community learns of my disability people might stop sending me clients, or some opponents would take advantage of it against me to win. I wonder if eventually I will be disabled but I love what I do, so I don't go there.
> —attorney with fibromyalgia and chronic myofascial pain, age 42

Although this chapter has spotlighted many challenges stemming from and detrimental aspects of CHCs, it is important to note that that many people report benefits of living with CHCs, such as increased resilience,[60] perspective, and empathy for others—all of which make them valuable employees that organizations would benefit from retaining. The following quotes from study participants help illustrate this point.

> So when I got diagnosed, I thought my life was over. Worst-case scenario, of course, went through my brain. I guess knowing that as long as you have a good support system, having the nutritionists and my doctor, and I really trust them, and they've really been helping me get to where I need to go . . . . Also, whenever I have a student that may have health concerns or anything like that, then they may come to me, I think I have a different perspective to provide, and can be a little more understanding.
> —graduate program director with type 2 diabetes, age 30

It's challenging and has created more depth in me. It's made [me] more thoughtful and more empathetic. That's the good part.
— office worker with multiple sclerosis, age 48

I am a medical professional and my empathy for people who suffer has increased greatly as a result of this chronic illness.
— healthcare professional with rheumatoid arthritis and depression, age 54

1.5 Takeaways

- CHCs include a wide array of long-term physical and mental illnesses, diseases, and ongoing symptoms that require ongoing management and/or lead to impairment.
- CHCs are highly prevalent in the US and around the world, and prevalence is expected to increase over time.
- CHCs lead to significant economic burdens to individuals, organizations, and society.
- CHCs lead to declines in well-being and quality of life for many affected individuals.
- CHCs have shared characteristics that can affect work, including:
  - CHCs require ongoing management.
  - Symptoms and/or disease activity are often not static, but intermittent, recurrent, or fluctuating.
  - Maintaining work ability can be challenging.
  - CHCs may require a worker to have career contingency plans.
  - Many CHCs are stigmatized, which can lead to discrimination.
  - Most CHCs are nonapparent/invisible to others, sometimes necessitating decision-making around disclosure.
  - CHC-related issues can be difficult to communicate with supervisors and others.
  - CHCs can create professional or work-related identity issues.
- CHCs pose common work–health challenges to workers that are typically not addressed by common workplace programs.
- Given the enormous productivity-related costs and large and growing prevalence of CHCs in the workplace, organizations stand to benefit significantly from upgrading their strategies for supporting their workers with CHCs in ways that help them stay productive at work.

Chapter 2
Disability and the Legal Landscape

In speaking with managers and leaders in organizations, I have learned that there is often confusion around CHCs in terms of disability; for example, *when do CHCs qualify as legally protected disabilities?* Many workers with CHCs also are unaware that their health condition may qualify as a legally protected disability. In addition, there are many misconceptions around disability protections and law in the United States (US). These conversations spurred me to include a chapter in this book dedicated to the intersection of CHCs, disabilities, and US law.

I begin by providing definitions of disability according to the two most common disability frameworks, the medical model and the social model and describe when CHCs may be considered disabilities. I then provide a brief overview of US laws pertaining to disability, including the Americans with Disabilities Act, the Rehabilitation Act, the Family Medical Leave Act, and the Health Insurance Portability and Accountability Act, with an emphasis on implications for leaders and organizations. In doing so, I provide examples of court cases to help illustrate ADA provisions, and examples of reasonable accommodations under the ADA. Readers will take away from this chapter an understanding of disability as it relates to CHCs, along with knowledge of US law pertaining to disability. A quiz at the end of this chapter will help readers check their knowledge of topics from this chapter.

2.1 Understanding Disabilities

Most people will experience disability in their lifetime. Over a billion people worldwide are currently experiencing disability[1] and in the US, an estimated 26% (61 million) live with a disability.[2] It is likely that *if you hold a leadership position, one or more of your subordinates lives with a disability*. And because many disabilities are nonapparent or invisible as noted in Chapter 1, *you may not be aware of it*. Workers with disabilities make up an important, yet underrecognized diversity category in organizations, and it is important to be up to speed on language preferences around disabilities, as well definitions of disabilities and applicable employment laws.

At the outset, it is important to explain the language used in this book. Sometimes I use *people/person with a disability*—in other words, "person-first" language—which, for decades, was generally thought of as the preferred way to refer to disability.[3] At other times I use *disabled people/person*, which is an increasingly preferred term for many disabled folks. Such "identity-first" language implies that disability is an identity characteristic to be embraced without shame—similar to how many who identify as LGBTQIA+ view their identity.[3] Language preferences are evolving. At the time I am writing this book, there is a slight preference for person-first language in the US—though younger people are more likely to prefer identity-first language.[4] As there is no consensus among those with disabilities as to preferred language, I will use both terms in this book interchangeably. Further, I will not use euphemisms such as "special needs" or "differently abled" to circumvent "disabled"—as I concur with many in the disability community that the term "disabled" is not something to be ashamed of, or otherwise avoid. Like my approach in this book, I encourage you to not only avoid such euphemisms, but also to consider individual language preferences and directly ask your subordinates who identify as disabled what they language they prefer.

Next, let's look at how disability is defined—what it is and is not. To that end, it is important to understand the two most common models for understanding disability, the medical model and the social model.

2.1.1 Medical Model

The *medical model*, also known as biological or biomedical model, of disability is an older model that states that disability is a characteristic of the individual person and is based on the trauma, health condition, or other medical factor that caused the limitation. As such, a focus of the medical model is medical intervention or treatment.[5] This model inherently assumes that disability is a defect, or "abnormal" and should be "fixed" by medical practitioners.

The medical conceptualization of a disability as something aberrant and defective can understandably be offensive to some people living with disabilities, particularly when those disabilities are important to their identities. The assumptions underlying the medical model may create reactions in others that both convey pity toward the person with the disability and heroize people with disabilities for accomplishing every day, mundane tasks.[6]

So-called inspiration porn, a term coined by disability rights activist Stella Young in 2012, refers to stories or memes of disabled people achieving goals or tasks ranging from the mundane (e.g., a news story about a developmentally disabled high school student attending a school dance) to the extraordinary (e.g., a Paralympian being pictured with a disabled young girl and the tagline "The only Disability is A Bad Attitude").[7] As it generates a positive emotional response among many people, inspiration porn is rampant on social media, television, and other forms of media. Yet it is seen by many in the disability community as a harmful manifestation of ableism that is condescending to disabled people and commodifies them to generate views and "likes."[7] To avoid unintentionally commodifying disabled employees in your organization, ensure that all accolades and awards are based on individuals' accomplishments and not their perceived hardships. Also, do not laud people with disabilities for doing typical or expected tasks, and do not convey pity or "other" those with disabilities by saying things like, "I don't know how you do it," "I could never imagine living with XX disease."

2.1.2 Social Model

Contrary to the medical model of disability, the more contemporary social model of disability states that disability is a product of social, cultural, and physical structures that interact with individuals' impairments. In other words, the social model states that the failure of structures to accommodate people with impairments creates disabilities, rather than health conditions. As such, a focus of the social model is changing societal structures and environments to enhance daily function through *universal design*.[6] Universal design is design that allows for maximum accessibility for all individuals, regardless of age, ability, or size. It applies to physical environments (e.g., including larger chairs and left-handed desks in classrooms, including ramps for wheelchair or stroller access, ensuring doorways and spaces are large enough for accommodating mobility devices), communications (e.g., ensuring text is large enough to read, using high-contrast font colors, using clear and simple language, and accessible web page layouts), and products and services.

The social model is generally favored over the medical model by disability studies and psychology scholars and practitioners because it specifically acknowledges the roles of cultural factors and the universal challenges they create for people with disabilities.[8] It also spurs political and social action to accommodate all individuals—adding value to society through allowing participation of all. Yet many see the social model as being incomplete on its own, as it ignores the biological components of disabilities, and in some cases, necessary medical intervention. To this end, the World Health Organization's (WHO) International Classification of Functioning, Disability, and Health (ICF) argues for synthesizing the medical and social models and not ignoring the complexities inherent to either model.[5]

2.1.3 Defining Disability

Have you ever wondered what qualifies as a disability or were unclear about what disability actually means? This is quite common, as there are inconsistencies across various definitions of disability, leading to confusion for both employees and those who manage them.[8] In the US, relatively recent legislative updates have made legal definitions consistent across federal laws and entities, including the 2008 amendment to the 1990 Americans with Disabilities Act (ADA), also known as the Americans with Disabilities Act Amendments Act (ADAAA), the Rehabilitation Act, and the Equal Employment Opportunity Commission (EEOC). These entities all define disabilities using language from the ADAAA; specifically, "A person with a disability is someone who 1) has a physical or mental impairment that substantially limits one or more major life activities, or 2) has a history or record of such an impairment (such as cancer that is in remission), or 3) is perceived by others as having such an impairment (such as a person who has scars from a severe burn)."[9] Importantly, per the ADAAA, "major life activities" are broadly defined and include not only activities such as eating and sleeping, but *also major bodily functions*, such as cognitive function of thinking and concentrating or operation of bodily functions such as circulation or reproduction.[9] Further, it stipulates that impairments currently in remission qualify as disabilities if they limit activities when active.[10] More information on the ADAAA and its expanded provisions is in Section 2.2. but for now, it is important to remember that the ADAAA broadly defines disability and includes limitations to bodily functions, which covers many CHCs.

Definitions of disability used in research and reporting often differ from the ADAAA definition. The US Bureau of Labor Statistics (BLS) uses data from the Current Population Survey (CPS) for its nationwide statistics on disability and employment. The CPS defines disability through a series of six questions as listed in Table 2.1,[11] which are notably more restrictive than the current definition of disability under the ADAAA. Another definition comes from the World Health Organization's (WHO) International Classification of Functioning, Disability and Health (ICF), which combines the medical and social models of disability to describe disability and is broader than the CPS definition (see Table 2.1).

Perhaps further leading to misconception is that the term "disability" is used in multiple, related but different ways in the workplace. Disability simultaneously refers to a(n):

- Impairment that leads to diminished work functioning.
- Impairment that makes one completely unable to work.
- Legally protected status in the workplace.
- Personal identity.
- Form of leave or descriptor of benefits (e.g., disability leave; disability insurance)

In organizations, the legal implications of disability and simultaneous association of disability with temporary or permanent leave may perpetuate some forms of stigma and general apprehension to fully embrace disability as a form

Table 2.1 Definitions of Disability

Source	Purpose	Definition
ICF[5]	Various clinical, research, economic, and policy purposes	An outcome of interactions between health conditions (diseases, disorders, and injuries) and contextual factors
ADAAA, EEOC, Rehabilitation Act[9]	US Federal Law	A physical or mental impairment that substantially limits one or more major life activities, a person who has a history or record of such an impairment, or a person who is perceived by others as having such an impairment
BLS and CPS[11]	Data tracking on disabilities and employment in the US	Endorsing one or more of the following questions: being deaf or having serious difficulty hearing, being blind of having serious difficulty seeing, having serious difficulty concentrating, remembering, or making decisions due to a mental, physical, or emotional condition, having serious difficulty walking or climbing stairs, having difficulty dressing or bathing, and having difficulty doing errands alone due to a physical, mental, or emotional condition

of diversity. I discuss issues of stigma and disability as a diversity category in Chapters 4–6.

2.1.4 Chronic Health Conditions as Disabilities

As I will detail in Section 2.2, the legal definition of disability and, consequently, whether certain CHCs may be considered disabilities under US law, has changed over time. The law is currently interpreted to cover physical or mental impairments, and impairments are broadly defined. Therefore, many workers with CHCs have legally qualifying disabilities. However, *many people with CHCs do not consider themselves to have a disability or be disabled.*

What leads people with CHCs to identify as having versus not having a disability? A *disability identity* is a social identity, or a part of a worker's self-concept that is defined by having a disability.[8] Disability identities at work are informed by several factors, including:[8]

- one's evaluation of their impairment as affecting their daily life and work,
- the relevance of the impairment to the work context,
- how stigmatized the impairment is at work,
- the climate of the employing organization for inclusion, flexibility, and accommodations,
- the societal-level legal and sociocultural context one is working in, and
- the attitudes of one's supervisors and coworkers. For example, if coworkers of a person with a CHC communicate negative attitudes about disabilities, they will be less likely to identify as having a disability at work.[8]

All of this is important for leaders like yourself to know because identifying as disabled has implications for self-identification/reporting of disability status in the workplace. As I will explain in Chapter 4, disclosure of a disability can be beneficial for both the employee and the organization by directing needed supports to help workers perform to their best capacity. And disclosure of a disability in employment records is helpful for organizations in terms of meeting federal reporting guidelines and ensuring a diverse workforce that includes workers with disabilities.

What percentage of people with disabilities identify as such? That is unknown, but evidence suggests that workers may be increasingly open to identifying as having a disability in employment records. Under US law, Section 503 of the Rehabilitation Act, the federal government, contractors, and subcontractors track percentages of workers with disabilities by asking job applicants and employees to voluntarily self-identify as having a disability using a form that explains what disabilities are and provides examples.[12] In 2014, 8.68% of the federal workforce reported having a disability, and that percentage increased to 9.52% in 2018.[13]

Similar trends in increased reporting have been observed elsewhere. Meg O'Connell from Global Disability Inclusion and Dr. Peter Rutigliano from Mercer have collected disability status data from engagement surveys of over three million employees in 66 different organizations around the world annually since 2011. They found that disability disclosure rates were stable at around 3% until 2017, when they began to increase, reaching 5% in 2019 and 6.2% in 2020.[14] Their lower disclosure rates compared to the Section 503 rates could reflect differences in information gathering and/or the inclusion of more private sector organizations in their data sample, for which regulations do not apply.

2.2 US Law

> I told the client and the project manager that I had health issues and would need accommodations and now 2+ years later "they didn't know" that the ADA applied or that they need to do anything. It's frustrating because I have a legal and moral case, but they're well known for getting nasty and finding reasons to fire people when they feel people are causing issues so I can't go in and tell them what they need to do. I have to hint around and ask questions rather than make a phone call to HR or someone who can help so they don't come after me ... I also know I could get compensation, but it would take too long and I've got a family to feed. I am very hopeful that I'll find a better place to work. I'm even hopeful that I'll find somewhere more accepting ... It's the anxiety of sitting here waiting for the other shoe to drop that's driving me nuts.
>
> —public relations associate with undifferentiated connective tissue disorder, age 38

In the following sections, I describe US laws that are relevant to CHCs in the workplace. It is important to remember that this information should not be used in lieu of working with an employment attorney.

2.2.1 Preventing Disability Discrimination: ADA and ADAAA

The ADA is US law, passed in 1990 by President George H. W. Bush, that prohibits discrimination on the basis of disability in employment, state and local government activities (e.g., education), public transportation (e.g., subways), public accommodations (e.g., restaurants), commercial facilities, and telecommunications.[15] Employment is covered under Title I of the ADA, which states that *all employers with 15 or more employees must provide qualified disabled individuals equal opportunities to benefit from employment that are available to others.* Title I prohibits disability discrimination in all employment functions, including recruitment, hiring, promotions, training, pay, benefits, job assignments, firing, layoffs, and social activities. Some of the most common disability discrimination complaints relate to harassment, reasonable accommodation, disciplinary action, terms and conditions of employment, and time and attendance issues.[13]

The ADAAA is an amendment to the ADA that was passed by US Congress in 2008 and signed by President George W. Bush. The ADAAA was created in response to a series of US Supreme Court decisions that made it difficult for plaintiffs with impairments such as cancer, epilepsy, and diabetes to demonstrate that their impairments qualified as disabilities under the ADA. A goal of the ADAAA was to refocus on the *discrimination*, rather than whether the disability "qualifies" as such under the law. The ADAAA emphasizes that "disability" should be broadly defined and is not limited to certain conditions, with the goal of making it easier for a person with a disability to establish that they have a disability and gain protections of the ADA.[16]

Specifically, the ADAAA *added "major bodily functions" to the existing "major life activities" provision* of the definition of disability, and these include (but are not limited to) functions of the immune system, normal cell growth, digestive, bowel, bladder, neurological, brain, respiratory, circulatory, endocrine, and reproductive functions. This is in addition to major life activities, which include (but are not limited to) caring for oneself, performing manual tasks, seeing, hearing, eating, sleeping, walking, standing, lifting, bending, speaking, breathing, learning, reading, concentrating, thinking, communicating, and working. The ADAAA states that such impairments are generally to be regarded as disabilities *regardless* of whether "ameliorating measures" such as devices or medications provide "mitigating effects" on the impairment.[10]

The ADAAA also changed how "substantially limits" is defined—stating that an impairment does *not* have to prevent or significantly restrict a major life activity to qualify as a disability—it only needs to *limit the life activity* compared to most people in the population. Determination of "substantially limits" is made from an individualized assessment, yet should not require extensive medical or scientific analysis, and should be construed in favor of expansive coverage.[17] Overall, it is important for organizations and individual leaders to recognize the legal landscape as expanded to be more inclusive/encompassing of what a disability is, and that consequently, CHCs are typically qualifying disabilities.

Although there is no list of CHCs that are automatically considered disabilities under the ADAAA, there are some impairments that will almost always constitute a disability due to their impacts on bodily functions (e.g., epilepsy, cancer, HIV, multiple sclerosis, major depressive disorder, cerebral palsy, muscular dystrophy, bipolar disorder, schizophrenia, post-traumatic stress disorder, obsessive compulsive disorder, and diabetes). For example, diabetes substantially limits endocrine function; long COVID affects lung, heart, brain, and circulatory systems.[18] In addition, the ADAAA specifies that an impairment does not need to be perceived by the employer to limit a major life activity to qualify for protections. This means that regardless of how you or others in your organization perceive the impairment, it may qualify for ADA protections, and it is best to work with human resources when receiving an ADA-related request to ensure fair treatment of the disabled employee.

Yet there are limits to what is considered a disability under the ADAAA. Impairments that are transitory—lasting six months or less—do not qualify under the ADAAA. Also, individuals currently engaging in illegal use of drugs do not qualify as disabled based on their drug use under ADAAA. Further, the ADAAA states that employers do not need to accommodate individuals who are regarded as having an impairment, yet do not actually have an impairment.[10] These limitations aside, the primary implication of the ADAAA revisions for workers with CHCs, those who lead them, and their employing organizations is that *most workers with CHCs will qualify for disability discrimination protection under the ADA.*

Disability discrimination under the ADA may be categorized as either unfair treatment in employment functions (e.g., hiring, promotion, termination) or harassment, when it is frequent or severe enough to create a hostile work environment. Harassment was the top alleged issue represented in EEOC complaints in 2018, with 2,011 based on physical disability and 1,252 based on mental disability.[13] Harassment can be perpetrated by anyone in the employing organization, as well as those external to the organization, such as customers or clients.[19] This means it is critical for organizational leaders to take a zero-tolerance approach to harassment and actively promote a culture of inclusion of people with disabilities. I detail strategies for this in Chapter 6.

Examples of cases in which organizations were found to violate the law through unfair treatment of employees with disabilities in employment functions or harassment based on a disability are provided in Table 2.2.

2.2.2 Other ADA Provisions

It is important for hiring managers to know that the ADA *prohibits pre-employment questions about the existence, severity, or nature of a job applicant's disability*. This may lead some to think that they may not ask about applicants' abilities to perform essential job functions. However, this is a myth—in reality, employers are free to ask about an applicant's ability to perform job functions, with or without reasonable accommodations.[19] For example, if a job applicant, Melinda, arrives to an interview for a job as an administrative assistant using a cane to aid mobility, the interviewer(s) may not ask why Melinda is using a cane or if she has a CHC or other disability. However, interviewers may ask Melinda whether she can perform an essential task of the job (e.g., lifting reams of paper to refill the copy machine)—with or without an accommodation.

Employers are required to *provide reasonable accommodations*: modifications or adjustments to the work environment, job tasks, or work structure to allow a worker with a disability to interview for a job or fulfill work role responsibilities, under the ADA. Reasonable accommodations are provided at *pre-employment*, to ensure equal opportunity in the hiring process for job applicants, and *during employment* to allow a worker equal access to performing job functions. A reasonable accommodation for a retail worker with a CHC that causes fatigue when standing is a stool they can sit on when not actively helping a customer. It is critical to ensure that workers who need reasonable accommodations can access them. Failing to provide reasonable accommodation was the second-most common complaint to the EEOC in 2018.[13] Examples of reasonable accommodations are in Table 2.3.

Importantly, ADA protections only apply to workers who can perform essential job functions with or without a reasonable accommodation. Employers are not required to remove essential job functions from a job to accommodate a disabled worker or job applicant. How are essential job functions determined? Primarily, job descriptions prepared for advertising positions are used to help determine essential functions.[24] As such, organizations should retain completed, updated job analysis information that is used

Table 2.2 Examples of Disability Discrimination Cases

Date	Company	Action	Determination	Settlement
2022	S & C Electric Company, Illinois, US	Employee of the company for 52 years was not allowed to return to his former position after taking medical leave to recover from cancer and a broken hip, despite medical clearance.[20]	Unfair termination	$315,000, plus requirements to provide the EEOC with records of similarly terminated employees and provide ADA trainings conducted by outside trainers to all managers and human resource professionals at S&C[20]
2022	Ranew's Management Company, Inc., Georgia, US	Employee experienced suicidal thoughts and informed the CEO that he needed help. The employee attended an outpatient program for five days, during which time he was diagnosed with major depression, and doctors recommended he take leave from work for treatment.[21] Initially, the CEO was supportive, but later terminated his employment, despite the employee receiving medical clearance to return to work.[21]	Unfair termination	$250,000, plus requirement to train managers and staff on ADA compliance
2018	Mine Rite Technologies, Wyoming, US	Iraq war veteran employee was subjected to repeated harassment for his PTSD. Supervisors referred to "Psycho Thursdays" because the employee attended therapy on Thursdays.[22] Supervisors also referred to the employee as "psycho," "crazy," and "loony." Business owners did not act to address the harassment.[23]	Harassment	$75,000, plus requirement to train all employees on ADA compliance and provide the employee with a letter of apology and a job recommendation

Table 2.3 Examples of Work Accommodations by Common Symptoms

Symptom	Examples of Accommodations
Fatigue	• Provide anti-fatigue mats for standing • Provide stools or chairs to allow sitting breaks • Provide flexible scheduling • Allow flexible breaks • Provide a nap area • Allow control over when to complete demanding tasks • Shorten the length of shifts
Pain	• Conduct ergonomic assessment and make needed changes to work station and work tools • Reallocate duties that require lifting and bending or twisting the body • Reduce the need for lifting by reorganizing items and/or providing lifting equipment • Provide mats to reduce impact of standing for long periods • Provide stools to allow breaks from standing • Provide flexible scheduling • Allow flexible breaks • Allow control over when to complete demanding tasks
Cognitive Issues (e.g., "Cognitive Fog" or "Brain Fog")	• Allow flexibility or leave time to attend counseling or coaching • Provide software or devices to help with tracking and remembering tasks and meetings • Provide work instructions in writing • Provide extra time for task completion • Allow flexible work breaks • Relocate workstation to a quieter part of the office • Allow use of noise canceling headphones • Restructure work to allow blocks of uninterrupted work time • Allow control over when to complete demanding tasks

to create job descriptions. Examples of other criteria that may be used to determine essential job functions include:[25]

- Whether the job exists to perform the function
- Whether there are limited or no other employees qualified to perform the function
- Whether the function is highly specialized and requires expertise or skill that person was hired to use
- The consequences of failing to perform the function
- The amount of time spent performing the function

Determining essential job functions and accommodations can be complex, and while supervisors are generally not trained on these issues, HR professionals are. Supervisors and hiring managers should work with HR on these issues and not try to go it alone. HR professionals are also trained in job analysis, which, as mentioned, is critical for determining essential job functions and reasonable accommodations. As a supervisor, you should generally know that there are processes to follow, and you can typically find support for these processes HR. You may need to ask questions and seek support when you have an employee with a CHC.

It is important to remember that when requesting an accommodation, employees do not need to use formal ADA language, and they do not need to request their accommodation in writing. This means you should be attentive to recognizing such requests and clarify whether the employee is asking for an accommodation when in doubt. Employees also *do not need to state what their specific CHC is*—however, they do *need to state their limitation*. For example, an employee could request an accommodation by saying, "I need to take one half day off work each month to attend a medical appointment." Ideally the request initiates an informal, cooperative discussion with the supervisor to help meet the employee's needs while ensuring job tasks are completed. The employer is *free to ask what type of accommodation is needed*. The employer must *limit the scope of medical questioning*, yet they *may request medical documentation* of the need for an accommodation if the disability is not apparent.[26] Again, this is likely to be handled through your organization's HR department, and you should work with them when receiving a request for a reasonable accommodation.

In contrast to myths that accommodations are costly to implement, *most reasonable accommodations are inexpensive*. The Job Accommodation Network found that of 1,029 surveyed employers who provided cost information, 56% said the accommodations *cost nothing*, and 37% said that they incurred a one-time only cost. Of those with a one-time cost, the median expenditure was $300.[27] Further, 67% of employers who responded stated that the accommodations they implemented were effective or very effective, with many saying they allowed them to retain a valued employee and increased the employee's productivity.[27] The Job Accommodation Network has lists of possible accommodations by disability, limitation, and work function on their website, listed below in Additional Resources.

An accommodation request may be characterized as imposing *undue hardship* if it requires significant difficulty or expense to implement, or if it is unduly disruptive or would fundamentally alter the nature of the business.[26] When evaluating whether an action is considered undue hardship, the nature and cost of the accommodation, overall financial resources of the organization, and the number of people employed at the organization are some factors to be considered. US court cases have demonstrated that it is not enough for larger organizations to show that local business units are affected by the expense of an accommodation—instead, they need to show a measurable impact on the overall larger business. Examples of cases with rulings against undue hardship claims are in Table 2.4.

Issues around essential job functions, undue burden and accommodations have come to light for many organizations as a result of the move to remote work during the COVID-19 pandemic and subsequent return to the office. When considering accommodation requests for continued remote work, organizations should consider whether being in-person is an essential job function. Certainly, some jobs require a worker to be present in-person to perform essential job duties. The EEOC maintains that "An employer should not, however, deny a request to work at home as a reasonable accommodation solely because a job involves some contact and coordination with other employees. Frequently, meetings can be conducted effectively by telephone and information can be exchanged quickly through e-mail."[29] Further, according to the EEOC, workers with qualifying disabilities who wish to remain working remotely after temporary telework ends may have a case against employers who refuse this accommodation, in light of

Table 2.4 Rulings Against Undue Hardship Claims by Organizations

Case	Reasonable Accommodation Request	Hardship Claim	Outcome
Searls v. Johns Hopkins Hospital (2017)	A deaf woman who was offered a nursing job requested an American Sign Language interpreter and was denied by the hospital.	The hospital claimed that the cost of providing an interpreter constituted an undue hardship to the local unit, and rescinded her job offer.	The court looked not just at the cost to the local unit but considered the hospital's full operational budget of $1.7 billion and ruled against Johns Hopkins' undue hardship claim.[28]
Kane v. Carmel Central School District (2014)	A teacher with multiple sclerosis who used a wheelchair needed a power door assist and a ramp to enter the building.	The school refused, claiming undue hardship based on cost.	The court criticized the broader school district for not considering its overall budget, as well as the benefits of providing these accommodations and court concluded that the school did not demonstrate undue hardship.[28]

their demonstrated ability to successfully perform work remotely during the temporary telework period.[30] This may make undue burden more difficult to prove. Ultimately, as the EEOC underscores, the accommodation process should be a collaborative one that seeks to meet the needs of both the employee and the organization.

2.2.3 Rehabilitation Act of 1973 and Sections 501, 503, 504, and 508

The US Rehabilitation Act of 1973 was signed into law by President Richard Nixon and amended by Congress in 1992. It outlawed disability discrimination in programs sponsored or funded by federal agencies and in employment by federal agencies and contractors of the federal government. The standards for determining discrimination and definition of disability are the same as described for the ADA and ADAAA in Section 2.2.1.

Section 501 of the Rehabilitation Act prohibits disability discrimination in the federal workforce, and unlike the ADA, does not have minimum employee numbers to trigger coverage. Section 503 prohibits disability discrimination in hiring, and requires affirmative steps to hire, retain, and promote people with disabilities, for all employers with federal contracts or subcontracts.[31] Section 504 extends protections for any program or activity receiving federal money or being run by a federal agency, and Section 508 mandates accessibility in information technology by federal agencies for all people with disabilities, including not only employees, but the general public as well.[31]

Section 503 is particularly important for employers, as it both extends legal obligations to federal contractors and requires affirmative action steps in employment functions for people with disabilities (e.g., hiring, retention, and promotion). It mandates a 7% representation goal and adds a requirement that job applicants and employees are invited to self-identify as having a disability.[31] Although failure to reach the 7% goal will not lead to fine, penalty, or sanction, when the goal is not met, the contractor must take steps to determine whether impediments exist and how to remedy them.[32]

2.2.4 Family and Medical Leave Act

The Family and Medical Leave Act (FMLA) of 1993, which was signed into law by President Bill Clinton, allows workers to take up to 12 weeks of unpaid leave in a year to care for their own serious health condition or to care for a family member (newborn, adopted or fostered baby or child; seriously ill child, spouse, or parent) without losing their jobs. All US employers with 50 or more employees within 75 miles of the employer are subject to FMLA.[33] Employee eligibility for FMLA leave is based on tenure and hours worked—the employee must have worked for the employer for 12 months and worked 1,250 hours during the 12 months prior to the start of leave to be eligible.[33]

Importantly for workers with CHCs, FMLA leave may be taken intermittently or to create a reduced work schedule when medically necessary. *Intermittent leave* allows a worker to take leave in blocks; a worker with lupus may need to take three weeks of leave to deal with an unexpected disease flare-up in March, and another four weeks of leave to deal with another unexpected flare up in October. As another example, a worker with rheumatoid arthritis who needs monthly infusions at a hospital may need to take one day of FMLA leave per month. Notably, employees must make reasonable effort to schedule planned treatments so not to disrupt business operations.[33] A *reduced schedule* refers to cutting back the employee's typical work schedule. For example, a worker with major depression may need to work six-hour days instead of eight-hour days while their depression is active. In cases of intermittent or reduced schedule leave, employers may temporarily transfer the employee to a different job that can better accommodate the leave schedule, as long as pay and benefits do not change.[33]

CHCs must be considered "serious" to qualify a worker for FMLA leave. This may be demonstrated by the need for ongoing medical treatment under the care of a healthcare provider, and the CHC causing periods of episodic disability.[33] Medical certification from a healthcare provider is required; yet this must be handled with privacy in mind, and direct supervisors may not contact healthcare providers for information on an employee's health. Instead, contacting the healthcare provider for certification should be done by human resource professionals or leave administrators. Employers also may not ask an employee to sign a waiver of their rights to medical record privacy.[33]

Additional complexities around FMLA leave exist; different coverage (Title 1) applies to certain limited US federal employees. Similar to the ADA, FMLA leave can be complex to administer, and supervisors should work with HR professionals in their organizations to ensure fair and effective administration of leave.

2.2.5 Health Insurance Portability and Accountability Act

Privacy and confidentiality, of course, are of the utmost importance when dealing with employees' health information. The US Health Insurance Portability and Accountability Act (HIPAA), enacted in 1996 by President Bill Clinton, is designed to protect patients' sensitive health information from being disclosed without their knowledge. There are many misconceptions about HIPAA, so let's cover the basics.

Some may be surprised that *employers and employment records are generally not covered by HIPAA*; instead HIPAA covers healthcare providers, insurance plans, clearinghouses, and business associates for healthcare-related transactions, including billing, payment, eligibility.[34] HIPAA only applies to employers in very limited situations, such as when they contact a health plan on an employee's behalf.[35] For example, if an employer contacts a hospital to ask about the status of an employee being hospitalized, the hospital is not allowed to disclose information about the employee's status unless the employee has signed a waiver consenting to the disclosure. If the hospital discloses information without the employee's consent, the hospital will be in violation of HIPAA, not the employer.[36] In addition, despite common misconception, asking for employees to submit proof of vaccination is not a HIPAA violation by an employer.[37] However, employers are subject to privacy and confidentiality rules set by the ADA and FMLA, and it is best practice to protect the confidentiality of workers' health information regardless.

2.3 Takeaways and Recommendations

- A person with an ADA-protected *disability* is someone who has a physical or mental impairment that substantially limits one or more major life activities, has a history or record of such an impairment, or is perceived by others as having such an impairment.
    - *Major life activities* also include bodily functions (e.g., endocrine function).
    - *Substantially limiting* is determined in reference to those without the impairment.
    - Impairments currently in remission qualify as disabilities *if they limit activities when active*.[10]
    - Although some workers with CHCs may not consider themselves to have a disability, most will qualify as having disabilities under the ADAAA.

continued

continued

- The ADA prohibits employment *discrimination* against workers with qualified disabilities for all US employers with 15 or more employees.
  ▷ *Discrimination* refers to unfair decisions or actions (e.g., harassment) in any employment function (e.g., hiring, pay, training, promotions, and termination).
  ▷ Discrimination also may occur when reasonable accommodation is withheld.
- ADA protections only apply to workers who can perform *essential job functions* with or without a reasonable accommodation.
  ▷ Organizations should be sure to have updated job descriptions based on job analysis information for determining *essential job functions*. This is a core HR function.
- The ADA prohibits *pre-employment questions* about the existence, severity, or nature of a job applicant's disability.
  ▷ However, hiring managers are free to ask about an applicant's *ability to perform job functions*, with or without reasonable accommodations.[19]
- Organizations are required to provide *reasonable accommodations*, that is, modifications or adjustments to the work environment or the job, to individuals with disabilities under the ADA.
  ▷ Accommodations must be provided both *pre-employment* (during the hiring process) and *during employment*.
- When requesting an accommodation, employees do *not* need to use formal ADA language. They also generally do not need to state what their specific CHC is, and they do not need to request their accommodation in writing.
  ▷ However, they do need to state their *limitation*, and employers may request medical documentation if the disability is not apparent.
- Most reasonable accommodations are *inexpensive* (< $300) and most employers report they are effective at improving worker retention and productivity.[27]
- Employers may claim a reasonable accommodation imposes *undue hardship* based on cost or disruption to the nature of the business.
  ▷ Organizations should only claim undue hardship based on cost if the expense has a *measurable impact on the entire business as a whole*.
  ▷ Organizations should carefully consider how essential it is for the employee to work without the accommodation when claiming undue hardship based on disruption.
- Section 503 of the Rehabilitation Act provides a 7% disability *representation goal* and mandates *data gathering for disability self-identification* for government contractors.
- The FMLA allows workers to take up to *12 weeks of unpaid leave* to deal with a *serious CHC* or care for a dependent or sick family member *without losing their jobs*.
  ▷ FMLA generally applies to all organizations with *50 or more employees*.
  ▷ Workers are eligible after one year of employment, with 1250 hours worked in the last 12 months.
  ▷ FMLA leave may be taken *intermittently* or to create a *reduced work schedule* when medically necessary.
- Managers should partner with trained HR professionals when determining accommodations and essential job functions and administering FMLA leave.

Quiz

1. Which organizations in the US are subject to ADA regulations?

    a. Those with more than 50 employees
    b. Those with more than 20 employees

c. Those with 15 or more employees, except for religious organizations
d. Those with 15 or more employees

2. Which of the following individuals would be considered to have a qualifying disability under the US ADA? Select all that apply.

   a. A person with a chronic disease that affects their immune system functioning
   b. A person with a hearing impairment
   c. A person with a health condition that is transitory (expected to last six months or less)
   d. A person who is suspected by their supervisor to have a neurological disorder

3. An employer may NOT ask a job candidate about _____, but they MAY ask a job candidate about _____.

   a. The candidate's ability to perform essential job functions with or without a reasonable accommodation; The existence, nature, or severity of a disability.
   b. The existence, nature, or severity of a disability; The applicant's ability to perform essential job functions with or without a reasonable accommodation.

4. What does an employee need to do to request a reasonable accommodation? Select all that apply.

   a. State the limitation they are experiencing in plain language
   b. State that they are invoking the ADA
   c. State their diagnosed chronic health condition
   d. Submit a formal written request

5. True or false: The EEOC maintains a list of chronic health conditions that are covered under the ADA.

   a. True
   b. False

6. Which of the following is/are true about reasonable accommodations in the US? Select all that apply.

   a. They are typically expensive to employers to implement
   b. They usually incur ongoing costs to employers over several years

c. They are typically inexpensive; most are one-time costs under $300
d. They are typically seen by employers as effective

7. Which of the following would likely be considered disability discrimination under the ADA? Select all that apply.

   a. Frequent and/or severe harassment of a worker with a health condition about their health condition
   b. Terminating employment of a disabled worker on the basis of their disability
   c. Failing to provide reasonable accommodation to a worker with a qualified disability
   d. Transferring a disabled worker who is unable to perform essential job functions with an accommodation to a different position for which they are able to perform essential functions.

8. True or false: When determining whether an accommodation will pose "undue hardship," the organization should look at their local business units rather than the business as a whole.

   a. True
   b. False

9. Which law extends legal obligations to federal contractors and requires a 7% representation goal for disability representation in their workforces?

   a. The ADAAA
   b. The FMLA
   c. The Rehabilitation Act Section 503
   d. HIPAA

10. The Family and Medical Leave Act (FMLA) is applicable to all organizations over _____ employees?

    a. 15
    b. 50
    c. 100
    d. 250

11. FMLA allows for 12 weeks unpaid leave for workers to care for an immediate family member or their own health condition. Which of the following are TRUE about FMLA? Select all that apply.

a. To be eligible for FMLA leave, an employee must have worked for the employer for 12 months and at least 1,250 hours in the year prior to the leave
b. FMLA leave may be taken intermittently throughout the year
c. Medical certification by a healthcare provider is needed for an employee to be eligible for FMLA leave
d. Direct supervisors of eligible employees should contact their employees' healthcare providers directly to discuss the employee's health condition.

12. True or false: HIPAA limits what an employer may disclose about an employee's health and work record.

    a. True
    b. False

Additional Resources

- Job Accommodations Network Listing of Disabilities and Accommodations: https://askjan.org/a-to-z.cfm
- Disability Identity Project: https://disabilityterminology.athersharif.com/#/
- About Universal Design: https://universaldesign.ie/about-universal-design

Answers to Quiz

1. d
2. a, b, d
3. b
4. a
5. b (False)
6. c, d
7. a, b, c
8. b (False)
9. c
10. b
11. a, b, c
12. b (False)

Chapter 3
Intervention Framework and Typical Approaches

Existing supports for workers with chronic health conditions (CHCs) in organizations typically center around wellness program offerings, job accommodations, and return-to-work (RTW) programs. While these supports are important and can be helpful to workers with CHCs, they are limited in that they are nonsystemic (i.e., focused on the individual worker and not the working environment, structures, or characteristics of the job itself) and/or reactive in nature (applied after work ability has declined to the point disability leave is necessary).

In this chapter, I start by providing a framework for understanding the different levels and targets of workplace supports/interventions. I then apply this framework to detail some of the more common supportive offerings to workers with CHCs, including wellness programs and RTW programs. In doing so, I point out some limitations of these common offerings and make a case for the need for more proactive and systemic approaches.

Because these more proactive and systemic approaches are detailed in depth in Part III of this book, I focus more on explaining existing approaches in this chapter—particularly around RTW. Readers will take away from this chapter an understanding of different categories of intervention, along with their potential benefits and limitations, and where they may be able to help make a difference in their organizations regarding these interventions. Readers will also gain focused knowledge of RTW programs, including how to help employees successfully return to work and remain sustainably employed.

3.1 Primary, Secondary, and Tertiary Intervention Framework

The public health model of intervention has three categories of intervention: *primary prevention* (preventing illness and injury), *secondary prevention* (risk-mitigating and reducing impact of existing disease or injury), and *tertiary prevention* (therapeutic and alleviating impact of existing illness and injury). This public health model of intervention has been applied to the workplace to categorize efforts to prevent workplace injuries and promote employee health and well-being.[1] Workplace primary prevention strategies apply to all employees in an organization and include, for example, efforts to decrease employees' exposures to hazards and stressors and offering flexible, predictable, or controllable work scheduling. Workplace secondary prevention strategies apply to employees at risk of stress, strain, and disease, and include, for example, providing stress management/resilience training and screening for early disease detection (e.g., diabetes screening). Workplace tertiary prevention strategies target employees with injuries, strain, or health declines, and include counseling programs, peer support programs, and return-to-work programs.

In turn, with some minor refinement, the public health model can be applied to explicitly highlight strategies that are supportive of workers with CHCs. In this refined model, the targets for secondary and tertiary intervention are employees with CHCs and the goals center around promoting work-related well-being and work ability as well as preventing disability leave and premature workforce exit. I highlight these strategies separately in this book because they are not currently part of dominant frameworks and intervention repertoires for employee health and well-being. The framework for strategies to support workers with CHCs is shown in Figure 3.1 and includes the following components.

- *Primary preventive strategies* are applied to all workers, and include strategies related to organizational culture, benefits, policies, and environment/design, as well as work design strategies to increase worker autonomy and supervisor support.
- *Secondary preventive strategies* are applied to workers with CHCs, and include job modifications/accommodations, individual coaching and mentoring programs, and group training programs.
- *Tertiary preventive strategies* are applied to workers with CHCs who have left work on disability leave and include return-to-work programs.

3.1.1 Primary Prevention Strategies

As reflected in Figure 3.1, primary prevention efforts are at the top of the lists to reflect their generally prioritized status to secondary and tertiary prevention efforts. Yet, despite their subordinate positioning, secondary and tertiary prevention efforts are integral pieces, particularly when primary

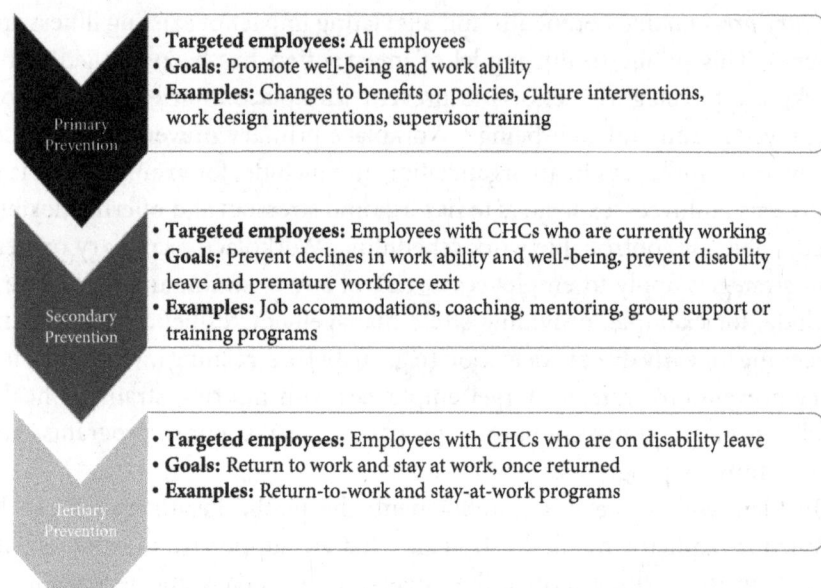

Figure 3.1 Framework for strategies to support workers with chronic health conditions

preventive factors are not able to be addressed and/or workers are at risk, as many workers with disabling CHCs are. Put another way, the subordinate status in Figure 3.1 of secondary and tertiary prevention efforts is meant to illustrate that that their effectiveness is somewhat dependent upon more systemic factors at the primary level. There are three reasons for this. First, primary prevention efforts have the potential to positively affect more workers than more targeted secondary and tertiary prevention efforts. Implementing changes to allow for flexible work arrangements can have a widespread positive benefit for most workers.[2] Second, primary prevention efforts address systemic issues that are often at the root of problems related to worker well-being and work ability, rather than the symptoms of such problems.[1] For example, flexible work arrangements can help workers more easily attend to family or health-related needs, reducing stress.[2] Third, without a foundation of organization and job-level supports, the utility of programs to help individual workers' well-being and work ability will be constrained. For example, coaching (secondary prevention) may help an employee build confidence to self-advocate to ask for an accommodation, but if the workplace culture (primary prevention) is unsupportive or the supervisor refuses to work with the employee, such efforts may result in backlash. Similarly, an employee may learn strategies to manage pain at work through periodic breaks to walk around and stretch but be unable to use them in a job that lacks autonomy to take breaks when needed.

I detail primary preventive strategies to support workers with CHCs in Chapters 6 and 7. For example, one worker with anxiety who participated in a recent study about strategies for maintaining work ability despite health-related hindrances stated that remote work helps her maintain her ability to work in her job as an administrative assistant despite her mental health condition.[3]

> My job right now is remote and depends more on completing the work by a certain time rather than sitting down at specified hours to do work. It's been really great for my mental health not having to go into an office all the time and work a fixed time period. I eventually start to grate up against any kind of forced structure and it starts affecting my sleeping and stress levels, so this has been wonderful.

3.1.1.1 Workplace Wellness Programs

Workplace wellness programs have elements of both primary and secondary prevention. These programs are commonly offered by organizations as part of employee benefits packages—54% of small firms and 85% of large firms in the US offer wellness programs.[4] Wellness programs typically promote healthy diets, regular exercise, and stress management in workers. They may also help workers quit smoking, and promote other behaviors that help prevent diseases and/or keep them in check (e.g., getting immunizations or early screening for preventable diseases).

Most firms are of the opinion that their wellness programs are effective in terms of improving worker health and well-being and that they are valued by workers as part of their benefits packages.[4] Unfortunately, rigorously designed studies have not found consistent evidence to suggest workplace wellness programs are providing a return on investment (ROI) in terms of reducing absenteeism or healthcare costs, or improving clinical health measures or worker job performance.[5,6] In their randomized controlled trial study of a workplace wellness program at BJ's Wholesale Club, a large retail company in the Eastern US, researchers Zirui Song of Harvard Medical School and Katherine Baicker of the University of Chicago found no significant differences in employee healthcare spending, healthcare use, clinical measures of health (blood glucose and cholesterol, blood pressure, and body mass index), or work outcomes (absenteeism, performance, and tenure) for wellness program participants compared to control group participants.[5] The researchers note that "to the extent that these results are representative of other wellness programs, they temper expectations of substantial improvements in health outcomes or financial returns on investment from wellness programs up to a three-year horizon."[5] Research findings such as these have led some experts to recommend that firms discontinue "overmedicalized" programs with extensive screenings, while continuing to offer lower-cost options such as healthier food options, exercise opportunities, and educational resources.[7] This might look like a wellness program offering with mental health support (e.g., access to a select number of free counseling sessions), gym membership reimbursement, exercise opportunities onsite (e.g., a walking track or paths), and healthier food options in vending machines or onsite cafeterias.

When interpreting these findings, it is important to note that it is remarkably challenging to properly evaluate wellness programs because, first, participation rates are generally low—particularly for health screenings.[8] And employees who self-select into wellness programs tend to be healthier to begin with and generally have lower healthcare costs (a key metric for ROI calculations) than those who choose not to participate.[6] Finally, participation of an employee in a wellness program might range from one immunization to full commitment to all aspects of the program. Collectively, these challenges may serve to obscure the potential impact of wellness programs.

Notable exceptions to the aforementioned wellness program ROI findings were observed for organizations with award-winning health and wellness programs. A series of studies of firms with the best-rated programs found that organizations with these award-winning programs enjoy improved financial gains in the stock market over firms that do not offer such programs.[9-11] While it is difficult to compare results from studies examining different outcomes (stock performance versus healthcare costs and worker productivity), a tentative takeaway is that the quality of the programs appears to matter in terms of the ROI.

Due to the primacy and foundational nature of primary prevention efforts noted at the start of this section, wellness programs will be limited in their effectiveness if they are not implemented within a broader culture and value of health in the organization. If jobs are not designed to be safe and promote well-being; if there is a lack of work–life balance; if mistreatment and harassment is allowed; if there is a lack of leadership commitment to worker health and well-being—then simply adding a wellness program is unlikely to yield benefits for firms. Employees are understandably cynical about efforts putting a sole focus on their behaviors to stay healthy and safe, while systemic structures and management go against such efforts. Wellness programs are also generally insufficient for supporting workers with existing CHCs in maintaining work ability, well-being, and employment longevity.

3.1.2 Secondary Prevention Strategies

Secondary prevention strategies are critical to support workers who are at risk of worsening outcomes, including declines in work ability and well-being, disability leave, and workplace departure. Many workers with CHCs are able to function well at work because they put most or all of their available cognitive, emotional, and physical energy resources into work. As such, they appear to be high-functioning and that they are not in need of support. Due to fears of backlash if they disclose their CHC, their own lack of acceptance of their current situation, a desire to prove themselves, or other factors, they may not ask for accommodations or other supports that could help them work more sustainably. Others may ask their supervisors for supports but not receive them or the supports may be inadequate. Prioritizing work, even when undersupported, may help them maintain employment for the short term, but puts them in a vulnerable state for worsening health outcomes, eventual declines in work ability, and possibly disability leave and turnover.

> I have learned to manage my illness in many ways, and have received excellent ratings in my job evaluations. My supervisor does not know about my illness ... My biggest health concern is that I am just managing everything, with little left over to really take care of myself. In particular, I don't usually have the energy to exercise and my family has a strong history of heart disease. I am concerned about the long-term effects of "living on the edge."
> —researcher with chronic fatigue syndrome, age 43

> It took everything I had to get up in the morning and push myself to get to that office and give it all I had, and when I came home at night I sometimes didn't even have enough energy left to eat dinner—I had to go straight to bed in order to get enough rest to get up and do it all again the next day. I gave up my social life for two years, had to forego holiday engagements ... I literally *had* to have those days off to rest and recharge, not to mention do my household errands like laundry and groceries and bills that I couldn't do all week, or I would end up missing even *more* days of work. I know I'm on my last legs with this job now and I'm on my way out the door ... was it only this particular job that was so difficult to manage with my illness, or is working at all going to be like this? Is this going to signal the end for me? Is this where I'm going to have to file for disability?
> —manager with rheumatoid arthritis and fibromyalgia, age 49

Secondary prevention strategies are specifically designed to help such workers avoid these outcomes, and leaders at all levels can play a pivotal role in these strategies—in terms of advocating for them to be implemented, suggesting them to employees who could use them, and helping facilitate employee access to them. As noted in Figure 3.1, they include work accommodations, coaching, mentoring, and group support or training programs. While such programs are most helpful when primary prevention strategies are in place, they can be effectively used to support workers even in the absence of primary strategies. This is important, because not all organizations are willing or able to change structural issues at the primary level. Secondary strategies can help workers cope, problem-solve, and plan in ways that allow them to work more sustainably and in a way that does not worsen their health and well-being.

Job/work accommodations are the most common secondary preventive strategy used to support workers with CHCs. And they are critical: as noted in Chapter 2, they benefit both workers and their employing organizations in that they help enable workers stay productive and perform to their greatest potential. Work accommodations can be formal, as requested and mandated through ADA protections, or informal, worked out in a cooperative manner between workers and their supervisors as needed. While the former have been associated with a more adversarial working relationship in some cases,[12] they are essential to ensuring workers have access to needed supports to continue working in all environments, even those that have less supportive cultures. Informal, creative accommodations worked out in a collaborative manner between workers and their supervisors are particularly beneficial for workers with CHCs[13] because, as noted in Chapter 1, most CHCs and their associated symptoms are intermittently disabling. Therefore, CHC-associated needs are likely to change over time, and in some cases, in unpredictable ways. As such, quality, supportive working relationships of employees with their supervisors is critical, as detailed in Chapter 7. Beyond working with employees on creative solutions to work challenges, supervisors can also help an employee feel comfortable disclosing a CHC so they can get the accommodations they may need. As noted in Chapter 2, formal accommodations will likely be implemented in conjunction with HR.

Beyond formal and informal work accommodations, other secondary preventive programs to promote work ability and well-being and prevent disability leave for employees with CHCs are very few, particularly in the US. Further, the ones that do exist are primarily small-scale ventures. One example of a secondary intervention aimed specifically at workers with CHCs to promote work ability and well-being is a coaching program I developed and tested with colleagues Rosalind Joffe and Dr. Joy Beatty. We provided 12 weeks of telephone-based coaching designed to help improve work ability and reduce strain through shared problem-solving, accountability, education, support, and reframing, in full-time workers with various CHCs in the US.[14] I detail this secondary preventive program and others in Chapter 8 of this book.

3.1.3 Tertiary Prevention Strategies

While it is preferable to avoid declines in work ability and disability leave when possible, through primary and secondary prevention efforts, some health challenges and working situations will necessitate disability leave, and accompanying tertiary prevention efforts. Tertiary prevention efforts focus on rehabilitation and return-to-work for those with CHCs who have had to leave work for some time due to disability. Tertiary prevention efforts are important to help workers recover and have successful reintegration with work. In addition to therapeutic rehabilitation they also may involve changing work, for instance, modifying the work environment, schedule, tasks, or other factors, or improving supervisor relationships to better accommodate continued work with the CHC once the employee returns. RTW and stay-at-work programs collectively are tertiary prevention efforts that provide early intervention to help workers get back to work as soon as possible after injury or disease and prevent another episode of disability leave.[15]

Although most people have probably heard of RTW programs to help workers who have left work on disability get back to work, fewer may be familiar with stay-at-work programs. Stay-at-work was added to the existing RTW vernacular around 2012, when the US Department of Labor recognized that social security disability insurance claims for permanent disability benefits were increasing at a rapid rate and that more preventive efforts were needed to help reduce social security disability insurance spending. One analysis found that US state governments would save an estimated $83,000 for each worker that was retained, versus replaced due to long-term disability.[16] Convinced that intervention was necessary, the US Department of Labor's Office of Disability Employment Policy was given funding to provide to states to develop and execute stay-at-work/RTW programs under the RETAIN initiative (Retaining Talent after Injury/Illness Network). These programs involve various stakeholders outside of employing organizations, including healthcare providers, state government entities, and insurance providers.

Stay-at-work represents an effort to expand thinking beyond RTW and to promote a more preventive focus for workers with CHCs who have experienced an episode of disability leave and are at risk for leaving again. As a newer concept, stay-at-work is not fully fleshed out or clearly defined;[17]

most research studies lump stay-at-work efforts together with RTW efforts, using the terms interchangeably or combining them as stay-at-work /RTW programs. Further, there is a lack of consensus among those who use the term as to what it means.[17] Some researchers focus on the length of time the worker has been back to work (e.g., four consecutive weeks) as a defining factor of stay-at-work; others view stay-at-work as more of a process, with periods of progress (rehabilitation and successful work) marked by periods of disability, leading to hopeful success where workers reach sustainable recovery and return to prior wages.[17] Regardless, it is important to note that to date, stay-at-work programs are mainly government-sponsored programs, and the uptake of these and other more preventive programs in organizations in the US is quite small. For this reason, the remainder of this chapter focuses solely on RTW programs instead of both stay-at-work and RTW programs.

3.2 Return-to-Work (RTW) Programs as Tertiary Prevention

Over two million workers in the US annually leave the workplace on disability, at least temporarily.[18] RTW programs aim to minimize time away from work and reduce the chances of the worker becoming permanently disabled and reliant on disability benefits (e.g., social security disability insurance in the US). Workers with CHCs in the US may take leave from work on a number of mechanisms, including FMLA (described in Chapter 2), through an ADA accommodation (also described in Chapter 2), worker's compensation (if the illness or injury is work-related), sick leave, and short- or long-term disability benefits (described in Chapter 6). However, if sick leave is brief (e.g., three days or fewer), it will not trigger disability benefits or the need for RTW programs.

RTW programs benefit individuals, organizations, and society. Maintaining employment is beneficial for *employees*, as it provides financial, social, and other important resources. Indeed, research finds that disabled individuals who are employed enjoy better quality of life than disabled workers who are not employed.[19-22] Additionally, a cost analysis findings suggest that workers who RTW after disability at age 50 stand to gain an estimated $422,000 USD in compensation and benefits versus leaving on permanent disability.[16] Returning employees to work also helps organizations in terms of retaining needed talent and spending less money on disability benefit payouts, and the economy by keeping people productively working, paying taxes, and off permanent disability benefits funded by taxpayers.

Managers play an important role in successful RTW for their employees.[23] Specifically, demonstrating inclusive behaviors when employees initially return to work (e.g., meeting with the returning employee and explaining RTW processes and any role changes, giving lighter or modified duties upon return) and displaying proactive support for employees (e.g., understanding the need for leave, making the employee feel they were missed when they were on leave, encouraging others to help, maintaining confidentiality, and remaining positive) are critical to successful RTW and linked to less sick leave, better well-being, and fewer work limitations for returning employees.[24] Additional supportive behaviors managers exhibit that help workers remain at work after returning include the following:[25]

- Reducing the employee's workload and encouraging the employee to adhere to workload reductions.
- Allowing for flexible work hours.
- Allowing for flexible work location.
- Having both formal and informal conversations about work and health.
- Providing long-term support through ongoing review of plans, graduated increases in workload, and increasing support during health flares.

Managers with lived experience of CHCs report having more empathy for returning employees, which helps them be supportive of returning employees.[25] Yet many managers experience significant challenges in providing support for returning employees. Lack of support from leaders and HR are commonly reported—senior managers are sometimes seen as focused solely on performance and being unsympathetic to the positions line managers are in regarding the need to support the returning worker.[25] Managers may also lack autonomy to implement supportive strategies to help returning workers or may face resistance from HR when implementing flexible supports for returning employees. This puts managers in a difficult position—unable to provide support in some cases, even when they desire to.

Another challenge managers face is a lack of knowledge of how to attend to the complexities of the RTW process.[25,26] Managers may not know what they can say to workers and end up not saying anything supportive out of fear. Managers may also not feel confident in determining and/or implementing work modifications or creating a positive team climate to support returning workers. Understanding the boundaries of support managers can provide is also critical—while they can't provide health-related advice or support, they can help make and implement work adjustments and provide work-related support.[25]

Thus, there is clearly also an important role for senior leaders in helping employees successfully RTW. Senior leaders should consider implementing training for managers on RTW processes and communication. In addition, senior leaders should be aware of and work through their own potential resistance to supporting returning employees and the line managers who desire to help ensure their successful transition back to work.

3.2.1 Components of RTW Programs

Reviews of RTW programs have identified the following common components across programs.[27-29]

- *Job accommodations.* These may include flexible working arrangements, an ergonomic assessment and changes to work equipment, or changes to working conditions or job duties. These may also include transitional or "light-duty" work as a worker recovers, before returning to prior job duties.
- *Information sharing*, typically through an *RTW coordinator* or case coordinator who facilitates communication between the worker and other stakeholders (physicians, insurance companies, and supervisors), helps the employee understand their benefits and responsibilities, and helps the employer understand their rights and responsibilities. This may also include technical assistance for a work adjustment or ergonomic modification.
- *Organizational policies* for workers and their supervisors related to, for example, when to report an injury or illness, cadence of communication between the employee and/or medical provider with the employer, training on the RTW program, and timely completion of forms.
- *Medical management* with a physician and/or other healthcare provider(s).
- *Other interventions* common to RTW programs for musculoskeletal disorders and mental health conditions include cognitive behavioral interventions focused on effective coping, improving self-efficacy, and facilitating problem-solving; educational interventions to promote self-care and/or pain management; and exercise programs to improve physical fitness.
- *Financial and other incentives and penalties.* Workers may receive wage replacement through workers' compensation programs or short-term disability benefits. Some programs include policies to counter "disincentives to work" including not allowing vacation time to accrue and only holding the job open for a predetermined length of time while the worker is out.

3.2.2 Effectiveness of RTW Programs

Are RTW programs effective in terms of return-on-investment and work outcomes such as successful return-to-work and stay at work, shortened sickness absence duration, and improved functionality and pain levels? Because RTW programs may divert investments away from other well-being efforts, is it critical to ensure they are cost effective.[30] Yet rigorous studies of RTW program effectiveness, including the "gold-standard" randomized controlled trials, are generally lacking, particularly in the US.[31] In addition, many studies have too few participants, and therefore low statistical power and unreliable results.[31] These research deficiencies are likely due to employers understandably being unwilling to have a sizeable group of workers in a control group not participate in a program that helps them RTW. In addition, employers may understandably be hesitant to allow researchers access to sensitive information.

Further, similar to the aforementioned challenges in studying wellness programs, there are different ways to define RTW programs. Programs may contain several of the components noted—or only one or two. Additionally, RTW programs tend to focus on one type of CHC (e.g., mental health disorders), and the majority of published studies examine programs for musculoskeletal disorders (MSDs) and mental health disorders.[31,32] It is unclear whether results from these studies would generalize to workers with other types of CHCs.[28] It is also important to note that individuals with greater levels of impairment are more likely to participate in such programs.[31] This is known as *selection bias*, and could possibly mask potential benefits from being realized in workers who have fewer functional limitations. In sum, we are only beginning to understand the effectiveness of RTW programs, and more high-quality research is needed.

Results of systematic reviews and meta-analyses (studies that aggregate findings across multiple independent studies of RTW programs) generally indicate that while some evidence exists for small effects of RTW programs on RTW, work absence, function, and pain levels, there is a lack of evidence for lasting effects of these programs in terms of staying at work and preventing future absences.[31-35] In addition, some researchers conclude that the overall evidence for effectiveness of RTW programs is generally weak and inconsistent.[31,32] This is especially true when looking at programs in the US, when looking at longer-term employment outcomes, and when considering returning and staying with the same employer versus including vocational training to find alternative employment.[31]

Research that examines specific components of RTW programs finds that contact with RTW coordinators is helpful for successful employee RTW.[36,37] This means that leaders should ensure their organizations have a designated

RTW coordinator to help ensure the success of their RTW programs. Organizational leaders can also help address the RTW evidence problem by allowing their programs to be rigorously evaluated and allowing such research to be published, contributing to the cumulative body of knowledge on RTW programs for a better understanding of what works and is worthy of investment.

3.2.3 Additional Factors That Affect Successful RTW

Beyond evaluating effectiveness of RTW and interventions, researchers have uncovered a number of personal and work-related factors that make successful RTW more likely for workers on disability. The amount of research on these factors is quite extensive; one meta-synthesis study revealed 94 systematic reviews on the topic—each integrating many individual studies.[38] Yet only some of the studied factors are modifiable, meaning they can be leveraged by organizations to help improve RTW outcomes, and I focus solely on these modifiable outcomes. The following modifiable factors are associated with more successful RTW and should be considered targets for intervention to improve RTW outcomes.[38]

- Individual worker factors:
    - Higher self-efficacy (i.e., confidence in one's ability to RTW)
    - Optimistic expectations for recovery and RTW
- Work factors:
    - Physical work demands (higher levels lead to worse RTW outcomes)
- RTW program factors:
    - Having an RTW coordinator
    - Using multidisciplinary interventions (i.e., those that target physical, psychological, behavioral, educational, and/or social aspects)

In addition, a growing number of researchers have found the following work and organizational factors facilitate RTW; these should also be considered as targets for intervention to improve RTW outcomes.[13,23,39,40]

- Work accommodations/modifications
- Supervisor attitudes, communication, and support for RTW (as detailed in the beginning of section 3.2)
- Coworker attitudes toward RTW and work group/team climate
- Human resource policies and practices (e.g., that promote motivation or allow for lateral career progression)
- Work design factors (e.g., autonomy, opportunities for breaks, avoiding high work pressure and high levels of physical demands)

In sum, this research points to several levers for leaders at different levels in organizations to facilitate positive RTW outcomes:

- Train supervisors on providing effective support and creating supportive team climates.
- Provide a RTW coordinator to directly interact with employees on leave.
- Examine work design factors, such as autonomy, the ability to take breaks, and intensity of work pace.
- Ensure alignment of HR policies and practices with successful RTW.
- Actively promote a supportive team climate for RTW.
- Implement appropriate work modifications or accommodations for returning workers.
- Provide coaching, mentoring, or training to build workers' confidence that they can successfully RTW.
- Ensure physical demands do not exceed a returning employee's abilities.

3.3 A Case for More Proactive Approaches

Of the three strategy categories, tertiary prevention is mainly reactive in nature—that is, RTW programs are meant to help workers with CHCs get back to work and stay at work once they depart due to CHC-related disability. While these programs are needed supports for workers with CHCs, and they appear to be at least somewhat effective in achieving their aims, they do nothing to prevent disability leave in at-risk workers who have not yet left due to disability. Considering this, alongside the unique work-health challenges listed in Chapter 1 that workers with CHCs face, it is clear that more proactive approaches to supporting workers with CHCs are needed.

Primary prevention efforts should be prioritized when possible, as they lay the foundation for successful secondary and tertiary prevention efforts. As detailed in Chapters 6 and 7, these include supportive organizational, supervision-related, and work design factors that benefit all employees when implemented. Secondary prevention efforts to specifically support workers with CHCs are also critical—yet beyond job/work accommodations, proactive approaches are currently sparse, particularly in the US.[13] In addition to benefitting employee well-being, taking a more proactive approach to preventing declines in work ability and disability leave may also benefit firms financially—potentially saving costs due to disability leave, hiring temporary replacements, and coordinating RTW. Chapter 8 will detail secondary prevention strategies, and Chapter 9 will provide a roadmap for an integrated proactive strategy, incorporating elements of primary and secondary prevention to help promote employee well-being and work ability.

3.4 Takeaways and Recommendations

- Strategies to support employees with CHCs include the following categories:
  - *Primary prevention efforts*, which focus on promoting well-being work ability of all workers.
  - *Secondary prevention efforts*, which focus on preventing declines in work ability and well-being, as well as preventing disability leave, turnover, and workforce exit for workers with CHCs.
  - *Tertiary prevention efforts*, which focus on helping employees with CHCs successfully return to work from disability leave.
- Establishing some primary prevention efforts first can help maximize success of secondary and tertiary prevention efforts to support workers with CHCs.
- Workplace wellness programs and RTW programs are insufficient to meet the work–health needs of workers with CHCs.
  - More proactive approaches incorporating primary and secondary prevention efforts are needed to support workers with CHCs.
- Job accommodations are important secondary preventive strategies.
  - Supervisors may work with their employees on informal, creative solutions to work challenges when appropriate.
  - Supervisors may help employees feel comfortable disclosing their need for supports.
  - Supervisors may work with HR to implement appropriate formal job accommodations.
- Managers can help their employees successfully RTW by:
  - Demonstrating inclusive behaviors when employees initially return to work.
  - Displaying proactive support for employees (e.g., making the employee feel they were missed when they were on leave).
  - Reducing the employee's workload and encouraging the employee to adhere to workload reductions.
  - Allowing for flexible work hours or location.
  - Having both formal and informal conversations about work and health.
  - Regularly reviewing plans, implementing graduated increases in workload, and increasing support during health flares.
- Organizations can help their employees successfully RTW by:
  - Providing training for managers on RTW processes and communication, along with providing effective support and creating supportive team climates.
  - Provide coaching or trainings to build workers' confidence they can successfully RTW.
  - Provide an RTW coordinator to directly interact with employees on leave.
  - Implement work modifications or accommodations for returning workers.
  - Ensure alignment of HR policies and practices with successful RTW.

PART II
CHALLENGES

Chapter 4
Work–Health Challenges for Workers and Practical Tips for Managers

Part II of this book contains information on challenges related to CHCs at work for employees, their managers, and their employing organizations. This chapter contains information on common challenges that are faced by *employees with CHCs*. I first provide information on two relevant theoretical models, the job demands–resources model and spoon theory, as organizing frameworks for understanding the challenges presented and how the proposed solutions in this book will be helpful. I then present workers' experiences related to work–health challenges, including those related to work–health management interference, maintaining work ability despite illness, experiencing stigma and discrimination, issues around disclosure and identity management, and career planning challenges. expanding on the information provided in Chapter 1. In doing so, I include quotes from participants in my studies to illustrate how these challenges play out in workers' lives. Alongside each challenge, I provide practical tips and considerations for managers and organizations. Readers will take away from this chapter an understanding of these challenges and how they affect employees, which will help set the stage for solutions presented both in this chapter and in Part III of this book.

4.1 Organizing Frameworks

Two frameworks are particularly helpful for understanding work-health challenges for workers with CHCs – the job demands-resources model and spoon theory. Before detailing challenges, I explain and apply these frameworks to CHCs and work.

4.1.1 The Job Demands–Resources Model and Work Ability

The job demands–resources model[1] is one of the most well-known and commonly used models of worker well-being.[2] The job demands–resources model categorizes working conditions into *job demands* and *job resources*, and proposes that each differentially predicts various worker *strains*, including exhaustion and disengagement (i.e., burnout) on the one hand, and worker motivation and engagement on the other hand. *Burnout* is a popular term that refers to *exhaustion* from work that stems from experiences of depletion. Like other forms of strain, burnout occurs in response to ongoing work stress that depletes an individual over time, particularly in the absence of adequate work resources. Therefore, burnout is different from experiences of work stress, which are more fleeting, but accumulate and can eventually result in burnout. The key and most critical feature of burnout is exhaustion, yet burnout is thought to also include *distancing one's self from work*, which has been alternately framed as cynicism or disengagement, or "quiet quitting."[3] On the other hand, *work engagement*, at least as it is defined in this model, is characterized by vigor (energy and willingness to exert energy in work), dedication to work, and absorption in work.[3–5]

According to the job demands–resources model, *job demands* are conditions that require ongoing exertion of effort to manage and are therefore depleting and can lead to burnout, particularly in the face of inadequate job or personal resources. Examples of job demands include time pressure, work overload, and exposure to environmental conditions, such as extreme heat or cold. *Job resources*, on the other hand, aid a worker in achieving goals, promote their growth and development, and/or mitigate high levels of job demands—and subsequently lead to work engagement. Examples of job resources include supervisor support, coworker support, and job autonomy.

The job demands–resources model states that job demands lead to strain, including burnout, and resources lead to motivation, engagement, and better job performance. Further, job resources are particularly important in the face of high levels of job demands, and can alleviate the negative effects of demands on strain.[6] The job demands–resources model was later modified to include *personal resources*, such as optimism and self-efficacy, which are thought to enable acquisition of more job resources and lead to work engagement and better job performance.[6] These basic propositions of the job demands–resources model are depicted in Figure 4.1.

The job demands–resources model has been also applied to understand worker's perceptions of their *work ability*, or their perceived ability continue working in their current job.[7–9] I will refer to work ability frequently in this book, as promoting and preventing declines in work ability is a main goal of the proposed intervention strategies herein (i.e., Chapters 6–9). This is

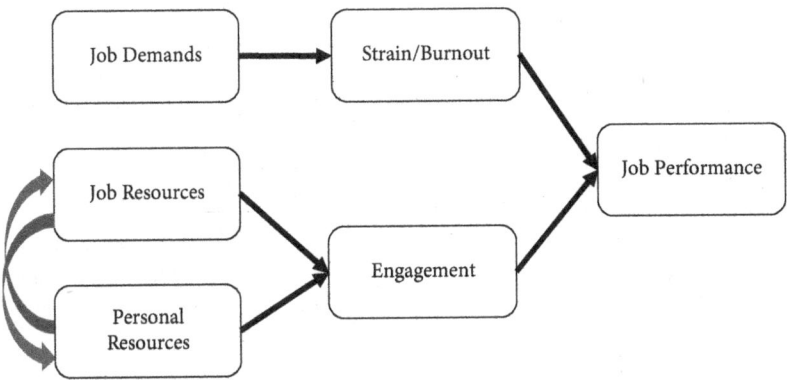

Figure 4.1 Basic propositions of the job demands–resources model

because research has consistently demonstrated that *work ability is a leading indicator of work absenteeism, disability leave, and early retirement.*[8,10–12] For organizational leaders such as yourself, intervening to improve work ability in the people you lead can help prevent some of these negative downstream effects.

This then begs the question of what types of factors can predict employees' perceptions of their work ability? Aligned with the job demands–resources model, *job resources and personal resources* are consistently associated with better work ability, and job demands are (to a lesser extent) associated with lower levels of work ability.[7–9,13] The following demands and resources are examples of those that have been found to relate to work ability.[7,8,14]

- Job demands associated with lower levels of work ability:
  - Harmful interpersonal behavior, such as bullying, and incivility.
  - Highly physically demanding work, such as heavy lifting.
  - Unfavorable body positions, such as bending or twisting.
  - Negative environmental conditions, such as extreme heat or cold.
- Job resources associated with higher levels of work ability:
  - Supervisor support, such as emotional support or practical support with work tasks.
  - Coworker support, such as listening to one's problems and providing advice or assistance with work tasks.
  - Autonomy, such as control over scheduling, work methods, or work decision-making.
  - Developmental practices, such as training or mentorship.
  - Perceptions of fair treatment at work, regarding decision-making and processes for decision-making.

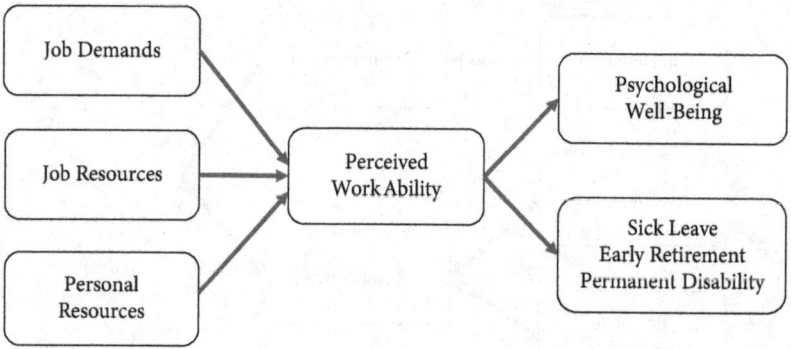

Figure 4.2 The job demands-resources model applied to work ability

- Personal resources associated with higher levels of work ability:
  - Sense of control (feeling like one has agency over their actions and outcomes)
  - Conscientiousness (degree to which one is detail-oriented, diligent, and organized)
  - Positive affectivity (degree of overall tendency to experience positive emotion)

An illustration of the job demands–resources model applied to work ability, well-being, and work withdrawal is in Figure 4.2. According to this model, excessive demands and a lack of work-related and personal resources will lead to lower work ability, which in turn will lead to declines in well-being and workforce exit. Therefore, *identifying ways to boost resources and prevent or mitigate the impact of excessive demands is important for intervention*, and I detail these approaches in Part III of this book.

Overall, the job demands–resources model is helpful for managers and other leaders in organizations to understand why their employees may be struggling and provides a lens through which to understand what effective supports may be and how they might help. The theory points to the need for managers and leaders to consider *boosting job resources* (Chapter 7) and providing *individual supports to help increase personal resources* (Chapter 8). Possible ways of doing so will vary significantly, depending on your organization and position.

Reflection Exercise 4.1

Take a moment to pause and think of ways you may be able to support one or more of your employees, in line with the job demands–resources model. Are there programs or other resources at your organization you may point employees to that could help boost their personal resources? Are there opportunities for you to work with employees to modify their jobs to either reduce demands or increase job resources, such as autonomy or support? Alternatively, if you are a worker with a CHC, think about potential ways you may be able to change your job or your working relationships to boost your job resources or reduce your job demands. Write your ideas here.

_____

_____

_____

_____

4.1.2 Spoon Theory

Spoon theory was coined by writer Christine Miserandino as a metaphor for explaining the physical and mental energy scarcity many who live with CHCs experience, and how it affects their daily lives.[15] Imagine a handful of spoons representing one's available energy for activities and tasks for a given day. Also imagine removing a spoon for each activity—for instance, bathing, grocery shopping, cooking food, caretaking, and work tasks. Each activity requires the use of one or more spoons and requires rest to replenish.

Many people with CHCs carefully plan their days to optimize the use of their spoons, requiring cognition and decision-making that many healthy people do not have to consider, and restrictions on activities many healthy people do not experience. For example, working full-time may mean having to restrict personal life activities outside of work. Further, unexpected activities requiring energy expenditure (e.g., an unexpected work shift; a work emergency requiring extra hours) may mean there is no energy left for self-care. To make matters worse, for many with CHCs, sleep may be difficult or nonreplenishing.[16] Fatigue-related issues are troublesome for many CHCs, including long COVID.[17] The participant quotes below illustrates energy-related issues.[18]

> It is very difficult to wake up exhausted and know you have to go into work for eight hours. I'm good for most of the morning, but then I feel the numbness in hands and legs (typing and sitting), my thoracic spine feels like there's a vice clamping on it, and I'm physically and emotionally exhausted. When I get home, I just sit there and try to recuperate for the next day, which is not near enough time.
> —**purchasing agent with ankylosing spondylitis, age 43**

While spoon theory did not originate from the scholarly literature, it is a valued framework in the chronic illness community. In addition to explaining experiences of energy use and fatigue, it helps differentiate the CHC community from the wider disability community. Namely, people with non-CHC disabilities often do not experience issues with energy scarcity and energy planning—at least not to the same extent as many people with CHCs. A main implication of spoon theory is that *unexpected depleting work activities, when chronic, are particularly detrimental to many workers with CHCs and should be avoided when possible or accompanied by adequate time for recovery*. If a worker is asked to stay late to meet a project deadline, for example, they should be encouraged to come in late the following day to allow adequate rest.

4.2 Work–Health Challenges

Now that we have gone through some common frameworks for understanding work ability, well-being, and stress in workers with CHCs, let's get into some common work–health challenges employees face. The categories of challenges in the following sections are those that are frequently represented in the research literature and that have been described by participants in studies my colleagues and I have conducted. I include several quotes from participants in my research studies in this chapter and throughout the book to provide nuance and perspective. To preserve participant confidentiality, I provide only some information about participants, including age, type of CHC, and job type.

4.2.1 Work–Health Management Interference

CHCs necessitate health management activities to prevent worsening disease, alleviate symptoms, and preserve functionality. For example, a worker with multiple sclerosis (MS) needs to be on a disease modifying drug to prevent worsening disease, which likely necessitates going to a facility for regular medication infusions or injecting oneself at home, alongside regular neurologist visits for medication management and follow-up. At the same time, the worker may also need to attend to their symptoms—such as going to physical therapy or occupational therapy to deal with muscle weakness due to nerve damage and/or pain, doing exercise or stretching routines at home to preserve physical function, going to counseling sessions to help manage stress and cope with and/or adjust to living with MS, and seeking complementary practices, such as acupuncture or massage therapy to address pain and fatigue. Many of these activities are only available during typical work hours, and further, require "spoons" (i.e., energy expenditure) and resources in line with the job demands–resources model (e.g., autonomy to schedule appointments during work hours and supervisor support to do so). A lack of such resources can create *conflict between meeting work performance expectations and adequately attending to disease- and symptom-management needs.*[18]

While health-promoting activities such as exercising, eating a healthy diet, and getting adequate and restful sleep are important for all people, they are especially important for those with CHCs. For example, sleep dysfunction is, not surprisingly, associated with chronic fatigue in people with MS.[19] Poor sleep can also lead to worsening chronic pain, and this relationship is reciprocal, such that pain exacerbations also lead to worsening sleep.[20]

My colleagues and I conducted a series of studies to examine what we termed "work–health management interference" in workers with CHCs. In a series of four samples of full-time workers with CHCs in the US, we found that work–health management interference is common amongst workers with CHCs.[18] Further, we found that work–health management interference includes time-based and energy-based interference, as time and energy are two critical resources that are allocated across life domains, including work and health maintenance for workers with CHCs. *Time-based work–health management interference* occurs when time or scheduling requirements of work interfere with health management activities for workers with CHCs.[18] *Energy-based work–health management interference* occurs when effort exerted to meet work roles and responsibilities exhausts energy needed to enact behaviors to manage a CHC.[18]

> My energy exerted in my job lowers my ability to treat my illness because I am mentally fatigued and physically fatigued at the end of the day. This causes me not to have the willpower or the energy to go to the gym or to eat healthy . . . This tiredness, time and energy spent at work causes me to want to overeat and not exercise and eat properly when I'm done with work, which negatively affects my diabetes and sleep apnea.
>
> **—video editor with type 2 diabetes and sleep apnea, age 39**

We found that high levels of work–health management interference is stressful, as it threatens maintenance of health (a critical resource), and is therefore associated with high levels of burnout and low levels of work ability. Fortunately, in line with the job demands–resources theory, job resources can help—job control has been found to mitigate some of the burnout workers experience from work–health management interference.[21] Due to the prevalence and negative outcomes of work–health management interference, organizations should be aware that workers with CHCs may experience it and *supervisors should work with employees to identify job modifications as* needed to help ensure sustainable work. As noted in Section 4.1, for example, after intense work to meet a deadline, *give workers time off to recover. Allowing remote work* is also likely to significantly help workers with CHCs, as it eliminates the need for commuting and requires less physical and social energy expenditure, which can then be reallocated to health management. Similarly, *allowing flexibility in scheduling* can permit workers to attend medical appointments during work hours, thus self-accommodating as needed.

4.2.2 Maintaining Work Ability Despite Symptoms

Workers with CHCs may also struggle to maintain work ability due to ongoing symptoms and the interaction of those symptoms with the nature or structure of work. In addition to time and energy depletion as discussed in 4.1 and 4.2.1, experiencing *chronic pain* can make work challenging for affected workers. Work-related challenges due to chronic pain may be classified into four categories: (1) activity interference, (2) negative self-perceptions, (3) interpersonal challenges, and (4) inflexibility of work.[22] In a study I conducted with Dr. Zachary Fragoso, we found that the first category, *activity interference*, was detrimental to workers in terms of emotional exhaustion, above and beyond somatic experiences of pain (i.e., pain severity).[23] Therefore, it is important to know that it is not just the experience of pain—though difficult to deal with—but the implications of the pain for work and other activities that drives distress in workers. *Giving your workers some control and flexibility over scheduling, breaks, and work task completion* can help with this, as it allows workers to self-manage (e.g., through stretching, walking, distraction from pain) and complete taxing activities when pain is at its lowest). It may also be helpful to *modify work and/or the working environment* to allow affected workers to minimize pain and continue working despite pain (e.g., provide an ergonomic setup and/or allow working from home).

In addition, work stress can exacerbate pain, creating a detrimental cycle.

> Work related stress and chronic pain diseases create a terrible cycle. Work creates stress which worsens pain. Worsening pain interferes with job performance creating more stress. I have an understanding employer but I disappoint myself constantly.
>
> —customer service representative with psoriatic arthritis and fibromyalgia, age 35

Researchers found that, for workers with rheumatoid arthritis who had high levels of job demands combined with low levels of job control, stressful events at work in the morning contributed to greater mid-day pain.[24] Yet when workers had *higher levels of control in their jobs, pain did not increase* with stressful work events—even when demands were higher. Further, the researchers ruled out neuroticism (propensity to experience negative emotion) as affecting the degree to which stress contributed to increased pain ratings. This study provides further evidence for the *importance of providing workers with autonomy/job control* to help them manage pain levels and stress, particularly in the face of high levels of demands (i.e., jobs that are fast-paced and/or require a lot of physical, cognitive, and/or emotional effort).

Another important work ability challenge is that CHCs often involve *intermittent* issues that are not resolved with a single period of disability leave or a single permanent work accommodation. So-called episodic disabilities arising from CHCs are temporary or transient, punctuated by periods of nondisability.[25,26] For example, a worker with major depression may experience a disabling flare-up, but once the flare-up is resolved, the worker is able to function as they were before the flare-up. In some cases, workers are unable to anticipate when disability flare-ups will occur, and the sudden disruption is difficult to cope with. In addition to dealing with a health crisis, workers may face financial challenges from having to take leave from work while incurring healthcare costs.

An important implication then for individuals working with and leading individuals with CHCs is that because they are many times unexpected, episodic disabilities are not well-addressed through more traditional, long-standing accommodations. This is where CHCs depart from many other types of disabilities, and where many challenges lie. An *understanding working relationship between supervisor and employee, characterized by open and effective communication around needs and informal accommodations* is critical in these situations for helping workers maintain work their ability and helping managers ensure work gets done. When possible, an employee-driven approach in which an employee and their direct manager work together and share responsibility for figuring out accommodations as needed and plans for work completion offers a more responsive solution than formal accommodations requests requiring medical provider input for workers with episodic disabilities/CHCs.[27]

4.2.3 Stigma and Discrimination

Many workers with CHCs face social challenges at work due to their CHC. These include decision-making and strategizing around disclosure of a CHC, effective communication about work-related needs, and impression management—desiring to appear healthy and capable. At the root of some of these issues is the legitimate fear of stigmatization, or devaluation at work based on their CHC, and the possibility of experiencing work discrimination based on their CHC.

Ableism refers to the devaluation of and prejudice and discrimination toward those with CHCs and other disabilities. Ableism occurs due to the inherent and mostly unexamined assumptions that ideal workers (and humans) are able-bodied and healthy. Values of productivity, independence, and resilience are fundamental and primary in most Western cultures, and disability is assumed to be counter to those values. As noted in Chapter 2, it is only when those with disabilities actively fight or "overcome" them (e.g., "cancer survivor" or "MS warrior") that they are lauded, and in those cases, they are often commodified as inspiration porn (as described in Chapter 2). There is a small, but growing cultural movement to explicitly reject ableism and promote love for one's self and body as they are,[28] but we will likely be in the grips of ableism for a long time.

How can one avoid ableism? As a first step, it helps to simply be aware that ableism exists. Everyone is ableist to some degree, as it is deeply culturally ingrained. Hiring managers may want to check their automatic reactions to job applicants, and all managers may wish to check their automatic day-to-day judgments of employees. For example:

- If you see an employee parking in an accessible parking spot, but they have no signs of visible disability, it is best to assume that they have a nonapparent/invisible CHC that requires use of accessible parking.
- If your employee is frequently absent or leaving work during the workday, ask them why without assuming ill intentions.
- If your employee has job accommodations, accept that the accommodations are needed, even if the employee appears to be healthy.

Ableism also tends to come out unintentionally in the language people use, so taking care to avoid certain words is also helpful—here are some examples that are commonly used but may be hurtful to people with disabilities:

- Using "dumb" to describe someone as unintelligent.
- Using "blind" to refer to someone as unaware.
- Using "insane" to refer to something as outrageous or nonsensical.
- Using "lame" to refer to something or someone as dry or boring.
- Using "victim" to refer to someone with a CHC (e.g., "cancer victim"), which is disempowering.
- Using "special needs" or "differently abled" instead of "disability," which implies disability is something bad or to be avoided.

Finally, I encourage you to consider going beyond ableism to *allyship* by being open and alert for opportunities to advocate for employees with CHCs. Research shows that effective allies at work demonstrate courage, perspective-taking, wisdom, perseverance, and patience—as well as intellectual humility (recognizing the limits of one's own knowledge, being willing to defer to the expertise of others, and demonstrating genuine respect for and curiosity about others).[29] Yet allyship does not have to be complicated or require specialized skills. I witnessed one form of allyship during the COVID-19 pandemic. Specifically, an organization called its employees back to the office at the height of the pandemic, and an employee with medical conditions that made her medically vulnerable to COVID-19 expressed concern to a supervisor about sitting in meetings, as no one else was wearing a mask in these meetings. Not only would she stick out for wearing a mask, potentially prompting questions or judgment, but she was afraid of getting sick from being in an enclosed area with many unmasked employees for long meetings. Her supervisor offered two potential solutions: she could call into the meetings remotely, or he would wear a mask to demonstrate allyship and in hopes others in the meetings would follow suit. His offering of these solutions meant a lot to this employee. How do I know? I am that employee, and I will never forget the kindness of these simple offerings from my supervisor. You can be that supervisor to your employees as well—if you pay attention and get to know your employees, you will find opportunities for allyship.

As noted, ableism is about discrimination, and unfortunately examples of *discrimination* against those with CHCs and other disabilities abound. One research study reported that *more than half* of the HR professionals and hiring managers surveyed agreed that employers discriminate against job applicants with disabilities.[30] Although we are well past legislation to outlaw more egregious and overt forms of work discrimination in the US (e.g., Civil Rights Act in 1964 and Americans with Disabilities Act, or ADA, in 1991), overt discrimination (unfair treatment at work, such as in hiring, promotion, or termination) still exists, in addition to more subtle forms of work discrimination (e.g., lack of verbal interaction or other social exclusionary behaviors).[31] In one study of 332 workers with CHCs, a graduate student and I found that 51% reported one or more experiences of work discrimination due to their CHCs.[32] Further, we found that experiences of discrimination were associated with compensatory behaviors to try to avoid discrimination (working harder and longer hours to prove one's self) and job-related strain.[32] These study findings align with those of many other studies that have found work discrimination to be generally associated with physical and psychological strains, along with negative work attitudes and behaviors in targets of discrimination.[33,34]

Examples of *subtle discrimination* in our study included others at work gossiping about the worker with a CHC, as well as ostracizing them or treating them with disrespect.[32]

> Because my illness is an invisible illness, many people think I am making it up or exaggerating. Having a fellow coworker who also has fibromyalgia has actually had a negative impact because she does not take care of herself, so other[s] expect me to also put work above my health. Because I choose to put my health first, I am seen as lazy, incompetent, and arrogant. I have become the bottom of the totem pole at work—often, others won't even talk to me anymore.
> —**unknown job title with fibromyalgia and depression, age 22**

Other examples of *subtle discrimination* in our study included lowered assumptions of capability and fewer opportunities for development.

> My work has been really accommodating in a number of areas. But they also seem to think I can do less than I actually can, or in different areas, and have changed my responsibilities to reflect that. They also stopped bringing me to meetings with members and clients, I think because they don't like the members to see me walk with a cane.
> —**administrative assistant with psoriatic arthritis, age 32**

An example of *overt discrimination* reported in our study is failing to accommodate a worker with a qualifying CHC-related disability (as discussed in Chapter 2).

> I am now a mail carrier . . . the Monday before this Christmas I had to work overtime in the dark with a headlamp. I believe the stress of being out in the dark, not knowing where the toilets are (and holiday eating no-no's) caused the current flare of my disease which is giving me a lot of pain and diarrhea. I want to take more time off when I am hurting but . . . my current supervisor . . . doesn't understand when people have to limit their overtime. What, will you turn into a pumpkin after eight hours?
> —**mail carrier with Crohn's disease, age 49**

> I am a teacher . . . and our new principal has shown no understanding or sympathy. It took two meetings with the assistant director of HR, along with union reps and doctor's notes, to allow me to have bathroom breaks and to be excused from late-night activities. The principal has not spoken to me since. The previous principal, after I had taken a day off to rest (covered under my FMLA form), passed along the information that other teachers thought I was taking advantage of my health

situation to get a day off. If she did not also believe that, why would she say that to me? As a result, I felt I had to push through my fatigue until I got so sick I needed a doctor's visit.

—teacher with chronic fatigue syndrome, fibromyalgia,
and ankylosing spondylitis, age 52

Other *overt discrimination* experiences in our study included threats to job security, termination, being scrutinized or otherwise treated differently.

I had unrealistic expectations put on me when I moved to another department. The supervisor said she needed to know what I was made of, the other person hired at the same time as me with the same experience did not have the same expectations. I get spied on. When I go lie down on my break (in the work meditation area) I am watched and timed... They tried to fire me by making up accusations but each and every investigation has proved I never did anything wrong... My work evaluations are always "meets or exceeds expectations" yet they don't leave me alone, they always try to find something on me... I think they just are trying to push me over the edge since I had to take time off for depression.

—unknown job title with clinical depression, anxiety, and chronic
fatigue syndrome, age 38

Further, due to the invisible nature of the CHC, it is unfortunately common for managers and coworkers to be skeptical that accommodations are needed, leading to discrimination.

My biggest issue is that I have no outward physical manifestation of my chronic illness. I look fine! My symptoms—pain and fatigue—tend to hit me hardest towards the end of the day and ruin my evenings... My accommodation has allowed me to work on projects in which I can pace myself, but some of my colleagues are resentful... despite my disclosure (they all seem to have forgotten about it) and my manager... says I may end up losing a level of seniority and HR is worried I am getting a free ride and working less than others, so they are making me track my hours while no one else has to! There are times it all just seems so silly and laughable. I am a professional—a lawyer—and at a relatively high level in the company, and I think they just don't know how to handle me. In this conservative [area of the US] town, invisible disabilities due to a rare disease no one has heard of I think just raise some skepticism, which just adds another burden to me, in addition to never knowing when or whether I will have another attack and whether or not it will paralyze or blind me... I never in a million years thought I'd be dealing with these types of issues. I think the invisible disability issue, especially for women, is a huge one.

—attorney with a neurological condition, age 53

Intersecting stigmatized identities, such as being Black and having a CHC, being gay and having a CHC, being a woman and having a CHC, being an older worker and having a CHC, or any combination thereof can pose increasing challenges and disadvantages. This is due to compounding effects of stigma and bias—for instance, ableism, racism, sexism, ageism, classism, weight bias, and homophobia. *Intersectionality theory* asserts that the various social identities individuals have intersect in complex ways and are affected by power structures. Evidence for intersectional challenges may be found in the health literature; for example, one study found that health disadvantages for Black women are attributable, in part, to overlapping effects of racism and sexism in daily experiences.[35] Another found that ethnic minority women experienced more workplace harassment than ethnic minority men, ethnic majority men, and ethnic majority women.[36]

> I have already been fired from one place because of depression and being gay (the combo is what did it, just like my predecessor). The last place I left because another manager who was an "internal customer" according to my boss began hassling me with hostile combative and very derogatory language. I was forced to apologize to her after she accosted me, and I was to apologize for not accepting her verbal abuse with kind words and a promise to make her happy.
> **—senior analyst with fibromyalgia and ankylosing spondylitis, age 42**

Anticipating discrimination may lead an employee to avoid disclosing a CHC, when *disclosing could benefit both them and their employer by allowing them to get supports they need to continue to work productively* and remain employed in their jobs or organizations. Discrimination is also illegal in many nations and may result in lawsuits with restitution as described in Chapter 2. It also perpetuates a hostile work culture and stifles work performance—for example, when people feel threatened and stressed, they may experience lower cognitive function[37] and weakened ability to innovate.[38] I discuss strategies to build a culture of inclusion and support and avoid discrimination of workers with CHCs in Chapter 6.

Some of the information presented in this chapter may understandably raise fears or concerns from the reader about unintentional discrimination, and perhaps even lead to inaction due to fear. I want to be clear that by reading this book, you are part of the solution. You want to do the right thing by people with CHCs, and this book is meant to help empower you to have a better handle on what you can do. Inaction will not be helpful; attentiveness to opportunities to reserve judgment, or even be an ally will. Don't let fear stop you from making a difference. If you mess up, or you think you may have messed up, don't be afraid to ask, admit it and apologize.

4.2.4 Disclosure and Identity Management

Because many CHCs are invisible/nonapparent to others, or concealable with effort, workers with CHCs face decisions around *disclosure*. CHC disclosure decisions are multifaceted and can be complex. Workers with CHCs may weigh the pros and cons of disclosure, and may also make decisions such as, to whom to disclose (e.g., to HR, supervisors and/or coworkers), when to disclose, and how much information to provide (e.g., "I have a condition that requires me to be out of the office for a half day once per month for treatment" or "I have ulcerative colitis and need unrestricted bathroom breaks due to my symptoms").[39] This is something you, the reader, may have struggled with or may be something someone you work with has had to deal with.

With that in mind, it is important to recognize that workers with CHCs may find themselves wanting or needing to disclose a CHC at work for many reasons. For example, they may need or desire:

- Attaining a formal or informal accommodation to help them stay productive at work.
- Avoiding misattribution of their behaviors to lack of commitment (e.g., frequently leaving the office for medical appointments).[40]
- Accessing other protections and rights to US workers under the ADA.[40]
- Accessing social support from other workers.[41]
- Maintaining congruence in their social identity across life domains (e.g., work, non-work community, and family).[42]
- Alleviating preoccupation, cognitive resource expenditure,[43] and feelings of isolation.[44]
- Educating others or being an advocate for others with disabilities or CHCs.
- Alerting others for safety reasons, for example if they could have a seizure or faint at work.
- Explaining dips in work performance.[25]

In one study, 51% of 896 participants who were working at least 15 hours per week in Canada with a CHC disclosed their disability to a supervisor.[25] Those who disclosed reported a greater need for support, had more absenteeism, more work-related stress, longer tenure, and a better psychosocial work environment.[25] Interestingly, *women reported fewer positive outcomes of disclosure* than men, suggesting intersecting challenges of gender and CHC status, wherein women face greater barriers to support.[25]

Despite the reasons to disclose and the potential benefits of disclosure, there are also reasons workers choose not to disclose—for example, desire for privacy, not needing or wanting accommodations, and fearing discrimination, including job loss, social rejection, or being overlooked for career-enhancing opportunities.[25,45] There are also potential immediate downsides to the act of disclosure, including unsupportive, negative, or harmful reactions to disclosure.

It is important to note that *disclosure is helpful to supervisors and organizations* in many cases, as it opens the door to productive conversations and problem-solving to help a worker with a CHC perform to their best capacity. Organizations can help workers feel comfortable disclosing by creating a culture where worker inclusion and well-being are valued and empowering supervisors to be supportive through their words and actions. I detail related strategies in Chapters 6 and 7. Supervisors can help workers feel comfortable disclosing by building supportive, trustful relationships with their employees—a point I return to later in this chapter.

Of course, working with a concealable identity such as a CHC involves more than the simple act of disclosing versus not disclosing, and there are varying *identity management strategies* workers use in the workplace. These strategies range from explicit acknowledgment to complete concealment of a CHC. Identity management strategies may be roughly grouped into *passing strategies*, which allow a worker to be assumed to be healthy by others at work, and *revealing strategies*, or disclosing an identity in some way at work.[45] Some examples of passing and revealing strategies are defined, with examples, in Table 4.1.

> It is incredibly difficult to come to work every day, sometimes in extreme pain and with a fever, and try to work in sales with customers and act like there is nothing wrong. It takes an enormous amount of energy to do this.
> —**sales associate with rheumatoid arthritis, age 46**

As this quote illustrates, identity management—in this case, concealing—can be exhausting. This worker undoubtedly is enacting large amounts of *emotional labor* in their sales position, not only suppressing signs of sickness and pain, but also displaying appropriate emotions required for success in a sales position. Emotional labor is the regulation of emotion and associated expressions of emotion as required by one's job.[47] Emotional labor can be exhausting, and some forms of emotional labor—particularly *surface acting*, or expressing an emotion that is different than what is actually felt—are strongly linked to worker strain and burnout.[48]

Table 4.1 Identity Management Strategies

Strategy	Definition	Example
Passing—Fabrication[45]	Deliberately providing false information	A worker is frequently leaving work to attend CHC-related medical appointments, and they tell others at work that they are caring for a sick parent.
Passing—Concealment[45]	Preventing others from finding out that one has a CHC	A worker maintains positive facial expressions and displays healthy posture around others at work, despite severe back pain.
Passing—Discretion[45]	Avoiding opportunities or situations to share	A worker provides vague personal information or dodges personal questions that may reveal a CHC.
Revealing—Signaling[45]	Dropping hints or social clues about a CHC	A worker states that their immune system "does not work well" to imply being immunocompromised due to a CHC, yet does not directly reveal a CHC.
Revealing—Normalizing[45]	Disclosing a CHC, and minimizing its significant and effects on work	A worker reveals they have diabetes and says, "It's incredibly common" and "It's well-controlled and is not a big deal."
Revealing—Claiming[46]	Disclosing a CHC and revealing positive aspects of the CHC	A worker reveals they have lupus and states, "Living with lupus has helped me become stronger and more resilient."
Revealing—Differentiating[45]	Disclosing a CHC, and presenting it as equally valued (not devalued), without minimizing it	A worker reveals they have diabetes and shares their health management activities and what they need at work to help them manage their diabetes while working (e.g., "I need to take lunch at the same time each day to avoid blood sugar crashes.")

Workers with CHCs experiencing symptoms, especially those in customer-facing roles, may be vulnerable to experiencing strain from both having to conceal their symptoms and portray positive emotional expression. Pain is known to be associated with negative emotion—and if positive emotional displays are required, this sets the worker up for frequently having to surface act, and possibly experiencing exhaustion and burnout as a result.

Managers can help alleviate some of the negative effects of emotional labor in their employees by *allowing employees to take breaks to recover from exhausting customer encounters*. They can also *provide emotional support* or create opportunities for team members to support one another in the wake of challenging customer interactions. They can also work to *create safety within their teams for emotional expression*; researchers found that a team "climate of authenticity" (being safe to show how one really feels among team members) was helpful in alleviating burnout from emotional labor.[49]

Beyond exhaustion, what are some other consequences of identity management? Concealment (and other forms of passing) is thought to lead to cognitive preoccupation, and some evidence suggests it may be associated with lower job performance in workers who conceal an identity as a result.[50] Some research also suggests that concealing is detrimental to workers' job satisfaction—particularly so for workers who value authenticity.[50] Additionally, concealing may hinder workplace relationships, in that failing to share personal information, or inadvertently signaling one is hiding something, may cause a person to be seen as untrustworthy or interpersonally "cold."

For these and other reasons, it is perhaps not surprising that some studies have linked concealing an identity at work with poor worker well-being.[50] However, that does not mean that every worker with a CHC should disclose their condition at work. It may be that concealing is an act of discrimination avoidance—and in this way, concealing a CHC at work may be an effective strategy despite some of its potential negative consequences, particularly in unsupportive work environments.

In sum, work-related identity management can be complex for workers with CHCs and may pose challenges for workers. In Chapter 8, I will describe coaching to support workers in this process. Ultimately, it is important for you to keep in mind that choices of identity management strategies and effectiveness of such strategies in achieving the workers' goals will vary by several factors, including the type of CHC, individual differences, including personality and values of the worker, type of job, organizational culture, and supportiveness of supervisors and the person to whom the worker is disclosing. I therefore recommend that workers consider their values around disclosure, and particularly, their goals for disclosure carefully, along with the supportiveness of their supervisor and the organization more broadly and select strategies that help them achieve their goals for disclosure while upholding their values. As noted earlier, I also recommend that managers *actively work to create a feeling of safety for their employees to disclose their CHC if they want to.* Beyond generally building trustful, reciprocal relationships with your employees, you may also consider disclosing your own struggles, to signal that it is okay for them to do the same. I provide practical tips for managers when responding to an employee's disclosure in Chapter 7.

4.2.5 Career and Work Identity Implications

> I'm not sure how to articulate this, other than to say that it is difficult to be a promising upwardly mobile professional who learns that she has an illness that is likely to kill her in the next 10 years—probably. It's so hard to plan one's career after that. Should one fight tooth and nail for tenure, or stop and smell the roses? It's a unique kind of stress for those working with chronic illness.
> —college professor with vascular-type Ehlers-Danlos syndrome, age 45

Being diagnosed with a CHC is a life stage event that may spur people to reexamine their life priorities and reassess the fit of their current job role and expected future roles to their changing physical or mental abilities.[51] It can also be a threat to one's identity more generally, as CHCs challenge core assumptions and expectations people have about their abilities and futures.[52] In the words of one of our participants (a 43-year-old researcher with chronic fatigue syndrome), "This illness really shakes my sense of self. And that is something I think is hard to articulate to people who haven't had that kind of a shift in their life." This disruption is particularly common early in a diagnosis, and for younger workers, for whom a CHC diagnosis is inconsistent with expectations of youth and health.[53] It may also become more salient during times of illness flare-ups or progression, and when health impacts work in a new way, for example, through a change in a work role. However, as you might imagine, it can affect workers at any time in their lives and careers, as we found through talking to participants.

In a study of career barriers and trajectories of workers with CHCs, Dr. Joy Beatty interviewed workers with epilepsy and multiple sclerosis, most of whom were diagnosed before age 30.[54] In line with what I reported previously in this chapter about stigma and discrimination, study participants reported career barriers that centered around *other people's misconceptions* about the CHC.[54] Participants reported that others made inaccurate assumptions about their abilities, which threatened their opportunities for advancement and resulted in fewer developmental and promotion opportunities.[54]

Participants' reported career paths were organized into the following categories.[54] It is helpful for managers to be aware of these career paths when considering what may appear on the surface to be disadvantageous career moves—such as job candidates who are *overqualified* for a position, employees who choose to *forgo promotion opportunities*, or employees who *leave promising careers*.

- *Redirecting* refers to changing to a new line of work. This strategy was based on anticipation of future issues with the current career path based on expected illness trajectory—often incurring pay cuts when doing so.
- *Plateauing* refers to remaining in the same role for an extended time such that promotion was unlikely. This was driven by multiple factors, including a desire for job security, wanting to retain benefits, including health insurance, and a desire to not have to explain their CHC to a new employer or attempt to receive accommodations from a new employer.
- *Retreating* refers to consciously reducing one's effort toward work, through switching to a lower-level position (e.g., going from a managerial role to an individual contributor role, and/or reducing hours (e.g., from full-time to part-time).
- *Self-employment* was the final strategy found in this study, and participants who used this strategy left conventional employment roles to start their own businesses.

In sum, CHCs may spur a need for identity reconfiguration and career reconceptualization. Further, career decisions are made more challenging and complex in the face of CHCs. This may be aided with therapy or coaching, and as described in Chapter 8, organizations can facilitate access to these supports through employee assistance programs or other benefits.

4.3 Final Points

While this chapter included many challenges and obstacles that individuals face in maintaining productive and satisfying employment with health challenges, it is important to note that working with CHCs is not all doom and gloom. Despite the challenges CHCs pose, work is vital to employee well-being, and many participants expressed appreciation for work and optimism for successful continued employment. As noted in Chapter 1, those who are able to continue working reap social and financial benefits of work, and some cite work as beneficial to helping manage their CHCs as well.

> However, it [working] works in a lot of ways because it gives me a feeling of accomplishment that I am doing something productive and it helps fight off the negativity that my anxiety and depression brings.
> **—web designer with anxiety disorder and depression, age 33**

4.4 Takeaways and Recommendations

- Work ability is an important leading indicator of work withdrawal, including absenteeism, disability leave, and early retirement.
  - Job and personal resources are protective of work ability, yet job demands can lessen work ability for workers with CHCs when job and personal resources are inadequate.
  - Boosting job and personal resources is a critical element of organizational support for workers with CHCs—for example, consider work design elements and job accommodations (Chapter 7) and provide individualized supports (Chapter 8).
- Many workers with CHCs face energy scarcity, rapid energy depletion, and fatigue, requiring them to carefully plan daily activities.
  - Unexpected depleting work activities, when chronic, are particularly detrimental to many workers with CHCs and should be avoided when possible or accompanied by adequate time for recovery.
- Many workers experience interference in attending to work and health management activities in terms of time and energy, and this can lead to burnout and low levels of work ability.
  - Increasing job control, giving workers time off to recover after intense work, and allowing remote work are some ways organizations can help alleviate this.
- Symptoms, such as chronic pain can decrease work ability and interfere with work activities, leading to distress in workers.
  - Giving workers control and flexibility over scheduling, breaks, and work task completion can help with this, as it allows workers to self-manage and complete the most taxing activities when pain is at its lowest.
  - It may also be helpful to modify work and/or the working environment (e.g., provide an ergonomic setup and/or allow working from home).
- Intermittent/episodic disabilities, which may be unpredictable, threaten work ability and are not typically resolved with traditional work accommodations.
  - An employee-driven approach wherein an employee and their direct manager work together and share responsibility for figuring out accommodations as needed and plans for work completion may offer a responsive solution.
- Stigma and discrimination are major challenges facing workers with CHCs—these are harmful to workers, but also employing organizations that may incur legal challenges and other consequences of an oppressive, unsupportive culture.
  - Managers can help prevent this by being aware that it exists, checking their automatic reactions, humbly asking questions, being careful with their language, not being afraid to apologize, and looking for opportunities for allyship, no matter how small.
- Disclosing a CHC at work is a difficult decision, yet in many cases, benefits both the worker and employing organization.
  - Organizations can help workers feel comfortable disclosing by creating a culture where worker inclusion and well-being are valued and empowering supervisors to be supportive through their words and actions.
  - Supervisors can help workers feel comfortable disclosing by building trustful, reciprocal relationships with employees, and possibly also disclosing their own struggles.

continued

continued

- Beyond disclosure, identity management at work can be complex and create challenges for workers. Further, CHCs may have implications for career decision-making for workers with CHCs.
  - Managers should be aware of these career challenges when considering what may appear to be disadvantageous career decisions—for example, job candidates who are overqualified for a position, or employees who forgo promotion opportunities.
  - Coaching can help workers with disclosure and identity management decisions and strategies, along with professional identity and career decision-making.

Chapter 5
Organizational Challenges and Hindrances to Supporting Workers

> Because of chronic health conditions of workers, it is difficult to keep an even workforce. People have to be put on light duty or FMLA. The paperwork is long and arduous, and this contributes even more headaches to the process. The schedules must be changed to compensate and if we don't have enough people to cover, then whoever is here has their workload doubled or tripled.
>
> It affects the employers and other workers because often times workers with a chronic condition needs time off for doctor appointments, treatments, hospitalizations or not feeling well enough to work, this puts pressure on employers and coworkers that may have to cover this person's job or shift with sometimes short notice or for long periods of time.
>
> Managing people with chronic health issues is a real challenge. The legal aspect with how you deal with employees is difficult. Knowing what you can or can't do is hard.

These quotes are from managers and HR professionals who completed a survey about challenges related to CHCs at work that I described in Chapter 1. As the quotes illustrate, challenges of CHCs go well beyond individual workers. Yet compared to research on challenges for workers with CHCs, there is far less research published on challenges faced by organizations and those who run them. This is especially true in the US—the little research that exists on organizational challenges related to supporting workers with CHCs has mainly been conducted in Canada and European countries. In an effort to better understand organizational challenges around and hindrances to supporting workers with CHCs in the US, graduate student Leah Bourque and I interviewed US managers, leaders, and HR professionals in large and small organizations about their perceptions of these challenges in their organizations. I combined the results of the interview coding using thematic analysis[1] with existing research findings on organizational challenges to determine several themes/categories of challenges as described in this chapter.

Chronic Health Conditions and Work. Alyssa K. McGonagle, Oxford University Press. © Alyssa K. McGonagle (2025).
DOI: 10.1093/9780197660669.003.0006

5.1 Operational and Other Practical Management-Related Challenges

It may not be surprising for you to hear that logistical and practical barriers to supporting workers with CHCs can be quite challenging and complex. In our interviews, we heard from managers, leaders, and to a lesser extent, HR professionals in both large and small organizations that *ensuring work gets completed while providing flexibility and support* for workers with CHCs is challenging. Whether to meet the expectations of higher-level leaders or to simply keep the business running, the work must get done—and managers are on the line for work completion. Worker absences, reduced or flexible schedules, and unexpected leaves are obstacles to work completion, which can be quite challenging for managers, particularly when the organization offers little or no leeway in work systems or staffing. These are demands, using terminology from the job demands–resources model in Chapter 4, and can obviously be stressful for managers, leading to burnout in the absence of support from the organization.

> Just the struggle to handle capacity when it comes to chronic healthcare needs if you have somebody on the team that has a flexible schedule or a reduced workload or intermittent leave. We don't often see immediate or even long-term relief in terms of like additional requisitions, and so for the team—the workload—a lot of times that becomes a challenge where you have somebody that's considered a full time [employee] on your team that isn't being utilized in that way.
> —HR manager, large organization, finance

These challenges are particularly difficult in *smaller organizations*, which have fewer employees and less leeway in their finances and operations to manage longer-term absences.

> Well, absenteeism is the main issue because we're a small company. Obviously, we operate on a shoestring budget, so having a call center, we can't overstaff in the event somebody is going to absent, we staff to the number of staff we need. I mean, that's just what we can afford to do. And so when someone is absent, particularly if they're absent for several days a month, it becomes challenging to meet the requirements that our customers expect of us.
> —vice president of operations, small organization, business services

When resources are scarce, work that needs to be completed often shifts to other team members, which can create management challenges around maintaining fairness for other workers, and further, not creating burnout for others.

> There's a lot of issues with just protecting employees who need additional support while not causing downstream effects in the team in terms of inequity, feeling like it's a burden to other people on the team... Most of the time, our teams are running with obviously less people and less resources than they would like to have. So then when you take out somebody else's capacity to a certain degree, it just puts more of a strain on a lot of those teams. And we don't right now have a great support system in place for when that happens. We don't offer additional contractors... you know, there's really no way to offset the work... And so I think a lot of times that's where we see the challenges—just some of the effects on other teammates, burnout, things like that just from managing multiple, multiple workloads. And then obviously in turn that affects their health... how do we continue to support everybody with the needs they have while still, kind of fulfilling the business side?
> —**HR manager, large organization, finance**

Relatedly, one of our interviewees described challenges with allowing hourly workers with CHCs to have paid time off, as it can cause other workers to feel resentful. However, not paying for needed time off can also lead to worsening health problems.

> It's kind of iffy when you pick and choose; who would you pay to be out? And here you don't, especially in the work downstairs in the plant because that always gets out, everybody always finds out... So that's a challenge for us. So a lot of times what I've seen companies do it and I've [done it] myself, this "scorched earth." This is the policy. That's it. Because once you let one person go home two hours a day and pay him, that's a whole other issue. So you say, well, we won't pay. But the challenge with that is if people don't get paid, a lot of times it can exacerbate health issues."
> —**vice president of operations, small organization, manufacturing**

The same interviewee described relatively greater challenges to supporting employees in blue-collar/manual labor positions, compared to employees in white-collar positions.

> For instance, ... the gentleman that operates the tow motor for trucks. It's going to be a lot harder to accommodate him. Supervisors are easier to accommodate, but there's some people that just use their hands... We have a small corporate office up in outside of [US city], and they can work remotely. I don't need to know sometimes

if they're there. If they pay the bills, pay the people, keep insurances going, they can do it anywhere... But the actual line workers downstairs... it's going to be hard to accommodate a lot of things, you know... So that's a challenge because you want to be equitable.

—vice president, small organization, manufacturing

These challenges can be stressful to frontline managers, who may feel stuck between wanting to support their employees on the one hand, and pressures from their managers or more senior leaders on the other. While seemingly intractable, there are some ways to mitigate operational challenges. Ideally, supervisors actively work to *build collaborative relationships* with their employees, characterized by *shared accountability for problem-solving* to meet CHC-related needs while getting work done. It is also helpful to *cross-train* and *build team cultures of support* where workers stepping in for each other is the norm.

5.2 Lack of Understanding and Compassion, Stigma, and Discrimination

Bosma and colleagues conducted focus groups and interviews with occupational physicians and organizational representatives (managers, leaders, and HR professionals) in the Netherlands to ask about barriers to supporting workers with CHCs. One main barrier to support the researchers found was "negative attitudes towards employees with chronic conditions" (p. 5).[2] These negative attitudes included an *unwillingness of managers, leaders, and HR professionals to support workers with CHCs*; some organizational representatives noted that they did not trust that employees needed the accommodations they requested—and that the workers requesting accommodations were taking advantage of the system to get unnecessary support.[2] Some stated desires or *attempts to lay off workers with CHCs due to their condition*.[2] Other researchers similarly found that negative attitudes and a *lack of compassion and understanding* were major barriers to supporting workers with chronic pain.[3] These findings around negative attitudes and mistrust are perhaps not surprising, given reports of discrimination faced by workers with CHCs as described in Chapter 4. Yet they are problematic, as discrimination is illegal in most countries, and further, positive managerial attitudes are critical to workers' continued successful employment with CHCs.[4] In our interviews, we also heard reports of negative attitudes, discrimination, and unwillingness to support workers with CHCs.

> I've been in one situation where the employee went above the manager. [They went] to their manager's director to kind of complain about not receiving an accommodation. They were granted the accommodation and there was retaliation from the manager and that was just ugly. I think about that... I wonder what could have prevented some of that. I think it goes back to manager training.
> —senior HR consultant, large organization, utilities

Beyond more overt discrimination, multiple interviewees spoke about a lack of perspective taking, understanding, and empathy around CHCs being problematic. This can stand in the way of effective communication, collaboration, and shared problem-solving between workers with CHCs and their managers.

> It's really just getting caught up with you know, the mission or the job of the day and ... someone coming to you with an issue like that disrupts the accomplishment of that, of that goal. So I've seen a lot of people get caught up in that mindset and ... not really understand or want to take the time to understand what the actual issue is and how to how to find ways around in order to address it. So everyone can do what they are supposed to do.
> —supervisor, large organization, manufacturing

Another interviewee discussed how lack of empathy can lead to workers not wanting to disclose a CHC for fear of being judged. This, again, gets in the way of shared problem-solving.

> I hear stories of people I know that just have dealt with managers that are not empathetic at all and just they don't realize, for example, that they're making microaggressions at their employees or, you know, that they're not sensitive to how comments about certain things [come across]. So it's almost like ... lack of empathy that keeps managers from wanting to discuss it [the CHC], or keeps employees, especially, from wanting to discuss it. Because they feel like they'll be chastised or, you know, maybe their opinion in the manager's eyes will be lowered.
> —senior analyst, large organization, finance

Several of the managers, leaders, and HR professionals we interviewed also stated *that mental illnesses and other types of nonapparent illnesses carry more stigma* than other types of CHCs. There are many reasons for this;[5] for one, some people may find it difficult to believe that a person with a mental or other nonapparent illness has a disability or needs an accommodation when they appear to be "fine." As one interviewee explained, this can also happen when the manager does not have the context due to the need for HR to protect the worker's health information.

> When it comes to the invisible and some of the mental health [conditions], I think a lot of times the managers—because it doesn't affect them, they don't understand and they often don't know, right? We don't share why somebody has a particular accommodation or need... A lot of times that I think is what causes the confusion. Like, I don't understand why I can only use this person for so many hours. They don't really know why they're always out... if the manager relationship is there and they've been given additional insight from the employee themselves, they tend to have less of that. But that's up to the employee, whether they feel comfortable sharing that information with their team, with their manager versus handling it through the HR function.
>
> —HR manager, large organization, finance

In Chapter 4, I suggested that when employees have not disclosed their CHC, managers try to suspend judgment and trust that their employees need the accommodations they have. It is understandable to want information about the disability, but it is important to respect employees' boundaries when they choose not to share those details. Leaders at all levels have roles to play in helping minimize the chances for discrimination by promoting a culture that values employee well-being and inclusion of all employees. As described in Chapter 6, this includes a range of efforts, including top-down commitments (e.g., resource investment and communication from top leaders), alignment of organizational policies, trainings/workshops for managers, and accountability at all levels.

5.3 Employees Not Disclosing CHCs

As mentioned in Chapter 4, disclosing a CHC can be beneficial not only to employees, but also their supervisors and employers.[6,7] Disclosing provides the employee's manager with context for behaviors that may, on the surface, appear to reflect a lack of commitment or dedication to the organization or one's job tasks. For example, a worker who is experiencing a new diagnosis or a flare-up of an existing CHC may need frequent time off for medical appointments during work hours to complete the diagnostic process and/or to get the disease under control. Such frequent absences could be interpreted as being due to lack of caring about one's role, or even job-seeking behavior.

Disclosure also helps the manager and organization because it opens the door to problem-solving that can help the worker perform to their full capacity. For example, a technical writer experiencing chronic fatigue due to a CHC may experience an inability to concentrate and brain fog at work due to energy expenditure from a long commute to work, and their performance may suffer as a result. However, with an accommodation they may work more effectively at home, and the energy they save from not having to commute allows them to perform better. Further, if they also have flexible hours as an accommodation, they may rest in blocks throughout the day, spreading their workload into the night. This all may allow them to produce better writing, still make deadlines, and take care of themselves while doing so.

For all the benefits disclosure can offer, it is often a difficult decision for the worker about whether to disclose, as discussed in Chapter 4. In line with other research findings,[2] our interviewees stated that nondisclosure was barrier to supporting workers with CHCs. One interviewee aptly observed that a manager cannot help an employee they don't know is struggling.

> Even if you are a really good manager and even if you ask a lot of really good questions, you may not know if your employee is struggling, you may not know if they need help . . . And so the biggest challenge to me is the amount of onus that's put on individuals that may have these challenges. And anyone who's struggling in any facet of life, they just may not be ready to ask for help or know what to ask for. And so that then just compounds the whole situation even more so.
> —VP of HR, large organization, technology

In Chapter 4, I suggested managers work to build trusting relationships with their employees to help them feel comfortable disclosing. This can also help build a supportive culture where employees feel safe to disclose their health challenges.[11]

> Not everyone wants to share their whole health story, but really increasing the safety and the level of dialogue around chronic health issues within the workplace. More normalizing where each person is or what type of experience everyone is having . . . Part of it is leaders in the organization really acknowledging everyone's coming from a different health standpoint and having open dialogue and conversation about that . . . There are so many things that could impact any individual that we just don't like, talk about or acknowledge, it kind of forces you to keep it a little hidden sometimes. So trying to make people feel comfortable, in a way that is very welcoming and inviting and acknowledging that everyone is dealing with different things as they are also working.
> —director, large organization, technology

In Chapter 4, I suggested managers disclose their own struggles when appropriate to help build a climate of trust in their teams. Participants in our study acknowledged that leaders' disclosures of their own CHCs, though rare, could send positive signals to workers that it is acceptable to disclose and get support if needed. To help encourage disclosure, organizations should work on building a supportive, inclusive culture and provide support for supervisors to build better relationships with their subordinates. Chapter 6 will include these and other strategies to help employees feel comfortable disclosing.

5.4 Lack of Knowledge and Skills to Handle CHC-Related Issues

In Bosma et al., interviewees attributed the negative attitudes discussed in Section 5.2 to managers, leaders, and HR representatives lacking knowledge about CHCs and that workers may perform well if they were accommodated; along with unfounded fears that accommodations were going to be financially burdensome.[2] This lack of knowledge was also cited as a cause of disability-related discrimination in Kaye et al., who surveyed HR professionals and supervisors working for employers known to be resistant to complying with the ADA's employment provisions. The researchers asked about reasons why their employers do not hire people with disabilities, and found that 81% agreed that not knowing how to handle the needs of a worker with a disability was a reason; further, over 80% cited myths about disabilities that are not true (e.g., accommodations are excessively costly; they would not be able to discipline or fire an employee with a disability).[8] Collectively, this research points to a lack of knowledge as one probable (but not sole) cause of negative attitudes and discrimination against workers with CHCs. I will discuss ways to increase managers' knowledge in Chapter 6.

In our interviews, we heard from several interviewees that a lack of knowledge and skills related to policies, legal obligations and communicating with employees about CHC-related topics were hindrances to supporting workers with CHCs. This includes lack of:

- Knowledge and understanding of *disability laws*,
- Knowledge and understanding of *HR processes and policies around disability*, and
- Skill in *initiating and having ongoing discussions with their employees about CHCs*.

> I would say one of the biggest challenges that I hear from a lot of managers really is not understanding ... what are the laws? What are the, what are the things as the manager I need to be aware of in terms of HR, processes, things like that? There's a big knowledge gap ... When should I be asking questions? When do I ask for information? When do I wait for it to be shared with me? A lot of times, they just gauge that based on their relationship with their team. But they don't have a general sense a lot of times of you know, what should I be doing? When should I be referring somebody? Do I have any follow-up questions?
> —HR manager, large organization, finance

> If there were more education, or if supervisors were more inclined to practice, talk with an HR professional, or kind of go through maybe scenarios that could happen, they would be better prepared because I feel like supervisors are more trained on disciplinary action and how to handle a bad employee. And so working with someone who has a disability or a condition ... they may not be trained [on this] as well, and they may not know what to do. Or they may not see the signs. This person has a lot of appointments—they may see that as an attendance issue. And so they because they don't know, they don't know what they don't know. So I think one of the challenges is not being educated in that space.
> —senior HR consultant, large organization, utilities

In addition, managers and HR professionals may lack knowledge about CHCs and the associated work-related challenges these employees face.

> Invisible disabilities, I would say, are difficult for individuals to understand, especially if they haven't experienced them themselves as a manager. Specifically, mental health, anxiety, and depression. So you're kind of doing almost like a sensitivity training, in terms of helping managers—if they've never experienced it or maybe don't have a family member or have seen it in their life—to really understand the impact. And that it's not just a way to get out of work. And so kind of working through—just first of all, the understanding, but then also the legal aspects of what they're required to do.
> —employee well-being coordinator, large organization, education

This lack of knowledge of CHCs, laws, and how to have discussions about CHCs was discussed as being due to managers being pulled in several directions, and a lack of time to attend to everything needed. Managers may also have their own health challenges to attend to and are under pressure and constraints from leadership above them. Many want to be supportive, but lack the resources (knowledge, skill, time) to do so.

> At my company, we promote a lot of managers who were individual contributors. So you go from being someone who's responsible for your own work to someone who's responsible for other people's work. And when you do that, there's a lot of training that is required in order to build a manager capability. And so you're asking one of many, potentially one of maybe 100 plus requests that will come across a manager's plate at any point in time. And although we do our best to educate, inform, the reality is some managers just either can't retain the information or forget about it because there's so much that comes across the plate.
>
> —vice president, HR, large organization, technology

While rectifying this lack of knowledge is critical to avoiding discrimination and successfully retaining workers with CHCs,[9] it is clear that organizations *should not expect managers and HR professionals to simply add more to their plates to support workers without broader system-level support.* Training supervisors and holding them accountable is one step, but meaningful support is also needed at higher levels, with concurrent changes to culture, policies, benefits, the working environment, and work design.

5.5 Unsupportive Organizational Culture

Supportive organizational cultures are the foundations upon which manager support and supportive team cultures are built. Supportive cultures and climates signal a value of employee well-being, and are important for setting expectations for what should be prioritized, rewarded, and tolerated by leaders and supervisors, trickling down to employees at all levels.[10] Leaders have a large impact on culture; it is said that a whisper at the top becomes a shout at lower levels in organizations.[12] Stigma against CHCs at top leadership levels is a perpetuating factor for poor culture around communication and support for workers with CHCs.

> Yeah, there's a look that a lot of people give if you say, I need a mental health day, there's, you know, there's a smirk and there's an attitude that a lot of people will get like, okay, yeah, I need a day off . . . giving people the benefit of the doubt is less common in high tempo operational environments . . . And then there's stigma at leadership levels . . . As a supervisor, I've had bosses who tried to come down on

me for maybe giving [an employee] the benefit of the doubt. So coming from both directions there's stigma to deal with.
> —supervisor, large organization, manufacturing

Culture signals what behaviors are encouraged or may be sanctioned. Therefore, in addition to a fear of disclosure and lack of open discussion about needs, an unsupportive culture will serve to *induce fear of using use of available benefits*, that is, a lack of perceived usability of supportive benefits or policies.[13] This is problematic, because the organization may be paying for programs that are not being used; further, employees are not being supported and may perform poorly or leave the organization as a result.

> I think the biggest struggle we see is really people are afraid to utilize the benefits. We have a lot of offerings for people to seek. And I think people don't utilize them because of kind of what I talked about with just the impact on the team, the manager judgment, the feeling like their career will be affected if they're utilizing accommodations, if they're utilizing, things like that . . . I think we do see a lot of people unwilling to even take advantage of things that would help them because the fear of just what that looks like . . . We do, we do talk a lot about how going on a leave does not impact you from a compensation or a performance opportunity perspective. But in reality, I think that isn't always practice.
> —HR manager, large organization, finance

Holding people in organizations accountable for acting in ways that go against organizational values is important to upholding culture.

> I mean, retaliation can take so many forms. It doesn't necessarily mean you have to treat someone bad. It can be not giving that person the same opportunities . . . So I just, I would love to see companies increase awareness and create space for security, safety, and transparency. But also hold people accountable. I mean, you have . . . data that's trackable. Those are metrics you can pull in—real managers that have complaints against them. Maybe ethical complaints that have come up through an ethics line or an employee engagement to hold them accountable for it.
> —senior HR consultant, large organization, utilities

Using best practices around promoting a supportive, inclusive culture that values employee well-being is critical; additional strategies for doing so are in Chapter 6.

5.6 Lack of Communication and Cooperation between Various Stakeholders

Employee-manager cooperation is an important factor for facilitating retention of workers with CHCs by line managers.[9] Yet another challenge we found in our interviews relates to communication and cooperation breakdowns between the various parties involved in supporting workers with CHCs—employees, their managers, and HR representatives. This can stem from some of the aforementioned issues around bias, personal beliefs, or lack of knowledge or skill.

> They work together. It's a dialogue. This is what works. This is what we can do. And they [managers] make it happen, and then it's documented. But, worst-case scenario, they [managers] make it work for some and not for others. Because maybe they don't understand the condition or maybe their own personal bias or their own, you know, what's most important to me? . . . I've seen some folks get dragged around and that's where I feel like . . . you need guidance to tell folks what to do step-by-step. Because there are folks who are mature enough in leadership and have experience in it and have had the variety of experience to provide good counsel and kind of have that dialogue. There are some folks who don't because they've just not been willing to give up their own personal beliefs, just not change their mindset.
> —senior HR consultant, large organization, utilities

Such problems between the employee and the manager can, unfortunately, exacerbate mental health or other health problems for the employee with a CHC.

> I think there's still some old-school management that happens from time to time. That is more so in not being fully transparent. And I think that that sometimes even creates or worsens mental health for individuals that, for example, that struggle with anxiety and they may have a manager that's not being fully transparent and giving them kind of indirect or passive aggressive feedback. That can be very difficult. I think when you have clear communication and things are transparent, it really helps both alleviate some of that anxiety and just prevent some of that spill over into the workplace.
> —employee well-being coordinator, large organization, education

Communication breakdowns can also happen between HR and management. This is problematic for managers in terms of their planning and ability to ensure work gets done when an employee with a CHC is out on leave, on a reduced workload, or has been reassigned. These challenges point to the *need for close communication between managers and HR professionals* in organizations around employee accommodations and leaves of absence.

> I think the biggest challenge is often just the communication chain, so to speak... Because it's confidential, oftentimes managers don't know what they can and can't tell HR. And then they feel out of the loop when HR knows, but they don't know. So I think, even with leaves of absence, they're expecting their employee back in two days. And then it turns out that the day before they are supposed to come back, they're not going to come back. And the employee is not purposely leaving out their manager. They have only been in contact with HR. And so I think most of the administration challenges and miscommunication... is because the individual will go to whoever they feel more comfortable with... And then we have to loop people back in.
> —interim HR director, large organization, education

We also heard from interviewees that more informal supports were, in some cases, not used by managers due to a perceived need to "go by the book" to avoid legal issues. While this may prevent some of the forms of discrimination, it may also prevent more one-on-one collaborative problem-solving and relationship building between employees with CHCs and their managers. Such informal supports can be integral to successful employment for workers with CHCs, and supervisors report that having flexibility in terms of *how* they implement policies, enact accommodations, or modify jobs is helpful in supporting workers with CHCs.[14]

> The bigger companies get, the more they sometimes feel like they have to have hard and fast rules... It's like a risk aversion thing, right?... And so I currently work for a very large company. And... managers are asked to stick very closely to the policies as they are written as to not open us up to potential lawsuits. That being said, I think... having a little bit more of a risk-taking manager can be helpful. Because I have seen managers that are... a little bit more willing to, to not do exactly what the company says. Say, like, I'm not tracking personal time. So you take 10 days break, you take 12. I'm not going to notice. You take 30, I'll probably start to notice.
> —HR specialist, large organization, manufacturing

You may have noticed that many of the challenges in this chapter can be at least partially mitigated through *training*. This issue of communication breakdowns and managers not knowing the process, or what they can and cannot know, say, or ask, is another example where supervisor training would be helpful. It would also be helpful for *HR representatives to clearly outline and communicate the processes, and/or have materials ready to send to managers at the times they are needed.* If managers do not have access to these materials from HR, they may want to create their own "cheat sheets" with information on processes and benefits available for when their employees approach them with CHC-related issues.

I end with an optimistic quote from a study participant that helps segue into Part III of this book, which will detail ways to help address some of these challenges.

> Chronic pain and other conditions pose challenges for both workers and management. These challenges can be overcome with positive communication, progressive policies and a willingness on both sides to work to find a solution that allows both to thrive.
>
> —HR manager with chronic pain, age 35

5.7 Takeaways and Recommendations

- Operational challenges are a major concern for many managers, including staffing issues when workers with CHCs need time off, shifting workloads to other team members, and causing feelings of unfairness and resentment in others.
  - Building collaborative relationships with their employees, characterized by shared accountability for problem-solving to meet CHC-related needs while getting work done can help.
  - Cross-training and building supportive team cultures that value well-being can also help.
- Lack of understanding, empathy, and compassion gets in the way of cooperative problem-solving between managers and employees to solve work–health challenges and can lead to discrimination.
  - Workshops, trainings, or other educational opportunities for supervisors can help.
  - Organizations should not expect managers to simply add more to their plates to support workers without broader system-level support. Meaningful support is also needed at higher levels, with concurrent changes to culture, policies, benefits, the working environment, and work design.
- Nondisclosure is a barrier to supporting workers with CHCs—further, disclosing to team members and supervisors may facilitate a trusting working relationship characterized by shared problem-solving.
  - To help encourage disclosure, organizations should work on building a supportive, inclusive culture and provide support for supervisors to build better relationships with their subordinates.
  - Managers and leaders at all levels disclosing their own struggles can help normalize disclosure.

Organizational Challenges and Hindrances 95

- Managers may lack understanding of CHCs and their impacts, disability law, and organizational HR policies and processes around disability. They may also lack skill in communicating with employees about CHC-related issues.
  - ▷ Timely and convenient trainings for managers on CHC-related management issues can help.
  - ▷ In the absence of trainings, managers may create their own "cheat sheets" to with information on legal and organizational processes and benefits for when their employees approach them with CHC-related issues.
  - ▷ Organizations should not expect managers and HR professionals to simply add more to their plates to support workers without broader system-level support, including changes to culture, policies, benefits, the working environment, and work design.
- Stigma and intolerant attitudes from leaders can trickle down to create an unsupportive culture, which both negatively affects employees' willingness to disclose a CHC to get needed supports, and negatively affects the willingness to use policies and benefits that could help.
  - ▷ Culture-building strategies include resource investment and communication from top leaders, alignment of organizational policies and HR practices, trainings/workshops for managers, and holding people at all levels accountable.
- Communication and cooperation breakdowns between the various parties involved in supporting workers with CHCs—employees, their managers, and HR representatives, are problematic.
  - ▷ It is helpful for managers and HR professionals to maintain close and ongoing communication around employee accommodations and leaves of absence.

PART III
STRATEGIES

Chapter 6
Organization-Focused Strategies

Supportive strategies span a range of organizational levels and targets, from *organization-wide* changes to culture, benefits, and policies to *job or work-specific* modifications or accommodations, to *individually focused* supportive programs. In Part III of this book I detail strategies at each of these levels, as well as an integrated approach across all levels. Recall from Chapter 3 the description of primary, secondary, and tertiary intervention approaches applied to supporting workers with CHCs. *Primary prevention* strategies seek to promote work ability and well-being of all workers, by changing aspects of work culture, work benefits, work policies, work physical and/or psychosocial environment, work tasks, work scheduling, organization leadership, and work supervision. By maximizing accessibility and promoting healthy, sustainable work, these primary strategies benefit all workers, not solely workers with CHCs, and they allow for self-accommodation, possibly precluding the need for disclosure of a CHC to attain a formal job accommodation. *Secondary prevention* strategies focus on preventing declines in work ability and well-being and preventing disability leave and premature workforce exit for workers with CHCs. As such, secondary approaches include changing the job (through accommodations/modifications) and/or the worker (e.g., through coaching, mentoring, or training). *Tertiary prevention* approaches focus on returning disabled employees to work and include return-to-work (RTW) programs, which are detailed in Chapter 3.

To organize a discussion of supportive strategies, I distinguish between *organization-focused*, *work-focused*, and *individual worker-focused* primary, secondary, and tertiary prevention efforts, as illustrated in Figure 6.1. As you consider these different approaches, I encourage you to recognize the layered nature of strategies; that is, where possible, higher ordered strategies should be prioritized as they have the potential to benefit a greater number of employees and are more preventive of declines in work ability and well-being than lower order strategies. Again though, as discussed in Chapter 3, as you will also hopefully see, collectively, that they are all important supportive efforts.

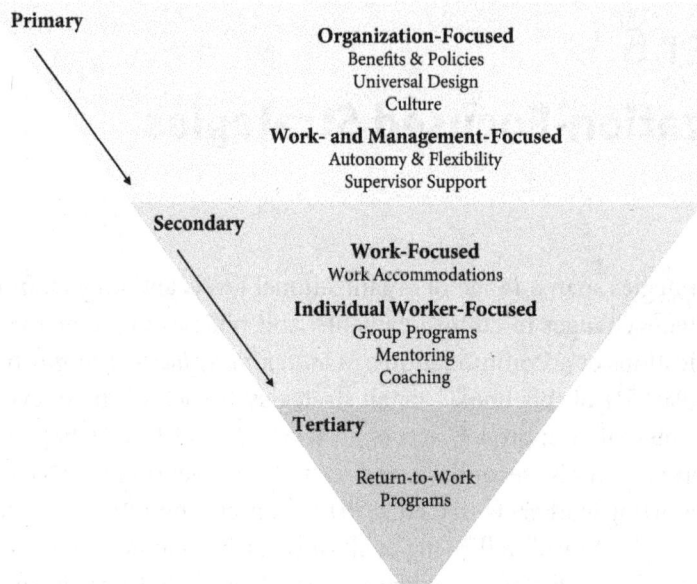

Figure 6.1 Hierarchy of support strategies to promote inclusion, well-being, and work ability for workers with chronic health conditions

6.1 Benefits

I start by discussing benefits that are important to all employees, and yet have particular importance for workers with CHCs. Box 6.1 contains a summary.

6.1.1 Healthcare Coverage

> We have recently been told that our health insurance for next year will change. We have not yet received many details but have been told that those who use the insurance more will pay higher premiums. I'm wondering how that will translate for me, considering that I receive Remicade infusions every other month at a cost of approximately $3,000 each plus I take two additional medications daily.
> —accounting manager with Crohn's disease, age 33

In our study on promoting work ability, we heard from many workers that healthcare benefits were a critical job resource, helping them maintain their work ability.[1] Healthcare coverage is essential for all workers, yet the consequences of poor coverage are more dire for those with CHCs. The US is one of the only industrialized nations that does not provide universal healthcare to its citizens. The passage of the US Affordable Care Act in 2010 has helped those without full-time employment attain healthcare coverage—however, *about half of the US population get their health insurance through their employers*,[2,3] and government-provided healthcare coverage is mostly limited to those over age 65 (Medicare) and those under 65 with no or limited income (Medicaid). Further, many low-income people who qualify to purchase health insurance under the Affordable Care Act cannot afford the monthly premiums.[4] The takeaway here is that while healthcare coverage is critical in terms of primary prevention for workers with CHCs—who comprise 60% of the US adult population as noted in Chapter 1—it is not always available or accessible to those who need it. Therefore, a layered approach, like the one I am presenting, is required to support workers with CHCs.

An inability to access healthcare while chronically ill can be fatal—studies consistently show that the US ranks poorly compared to other nations in healthcare outcomes, including life expectancy. One study showed that the US ranked last in life expectancy of those under age 65, compared to 17 other nations.[5] Interestingly, mortality rate improvements are dramatic for those over 65, including those over 65 with multiple CHCs, as Medicare provides access to healthcare for those individuals.[5] In short, it is not an overstatement to say that access to adequate healthcare coverage is a life-or-death necessity for those with CHCs.

Even with health insurance coverage, attaining healthcare is expensive in the US, with premiums for employer-sponsored health insurance plans increasing at a rate that outpaces inflation. For example, average yearly premiums were up 7% from 2022 to 2023, costing $8,435 for a single individual and $23,968 for a family in 2023.[6] In addition, the average annual deductible before insurance covers costs was $1,735 for single coverage; the average coinsurance rate was 20% for hospitalizations and specialty care; and the average copayments for office visits were and $26 for primary care visits and $42 for specialty office visits in 2023.[6]

Many employers offer workers choices between different types of plans, and the quality of employer-provided health insurance plans varies widely. High-deductible health plans may be attractive to individuals because they offer lower monthly premiums—yet in many cases they are not a favorable option for those with CHCs. High insurance deductibles are a barrier to accessing medication, disease monitoring, and routine medical care—and are therefore associated with worse health outcomes, including increased emergency hospitalizations, particularly among lower-income individuals.[7] However, some organizations with high deductible health plans provide employees with a contribution that workers may apply to their deductibles, reducing costs (7% of organizations with high deductible plans in 2023).[6] Compounding these issues, many health insurance plans are complex and difficult to understand, leading employees to choose between plans based on incomplete or inaccurate interpretations of plan coverage information.

Organizations can help with these issues by *providing quality health insurance plans with affordable deductibles and low out-of-pocket maximums* so workers do not forgo needed care to maintain their health. Organizations should also provide *clear, transparent plan information* to allow workers to both understand their benefits and select a plan that meets their needs, if they have a choice between plans. Organizations should also *clearly communicate that the monthly premium should not be the driving factor in selecting an insurance plan*, as lower premiums often come with higher out-of-pocket costs which may discourage accessing needed care.

Needless to say, the above is easier said than done. As such, a potentially more actionable recommendation is for organizations to *provide, and encourage employees to use, flexible spending accounts* (FSAs). FSAs are an important adjunct to health insurance plans, as they can help cover out-of-pocket medical expenses through pretax payroll deductions. Employees may use their FSA for any amount up to the yearly total at any time during the year, even before they pay into it at that amount through their payroll deduction. So if an employee needs an expensive medical test or procedure in the beginning of the year, they may face very high out-of-pocket expenses due to not yet working toward their deductible. To help cover this expense, they can use their full FSA funds, even before their payroll deductions have covered that amount.

FSAs are gaining popularity; over 60% of US employers currently offer FSAs to their employees.[8] Yet they are more frequently offered in larger organizations and to higher-wage workers.[9] Compounding accessibility issues, higher-income workers are more easily able to afford the payroll deductions to attain the tax benefits. FSAs are also complicated to use and difficult to understand. In sum, organizations should therefore consider offering these to their employees if they are not already, as well as supporting their employees in learning how to effectively use them to their advantage (e.g., group training and Q&A sessions and accessible materials that break down complex information).

If you are person managing a CHC in the US, you are likely already well aware that insurance plan formularies may exclude certain medications or require that a person "fails" other drugs to treat their CHC before allowing a prescribed medication.[10] If this phenomena is new to you, it is important to recognize that the drugs that the insurance company insists patients use to treat their CHC may be lower in efficacy, or may be drugs that the person has already tried and failed.[11] This is a major problem for people with CHCs, who, alongside their medical providers, want to access the best possible treatment for their CHCs. Even if a person with a CHC ultimately ends up getting the drug covered, they will often spend several hours working within the system to advocate for themselves.

In addition, coding errors and surprise insurance exclusions often lead to unexpected large bills, the need to self-advocate, and possibly long-term debt. Employees facing such issues often do not realize their organizational benefits representatives may be able to assist with these issues. Organizations should therefore clearly *designate a point person in HR who can assist a worker with navigating the insurance plan* and make workers aware that they can help with these issues. In addition, they should be sure to have *clear and accessible information about benefits* on their employee benefits websites. Finally, because insurance issues are complex, and employees may not be able to get all the assistance they need from their employers, I suggest organizations make employees aware of *external resources that can assist with insurance issues*, such as the Patient Advocate Foundation, which can provide assistance with copays and other issues.[12] Telemedicine also became popular during the COVID-19 pandemic and will be important going forward to provide access to care for many employees.[13] Organizations should therefore *advocate for and support continued coverage for telehealth with their health insurance providers*.

6.1.2 Life Insurance and Long-Term Care Insurance

In the US, people with CHCs are often denied coverage when trying to purchase some insurance policies. Insurance companies may deny life insurance and long-term care insurance policies to those with diabetes, obesity, cancer, heart disease, and other serious CHCs.[14,15] Further, life insurance denials are more common amongst those with CHCs who are Black, mixed-race, or Hispanic compared to those who are White.[16] Therefore, many with CHCs rely on employer group plans to attain needed life insurance and long-term care insurance —yet they need to sign up during a period (typically, when first hired) when no medical evidence is necessary to attain coverage. Organizations should *offer life insurance plans to all workers, and clearly communicate the deadlines for enrolling in coverage without a medical exam or providing medical information*.

While people with lifelong health conditions are more likely to need long-term care at some point in their lives, not everyone can benefit from long-term care insurance. For example, people with very little money when they need care will be covered by Medicaid, and those with significant financial resources at the time care is needed may be able to afford care for themselves, without paying costly insurance premiums over a lifetime.[17] Further, plans are complex and some are not worth the money paid into them. If organizations offer long-term care insurance, they should *ensure plans provide value, provide counseling or other resources for employees to make informed decisions, and clearly communicate deadlines for enrollment without a medical exam or providing medical information.*

6.1.3 Time Off Benefits and Policies

Based on your own lived experiences, as well as the research reviewed in previous chapters, it should be quite apparent that workers with CHCs will need to use sick days or vacation days to attain treatment, medical procedures or diagnostic testing, or recover from disease flare-ups. Further, it is common for those with CHCs to have a "regular" sickness such as a common cold or the flu last longer or spur complications (e.g., secondary infections), necessitating additional time off. Providing access to paid sick time can help ensure workers do not forgo needed medical treatment or pass communicable illnesses to others. Taking needed time off can also be helpful with reducing presenteeism, allowing workers to address their symptoms, rather than additionally depleting their resources to keep working when they are not feeling well. Finally, allowing needed time off signals support.

> So I just use my vacation, [and] communicate with them that I just need to rest. And they agreed and their response is it is there for you to feel better because it helps us. We want you to be productive, so whatever it takes for you to do that, you should do that.
>
> —research assistant with multiple sclerosis, age 29

One detrimental recent trend in paid time off (PTO) I have heard about anecdotally from workers with CHCs is a requirement that the employee take a full day of PTO if they leave work for a medical appointment, even if the appointment only takes a few hours out of the workday. Employees resent these policies because it often means they must use all their PTO for medical care, and therefore cannot take a needed vacation. Also, when employees often work nights and weekends to meet work deadlines, yet their employers are unwilling to afford them flexibility when they need it, it understandably creates resentment and hurts employee motivation.

Another detrimental practice, though seemingly well-intentioned, is having other employees donate their own personal leave to support a coworker with a CHC. Many employees resent such policies, as they need their leave for their own health and well-being, and many see it as the responsibility of the organization to provide additional leave for the sick employee. I have seen such leave donation requests lead to cynicism among employees.

Yet another recent trend is for organizations to offer unlimited PTO, and there are pros and cons to this approach for workers. First, employees may be afraid to use their time off, as they feel uncomfortable taking the time without having a designated number of days allocated. If organizational culture does not support taking time off, and workers see others not using their PTO, they also may be reluctant to do so. One study found that those with unlimited PTO took 13 days of leave on average per year, compared to those with traditionally allocated PTO, who took 15 days of leave on average per year.[18] *Organizations should help encourage workers to use PTO by instituting minimum requirements for days off, and having leaders and supervisors use their PTO, signaling to workers that it is okay for them to use it as well.*[19] Importantly, PTO is not only important for workers with CHCs—it positively affects all employees. Vacations have been positively associated with worker health and well-being—more specifically, lower levels of exhaustion, fewer health complaints, and higher levels of life satisfaction.[20]

Notably, these recommendations are likely beyond the scope of what most managers and HR professionals can affect in terms of change in their organizations. Yet bringing them to light as affecting workers with CHCs (which comprise a large proportion of most organizations) is important, nevertheless. Organizations that desire to do their best for their workers with CHCs should consider these and the other benefits and policy recommendations in this chapter.

6.1.4 Disability Benefits

When first diagnosed, or when CHCs worsen or flare, workers may need extended time off from work to attain treatment and recover. For this, many rely on short-term disability insurance that pays some or all their wages while they are recovering. If their condition requires longer-term absence (e.g., more than 12 weeks), they may use long-term disability insurance. Similar to life insurance and long-term care insurance, workers with CHCs may be denied individual disability policies, and therefore rely upon organizational group insurance for needed coverage. *Organizations should offer short- and long-term disability insurance to employees.*

6.1.5 Employee Assistance Programs

Employee Assistance Programs (EAPs) are designed to help employees resolve personal problems that affect their work. As such, the goal and focus of these services is restoration of work functioning.[21] Most large and medium-size organizations in the US provide access to EAPs and they are also common in Canada; though EAPs are less commonly provided by smaller firms in the US and by organizations of all sizes in European countries.[21] Examples of issues that EAPs may assist with include child or elder care, relationship problems, legal issues, mental health challenges, and alcohol or other substance misuse.[22] EAPs may also provide group training sessions on topics such as conflict resolution, and may assist after a traumatic workplace event. Yet the most essential and common EAP function is to provide free counseling as needed to workers and their family members.[21] Employees typically voluntarily self-refer to EAPs, though managers may suggest EAP resources when an employee discloses a CHC. Organizations have a responsibility to *ensure any relevant services offered through an EAP are accessible and helpful*; one way to do so is to survey employees for their feedback.

Efforts may also be made to tie EAP utilization to the bottom line. Return-on-investment (ROI) for EAPs are typically based on reductions in costs related to healthcare claim, disability claims, absenteeism, and presenteeism. ROI for EAPs varies by program costs, number of employees, utilization rates, and average employee hourly wages. Estimates of ROI range from $3.00 USD to $10.00 USD per dollar invested[21,23] A systematic review of EAP effectiveness found that they were effective in terms of decreased presenteeism and improved work functioning—though not reduced absenteeism.[24]

Despite their apparent effectiveness, not many employees make use of EAP benefits. External (vendor) EAPs in particular are often not well-known to employees and have utilization rates ranging from less than 1% to 5% of employees.[21] To counter this, *organizations should promote relevant services offered through EAPs effectively and widely, both to supervisors and their employees*. Stigma may prevent employees from using EAP services; some organizations have countered this by rebranding them as "work–life" programs with more modern and responsive approaches to employee mental health support.[24]

6.1.6 Wellness Programs

Wellness programs are typically considered part of employee benefits packages, and are designed to promote healthy diets, physical exercise, stress management, smoking cessation, immunizations, and other individual behaviors that help prevent diseases. As noted in Chapter 3, wellness programs are prevalent in the US—yet despite their popularity, evidence to support their effectiveness is lacking. Organizations implementing wellness programs may do so to help *signal support for worker well-being*; however, they should also pay attention to other supportive primary preventive efforts, including offering developing and sustaining a workplace culture that values employee health and well-being.

Summary of Recommendations: Benefits and Policies

- Provide high-quality health insurance, life insurance, long-term care insurance, and disability insurance, along with paid time off.
- Provide user-friendly, accessible, comprehensive benefits information online; follow web content accessibility guidelines in doing so.
- Clearly state deadlines to obtain life insurance, long-term care insurance, or other benefits without medical examination or medical information disclosures.
- Train supervisors on relevant available benefits and resources and encourage them to share sponsored benefits and resources with their subordinates.
- Promote relevant services offered through EAPs widely.
- Continuously assess the value of EAP and other services, including user experiences with such services.
- Understand limitations of wellness programs, particularly when the broader organizational culture, work design, and supervision is not supportive of employee health and well-being.

6.2 Universal Design

Universal design is design that intentionally considers the needs of all people, and as such, is accessible to all. For readers unfamiliar with universal design, I have included a link in Additional Resources (Seven Principles of Universal Design). Universal design may be contrasted with traditional design, which is made by and for people without disabilities, and requires added accommodations. An example of universal design is a workspace that includes plenty of quiet, private spaces for workers who need them to be productive and avoid sensory overwhelm, including workers affected by CHC-induced fatigue or cognitive fog. To the contrary, open office spaces lacking walls are inaccessible to many employees with autism, attention-deficit/hyperactivity disorder (AD/HD), sensory processing disorders, and other conditions.[25] Research shows that open-office arrangements are generally associated with negative health, satisfaction, productivity, and social outcomes compared cellular office designs,[26] and in direct opposition to their intended goals, open-office arrangements actually reduce in-person interaction and collaboration.[27] Other examples of universal design in the workplace include:[28]

- Adequate space for maneuvering
- Accessible entrances and exits
- Minimal noise levels and effective lighting
- Limiting strong smells
- Accessible door handles
- Ergonomic, adjustable seating and workstations
- High contrast signage
- Multisensory alarm signals
- Accessible web design

Universal design in the workplace reduces the need for individual accommodations and promotes inclusion and productivity of all workers, regardless of disability status.[29] As such, universal design is considered "mainstreaming" support for workers with disabilities, in contrast to "specialization," which refers to tailored supports.[30] Examples of specialized supports include targeted recruiting and hiring initiatives and employee resource groups, whereas mainstreamed supports include universal design, flexible scheduling, and other work design elements as discussed in Chapter 7. While both are important, principles of universal design have been slow to catch on in organizations; I therefore recommend that *organizations should be aware of and incorporate universal design principles in work environment, work communications, and work policies.*

6.3 Organizational Culture

Organizational culture reflects explicit and implicit enacted values of organizational members, particularly founders and high-level leaders. Culture is perpetuated through policies, practices, decisions, language, actions, and inactions of leaders and supervisors at all levels. Culture lays the groundwork for climate, which affects employees' day to day experiences by indicating priorities, thus directing their attention and action and shaping the physical and psychosocial landscape in which they work.

Two elements to organizational culture are particularly critical to supporting workers with CHCs: *valuing diversity, equity, inclusion, and accessibility (DEIA)*; and *valuing employee health and well-being*. Of course, these two elements are important beyond workers with CHCs—they support all workers and the organizations that employ them. Yet as discussed in Chapters 4 and

5, workers with disabilities face various forms of work discrimination, and most CHCs are nonapparent or concealable, which spurs challenges around disclosure decisions and identity management at work. Thus, promoting a culture that values inclusion and well-being is important for:

- Helping workers feel safe to disclose often-concealed CHCs in order to attain needed supports or accommodations can improve their work ability, safety, and work performance.
- Helping organizations retain talented workers, as employees who feel valued and supported tend to be more committed to their organizations.
- Helping organizations uphold disability laws, potentially avoiding disability discrimination claims.
- Providing a context in which supervisor training, worker coaching, mentoring, or other programs to support workers with CHCs can be more successful.

6.3.1 Values of Worker Well-Being and DEIA

A culture that values employee well-being is a foundation upon which many other, more specific forms of strategic or focused climate may be built (e.g., safety climate, diversity climate). A culture valuing employee well-being is also ultimately critical to an organization's success, through its ability to recruit and retain talent.[31] Inclusion is an important component of well-being, and (recent backlash notwithstanding), there has been a growing recognition of the importance of workplace DEI efforts since the murder of George Floyd in the US. Yet disability has been relatively underrepresented as a diversity issue in organizations, and tend to take a backseat to other diversity categories such as race and ethnicity, gender identity, and sexual identity.[30,32,33] A critical first step toward building a culture that supports workers with CHCs, therefore, is *explicitly recognizing disability as a diversity category*—one that is valued in the organization alongside, and in combination with, other diversity categories.[32]

To this end, professionals are increasingly using the term "DEIA" instead of "DEI"—to explicitly include accessibility, which is critical to inclusion for those with disabilities.[34] Yet there is much more work to do. A study of employee engagement survey data over 10 years with 12 million data points found notable discrepancies in perceptions of fair treatment and workplace culture between those with and without disabilities.[35] For example, 82% of employees without disabilities, but only 72% of those with disabilities agreed that their organizations treat workers fairly regardless of age, family/marital status, gender, disability, race/color, religion, or sexual orientation.[35] Similarly, there was an eight-point discrepancy in agreement with the statement "My company creates an environment where people of diverse backgrounds can succeed" between employees with and without disabilities.[35]

6.3.2 Culture Strategies

To help promote a culture that values inclusion and employee well-being, organizations must communicate these values, both in internal and external communications, and with decision-making and actions—while connecting them to the broader organizational strategy.[36] Among organizations that have received national attention for disability inclusion efforts, a common strategy to this end is *including diversity statements that specifically include disabilities* in corporate social responsibility reports.[30] These statements may generally affirm the value of diversity, including disability specifically, or may describe how they will make investments to support accessibility.[30] Additionally, some organizations, such as Johnson & Johnson, include employee health and well-being as values in their credos.[37,38]

Frontline managers in organizations have responsibility for *transmitting and translating organizational culture* to their employees through their daily interactions with their subordinates. For example, frontline leaders can uphold a value of employee well-being by encouraging workers to use their PTO and taking their own PTO to role model caring for their own well-being. Top leaders in organizations should *explicitly communicate commitment to DEIA and worker well-being*. Upper leaders have a responsibility to communicate this to supervisors at all levels in the organization, along with expectations they have for supervisors related to upholding these values through their own actions and communications with subordinates. It is not enough to communicate expectations, however—in addition, *leaders at all levels should be held accountable for upholding these values* in performance management processes. Simply verbalizing a value of DEIA and worker well-being without investing in it is hollow and will generate cynicism. Therefore, organizations should also *invest financial and time-related resources into infrastructure, partnerships, work changes, or activities that promote inclusion and well-being*, such as:

- *Implementing universal design or work design recommendations* in Chapter 7.
- *Supporting and partnering with disability advocacy organizations* such as those that prepare students with disabilities for success in the workforce.

- *Offering worker-focused programs* like the ones discussed in Chapters 8 and 9.
- *Empowering employee resource groups* (ERGs) to carry out work in this area. For example, Northrop Grumman, which was named a 2022 Best Place to Work for Disability Inclusion, has a VOICE ERG for workers with disabilities,[39] and Nestlé has a THRIVE ERG for workers with disabilities and critical illnesses, as detailed below.

In addition, organizations should offer *policies that help with work–health issues, and importantly, ensure that policies and benefits offered are usable*. It is not enough to offer flexible work policies, or other supportive policies, if workers cannot use them without social- or career-related consequences. To promote their use, leaders should walk the walk and act as role models for other employees as noted earlier. For example, leaders should demonstrate that it is acceptable to use organizational policies around flex time and flex place by *using these policies themselves*, thus normalizing their use and increasing usability of such policies for all workers. Leaders may choose to *disclose their own CHCs*, which signals to workers that it is safe and acceptable to do so. One study of 1,000 employees found that 62% of respondents said having a leader in their organization speak openly about mental health would help them feel more comfortable disclosing their own mental health conditions.[40] Aaron Harvey, cofounder of Ready Set Rocket, disclosed his mental health struggles and suicidality. He later launched a campaign, an app, and a workplace manual on how companies can assist workers with mental health conditions.[41] While this is a notable example, simply being open about your own struggles as a manager or leader may go a long way toward helping de-stigmatize CHCs at work. I provide another example of this later in this chapter (Section 6.2).

To sustain culture, it is important for *HR practices to align with values*. Beyond holding leaders accountable as mentioned, other examples include:

- *Include disabilities in recruitment efforts and materials*. Given the stigma against and reluctance hire people with disabilities,[42] disability-specific recruitment plans are needed.[30] For example, Northrop Grumman has partnerships with Student Disability Offices on college campuses for recruitment.[39]
- *Use fair and inclusive practices for selection and staffing*, including standardized selection systems based on job analysis results; use multiple raters in interview settings; use structured interviews; and train hiring managers on inclusive, fair hiring practices and legal rights and responsibilities.[43]

- *Use fair, inclusive, and accurate practices for talent management,* including standardized systems for performance appraisal; monitor compensation systems for discrepancies and correct them; and provide opportunities for lateral or downward career movements when desired.[43]

A seemingly minor aspect of culture that is often overlooked but emerged as important in a study I am currently conducting on workers with type 2 diabetes, is around food. Many participants felt socially excluded from events that only had food they could not eat.[44] Having accessible food options for a variety of dietary restrictions can help employees with invisible disabilities such as diabetes, celiac disease, or irritable bowel disease, feel included. As someone who lives with multiple dietary restrictions, I understand firsthand that this is not easy—here are a few recommendations.

- Include a platter with vegetables and dairy-free dip (e.g., hummus).
- Include salad mix and/or brown rice for a build-your-own salad or rice bowl option, with different vegetables, beans, and other proteins for people to add.
- When ordering sandwiches or burgers, include lettuce wraps or gluten-free bread.
- Pizza is easy and cheap, but is bad for several health conditions, so skip it and include build-your-own tacos with corn tortillas or salad or rice bowls instead.
- Include flavored sparkling water or plain filtered or bottled water instead of sugary sodas.

Another specific, concrete culture recommendation that in my experience is not on the radar of many professionals, is to *include disability status question(s) on employee engagement surveys.* Most companies use regular engagement surveys to assess employee perceptions, attitudes, engagement, and intentions to remain with the organization, and most include demographic questions so that results may be examined for discrepancies between demographic categories. However, most do not ask about disability status. Organizations could include the question as an optional self-report, "*Do you have an apparent or nonapparent disability*? (Yes/No/Prefer not to say)."[45]

Dr. Peter Rutigliano of Mercer Consulting and Meg O'Connell of Global Disability Inclusion, Inc. examined over three million employee responses from 66 organizations from 2011 to 2020, and found that only 9.6% of companies in the US and Canada included disability status in their surveys in 2020, compared with 90% that included gender and 75% that include ethnicity.[45] They also found notable differences between people with and without disabilities in survey responses to questions about fair treatment, being valued, and company concern for employee well-being. The largest discrepancies were seen for items assessing perceived opportunities for advancement, recognition from management for good performance, the ability to express ideas without fear of negative consequences, job security levels, the job making good use of one's skills and abilities, and fairness of treatment regardless of demographic categories.[35,45] Interestingly, these discrepancies do not exist for new employees, but *increase with increasing years of tenure with the organization*. In contrast to stark differences by disability status, the researchers found no meaningful differences in responses by age, gender, ethnicity, or sexual orientation.[35,45] These data clearly point to a stark need for disability to be a greater target area for organizational inclusion efforts. Companies cannot understand their own workforce discrepancies by disability status if they do not gather data on it; *including disability status on surveys is therefore imperative.*

Deloitte recommends taking this a step further, and disaggregating disability types to understand unique equity barriers in outcomes based on type of disability, such as physical disabilities versus learning disabilities, along with intersectional analyses, such as people with disabilities who are LGBTQIA+.[46] Of course, this would require a high level of trust, and thus would not be recommended for all organizations. Further, it would only work in large organizations, as these types of analyses could identify specific individuals in smaller organizations. It also requires developing trust with employees, who will likely be wary of disclosing disability or CHC status on a survey. All information provided by employees should of course be collected voluntarily, kept confidential, and only reported on an aggregate level.

It is important that this effort does not stop once the data is collected—*results by disability/CHC status should be reported transparently*, and the organization should *state what they intend to do to improve* if the results indicate a problem. The organization should also follow up and implement those steps and measure their success through repeated surveys over time.

Language matters in culture, and preferences are important. As noted in Chapter 2, some people prefer to be referred to as "disabled" (identity-first) whereas others prefer "person with a disability" (person-first). When in doubt, just ask how someone would like to be identified. However, *avoiding ableist language* is imperative, as noted in Chapter 4. Chapter 4 provides a full list of terms to avoid—such as "they're so OCD" and "fell on deaf ears," which are unintentionally harmful to the disability community,[47] and euphemisms for disability such as "special needs," which are offensive in that they imply disabilities are something bad to be avoided.

As noted in Chapter 2, organizations should also *be aware of ableist practices*, most of which are unintentional. One organization routinely gave "inspiration awards" to those facing what the award nominators perceived as challenges—including disabilities. The awards were not for superior achievements, but instead were for simply showing up and completing expected tasks despite having a disability or facing another perceived hardship. This is an example of "inspiration porn" that creates a feel-good emotional response from those who are "inspired" by disabled people simply living their lives,[48] but is de-humanizing and infantilizing to people with disabilities. Such practices do nothing to improve accessibility or inclusion more broadly. Further, praising someone for doing something routine, sends the message that lesser is inherently expected of them.[48] To the contrary, *always presume competence*, and *recognize people for their achievements* and not their perceived hardships.[48]

Reflection Exercise: Culture Strategies

1. Take a moment to reflect on your organization's culture, specifically the extent to which it values employee well-being and inclusion. How would you describe your organization's culture for well-being and inclusion? What factors led you to describe it in this way?
2. Given your role in your organization and your answers to #1, what are some steps that you could personally take to help promote the value of employee well-being and inclusion in your organization? Feel free to use the examples from this chapter as inspiration, but don't limit yourself to these examples.

_____

_____

_____

_____

6.3.3 Examples of Culture-Related Strategies

Next, I provide examples of strategies to improve culture, including employee resource groups and trainings.

6.3.3.1 Employee Resource Groups

Nestlé USA has an innovative ERG called THRIVE Ability Network, which helps support its inclusive workplace culture. The group was started in 2019 by employee Christine Hambleton, who returned to work following cancer treatment and was mentored through the experience by a colleague who was also a cancer survivor. After experiencing the benefit of this type of peer support first-hand, Christine was inspired to launch THRIVE, which now includes over 900 employees. THRIVE provides a forum for employees to share experiences and receive and give support with the aim to reduce stigma and provide education and support. ERG activities include:

- Offering peer-to-peer connections, which I will discuss in Chapter 8;
- Opportunities to connect via shared lunches and "mindful moments;"
- Amplifying benefits and other resources sponsored by the company (e.g., mental health support);
- Weekly messages created by and sent to network members, including leaders, sharing stories of related challenges and associated empowerment.

THRIVE's success, and its ability to help drive culture is achieved, in part, through its support and participation from company leaders. For example, during the pandemic in 2020 Brian Schoo, who currently serves as the Director of People Analytics at Nestlé, began sharing a weekly message with the network about his struggles with AD/HD and dyslexia while navigating the quick switch to remote work. He did this both as an accountability tool to himself and to encourage others who may be struggling to feel less alone. He also wanted his employees to feel free to come to him with their challenges when they needed support. This became an ongoing weekly message where employees in the network can sign up to share their own stories via messages to the network. Messages can include the writer's story of challenge, along with what the writer is doing to empower themselves through the challenge, as well as reflective questions for the reader.

By voluntarily disclosing his own challenges, Brian modeled that it is okay to share challenges, which opened up the doors to help employees feel open to connection and create an authentic environment at work. Other leaders have similarly shared messages since then. Further, Nestlé North America CEO Steve Presley signaled his support by awarding THRIVE a prestigious organization-wide True North award in 2021, which celebrates the work of individuals and teams that drive the organization forward. Combined, such leadership support helps ensure the success of THRIVE and helps embed and sustain a supportive culture more generally. Leaders I spoke with at Nestlé state that THRIVE is not only helpful for employees—it also helps the company retain valued talent and facilitate agility through employee authenticity, support, and connection.

6.3.3.2 Trainings

Trainings, workshops, and other programs are commonly promoted as efforts to foster an inclusive work climate through shifting employee attitudes and decreasing the stigma of marginalized groups at work. Trainings may be general, promoting inclusion of all marginalized groups, or specific to certain groups, including disabilities. Interestingly, in a meta-analysis, researchers did not find differences in effects for more specific trainings (e.g., on gender or disabilities) compared to more general trainings.[49] What did make a difference was length; longer trainings were more effective than shorter ones.[49] When considering these findings, it is important to note that studies of diversity training for disabilities in the workplace are virtually nonexistent; in the aforementioned meta-analysis, only four of 260 included studies were on disabilities.

In an attempt to fill this gap in disability-specific trainings, Dr. Enrica Ruggs and I designed and tested the effectiveness of brief video trainings to mitigate disability bias. In the videos, workers with disabilities (bipolar disorder, multiple epiphyseal dysplasia, and epilepsy) share knowledge/facts about disabilities to combat common myths about disabilities at work, along with their personal stories and experiences to provide socialization to individuals with disabilities.[50] We found evidence for the videos' effectiveness in raising awareness and improving attitudes in the short term; however, given their brief nature it is unlikely these benefits would be long-lasting.[50] Therefore, we recommend that organizations use these as one piece of a multi-pronged effort to improve culture of inclusion for workers with disabilities. The videos may be accessed via the link in Additional Resources.

In contrast to our video approach, diversity trainings are typically delivered in lecture format by an outside consultant, with a presentation followed by interactive group activities.[51] Some studies have found evidence that diversity trainings are associated with short-term improvements to employees' perceptions and attitudes toward marginalized workers.[52] Yet others have found diversity trainings to result in a backlash effect, particularly when trainings are mandatory or participants feel they were referred to training due to complaints of biased behavior.[53] Taken together, study findings have led researchers to state that evidence for diversity trainings' effectiveness is mixed, conflicting, and inconclusive.[51] Instead of training, the researchers recommend targeting socially connected individuals within an organization to enact change, and monitoring hiring, retention, and perceived belonging for marginalized groups over time (as I described in section 6.2.2).[51] Further, the authors recommend only *implementing diversity training when it is embedded within larger, systemic workplace initiatives such as changes to policy, with strong support from top leaders.*[49,51]

6.3.3.3 Summary of Recommendations: Culture

- Organizations use principles of universal design to inform decisions about technological, physical, and social infrastructure, along with benefits, policies, and practices, to meet the needs of all workers to the extent possible.
- Organizations offer policies that help with work–health issues, and importantly, ensure that policies and benefits offered are usable.
- Organizations include diversity statements that reference disability among other protected groups in corporate social responsibility reports.
- Top leaders explicitly communicate commitment to DEIA and worker well-being.
- Top leaders hold leaders at all levels accountable for upholding values of DEIA and well-being.
- Top leaders invest financial and time-related resources into infrastructure, partnerships, work changes, or activities that promote inclusion and well-being.
- Top leaders align HR practices with values of DEIA and worker well-being.
- HR and leaders gather data to assess standing and progress—include disability status question(s) on employee engagement surveys alongside other diversity categories. But don't just gather data—act on the results.
- Leaders and employees at all levels avoid unintentionally ableist language and practices.
- Frontline managers uphold culture in their daily behaviors and interactions with subordinates by, for example, role modeling self-care behaviors for employees by using PTO and other benefits.
- Remember that diversity trainings should only be implemented within the context of larger, systemic workplace disability inclusion efforts and with support from top leadership.

Additional Resources

- Brief Videos used in Disability Bias Study: https://pages.charlotte.edu/hiringbias/
- Cancer and Work Site for Employers and Cancer Survivors: https://www.cancerandwork.ca/
- Epilepsy @ Work Site (Training and information on supporting workers with epilepsy in the workplace): http://www.epilepsyatwork.com/en
- Guide to Investigating Disability Issues: Language and Interviewing: https://gijn.org/2023/03/07/investigating-disability-issues-language-interviewing/

- Harvard University Work and Well-Being Initiative Employer Toolkit: https://workwellbeinginitiative.org/employertoolkits/Overview
- Lime Connect (Disability Advocacy and Mentoring): https://www.limeconnect.com/
- Patient Advocate Foundation (resources for patient advocacy for healthcare and financial aid for treatment): https://www.patientadvocate.org/
- Seven Principles of Universal Design: https://design.ncsu.edu/research/center-for-universal-design/
- White Paper on Telecommuting: https://www.siop.org/Portals/84/docs/White%20Papers/ScientificAffairs/telecommuting.pdf
- Web Accessibility Initiative's Essential Components of Web Accessibility: https://www.w3.org/WAI/fundamentals/components/
- Work, Family, & Health Network Workplace Change Toolkits: https://workfamilyhealthnetwork.org/toolkits-achieve-workplace-change
- Workplace Strategies for Mental Health: https://www.workplacestrategiesformentalhealth.com/

Chapter 7
Work- and Management-Focused Strategies

This chapter is one of the longest in the book, and rightly so. It is an important one, so I encourage you to get through as much of it as you can and return to it as needed. It continues the discussion of primary preventive strategies that positively affect all workers from Chapter 6. Moving down a level from the organization to the work/job and management, this chapter focuses on primary preventive *work design and management strategies*. Specifically, I provide work design and management/supervision considerations that are particularly relevant to the health, stress, well-being, and work ability of workers with CHCs, starting with *autonomy and flexibility*. I then detail *management strategies* to support workers with CHCs, including tips for providing emotional support, practical support, building trust with employees, and role modeling health-focused behaviors. Relatedly, I discuss how managers can *avoid pitfalls to supporting workers*, and how they can *respond to a CHC disclosure at work* in a supportive manner. Following this, I provide information on some existing primary preventive work design and management support *interventions*. I close the chapter with a discussion of secondary preventive work-focused strategies, including *job accommodations* and *reduced-load work*. I also include two exercises in this chapter that encourage you to reflect on ways you may support your employees.

7.1 Work Design Strategies: Autonomy and Flexibility

Work design refers to how work is structured and organized in terms of its associated activities, tasks, and relationships.[1] As such, work design includes the tasks workers complete, how tasks and jobs are structured, how much freedom workers have over various aspects of their work, and the social structure of work, such as how interdependent team members are, and how much social interaction is afforded or required through work. As you might imagine, effective work design is a key driver of employee motivation, performance, innovation, safety, well-being, and health.[1]

Feeling that one has control over their own behavior is a fundamental human psychological need;[2] therefore it is not surprising that autonomy is a critical element of work design. The degrees to which a worker has discretion or control over their *work schedule* (i.e., when they work), their *work methods* (i.e., how they complete tasks, the order in which they complete work tasks, and when they take breaks), and their *work decision-making* (i.e., using their judgment in completing work) are collectively known as work autonomy.[3] All of these components are known to positively and strongly relate to satisfaction with work,[3] and various theories support this notion, including the job demands–resources model introduced in Chapter 4. According to the job demands–resources model, autonomy is a job resource that promotes worker motivation and engagement and helps lessen strain experienced with high levels of job demands. Autonomy also signals that a supervisor *trusts* the worker, which is also an important motivating relational factor. For example, in response to a question in our study asking about what helps them maintain work ability despite a CHC, one Sales Manager with chronic pain said, "My employer allows me freedom to choose what I want to do in my job, which makes me feel like they trust my choices and abilities."[4]

It may be helpful for you to think of autonomy as having two main categories—autonomy related to work methods, order of task completion, breaks, and work decision-making, which are also collectively referred to as *job control*; and autonomy related to work scheduling, timing, and location, which is also referred to as *flexible work arrangements*.[5] I will first describe the former—autonomy related to work methods, order of task completion, breaks, and decision-making.

7.1.1 Job Control

Beyond the noted motivational benefits, the first category of autonomy (related to work methods, order of task completion, breaks, and decision-making; i.e., job control) is particularly important to workers with CHCs, first because it is *necessary for workers to implement individual strategies to maintain their work ability*.[4] If you are a worker with a CHC, you are likely well aware of the importance of having job control. If you manage employees with CHCs, allowing job control helps you in that you will not need to approve minor work changes for your employees—instead, they can "self-accommodate." This can help them perform better, maintain their work ability, and ultimately stay employed in their job longer.[4] For example,

- An employee with chronic pain may rely on autonomy to take breaks to rest, stretch, or walk around to alleviate pain when needed.[6] When asked what helps them maintain their ability to work in their current job, a manufacturing worker with scoliosis, endometriosis, thyroid disease, and chronic migraines, age 31, responded, "Allowing rest when it is needed. I am allowed to stop and get pain medicine or take a breather when I cannot handle the pain any longer."
- An employee with chronic fatigue may rely on autonomy to allow coffee or walking breaks to stay focused in the face of heightened fatigue. An information technology support worker with hypertension, and chronic pain, age 23 reported, "My employer will always allow me to grab a coffee if I need to, and if we're out of coffee in our facility, he doesn't mind if I go to the store on campus to grab an energy drink or something of the sort."
- An employee with diabetes may rely on autonomy to take breaks to eat at certain times of the day to keep blood sugar levels stable or do physically laborious tasks as needed to help decrease blood sugar levels. An assistant nursery manager with type 2 diabetes, age 54 said, "I will get suggestions, 'Oh, why don't you do that that way? That'll be easier.' And I say, 'Nope, I am bringing my blood sugar down.'"
- An employee with cognitive dysfunction may rely on autonomy to select optimal times of day to complete more demanding work tasks when their cognition is at its best. A sales manager with a herniated disc and chronic pain, age 35 reported, "For the most part I'm free to determine how to do my job and processes and strategies to use which helps me in working around and preventing difficulties."

Unfortunately, there is a gap in job control between workers with disabilities and those without—73% of employees with disabilities say they have freedom to use their judgment in accomplishing work tasks, as opposed to 86% of employees without disabilities.[7] Put another way, if you are leading people with a CHC, it is likely they feel they have less job control then the people you lead who are not managing a CHC. Alternatively, if you are someone yourself with a CHC, and you feel like you have less control on the job than your coworkers, you are not alone. Yet as noted, job control allows employees to work in optimal ways that maximize their work ability—helping them address some work–health challenges on their own. The discrepancy, combined with its benefits, makes job control a *critical target for intervention to support.*

Reflection Exercise: Job Control

Take a moment to reflect on the level of job control you have, or your subordinates have, if you are a manager or leader. Try to think of ways you can work to increase your own level of job control, and/or the amount of job control that your subordinates have in their roles. You may be thinking that allowing employees more job control is difficult—yet in most cases, it can be increased with creative thinking. Feel free to use the examples in this section for inspiration, but also try to think outside the box.

_____
_____
_____
_____
_____

7.1.2 Flexible Work Arrangements

As you are most assuredly aware, in the past four years there has been an unprecedented increase in flexible work arrangements, spurred by the global COVID-19 pandemic. You yourself may be working a flexible work arrangement. With that in mind, it is important to recognize that flexible work arrangements include both flex time (flexibility regarding *when* work is done) and flex place (flexibility regarding *where* work is done). Examples of flex-time arrangements include adjusted start and end times (e.g., 7:00 a.m. to 3:00 p.m. instead of 9:00 a.m. to 5:00 p.m.) and compressed work weeks (e.g., four 10-hour days instead of five eight-hour days). Examples of flex-place arrangements include telecommuting or working from home and working from different company locations.[8]

Flexible work arrangements have been linked to fewer somatic symptoms, reduced absenteeism, and better physical health, and are thought to facilitate employees maintaining their health with time and energy saved from a reduced or eliminated work commute.[8] They also play a critical role in helping many workers with CHCs maintain employment. How do they support workers with CHCs? First, flex-time arrangements, such as an adjusted schedule or compressed work week, may allow a worker to attend medical appointments during typical working hours without taking a day off from work. Allowing reduced work hours, which I discuss later in this chapter, may allow a worker with a CHC to allocate time and energy to necessary health management behaviors such as exercising, preparing healthy foods, getting adequate rest and sleep, attaining and administering medications, and attending physical therapy and/or counseling sessions.

Remote work arrangements may similarly allow a worker with a CHC to better manage their health condition with saved time, energy, and money that would have been spent on commuting. Working at home also allows workers to work comfortably, perhaps in less formal clothing and in a setting that meets their pain-related needs. Workers with fatigue and/or cognitive fog may find working remotely to be less draining if they have a quiet space with fewer distractions than are typically present in an office setting. Further, workers who are immune-compromised benefit from working remotely to avoid potential exposure to illness.

Several participants in our study shared with us how flexibility has helped them maintain their work ability despite their CHC; examples include:[4]

> He's allowed me to come in earlier and work later so that I may expand my break times to ice/heat my back and rest it.
> —web services manager with a slipped disc in the spine, type 2 diabetes, and hypertension, age 45

> I'm allowed to work remotely occasionally when my condition prohibits me from coming into the office physically.
> —business analyst with gout and chronic pain, age 41

> My employer ... allows me the freedom to do my job how I see fit and I'm able to do it from home so when I'm not feeling well (I have auto immune disorders so this happens a lot) I can work from the comfort of home at my own pace.
> —teacher with fibromyalgia, degenerative disc disease, migraines, and anxiety, age 35

> I haven't much immune system so being virtual allows me to stay somewhat secluded.
> —customer service representative with asthma, COPD, and chronic pain, age 44

> If I am having a difficult time concentrating on my work at the office, I am able to take some of the work to home to finish.
> —data entry clerk with depression and chronic pain, age 35

Although flexible work arrangements are typically thought of for white-collar workers, flex time is also relevant to shift workers. A recent study found that the availability and use of *shift flexibility* in shift workers was related to lower levels of tension, presenteeism, and turnover intentions and higher levels of work engagement and job satisfaction, along with more health maintenance behaviors.[9] Shift flexibility is helpful for workers with CHCs who may experience sudden symptoms or a need to access medical treatment. Organizational leaders can help facilitate shift flexibility by *allowing shift swaps without managerial approval*. They can also *cross-train employees* so they can easily swap shifts for each other as needed. Of course, workers may be more willing to swap shifts if they have positive working relationships with their coworkers, so *facilitating a supportive team culture* is also critical.

Beyond flexibility, shift schedule *predictability* is a helpful job resource to promote worker health and well-being. For workers with CHCs, predictability allows for planning health management activities, including rest, exercise, dietary needs, and medical appointments. In 2017, Seattle passed Fair Workweek legislation, which increased schedule predictability by requiring employers to provide two weeks' notice of work schedules. Researchers found that compared to similar shift workers unaffected by the legislation, those workers with predictable schedules had improved subjective well-being, sleep quality, and economic security over time.[10] Yet others note that legislation requiring predictability often leads workers to have less flexibility and makes it more difficult for organizations to respond to changing personnel needs. A perhaps ideal approach would be for *managers to work with employees one-on-one while maintaining schedule predictability to the extent possible*. Practically speaking, research shows that it is helpful for managers to consult with their employees, allowing them to provide input into work schedules, while setting work schedules two weeks in advance.[11]

7.1.2.1 Best Practices for Flexible Work Arrangements

Dr. Kristen Shockley and colleagues studied the rapid transition to remote work during the COVID-19 pandemic,[12] and their findings inform best practices around remote work. The researchers examined factors that predicted overall adjustment to remote work, stress level during remote work, and job performance relative to prepandemic levels. *Feelings of social isolation* predicted all three outcomes—indicating that *managers should make efforts to help their remote employees maintain social ties.* Further, managers should ensure workers have *access to needed equipment* at home. More specifically, managers can:

- Communicate with subordinates frequently, for instance, on Zoom or by phone.
- Set up remote lunches or coffee breaks.
- Ensure employees have access to a proper desk, chair, and office-quality computer equipment at home.

While flexible work arrangements can be very beneficial to workers with CHCs, as detailed in Chapter 6, these benefits are unrealized if the work culture does not support their use. If employees face negative career outcomes or hostile attitudes from supervisors or coworkers for using flexible work arrangements, others will be less likely to use them, and they will be less effective when they are used.[13] Leaders can *set positive norms for using flexible work arrangements* by:

- Shifting norms from face time to output and quality of results.
- Demonstrating buy-in by using policies themselves and/or actively promoting their use.
- Tracking compensation and talent management systems to ensure they are not biased against those who use flexible work arrangements.

Post-COVID return-to-office mandates are distressing to many workers, particularly those with CHCs who are more vulnerable to illness exposures and those who found working from home to be more sustainable in light of their health needs.[14] Years after the height of the pandemic, this continues to be an issue. As one study participant stated,

> We develop strategies, we develop an ergonomic workstation that works for us. It's comfortable, we can see properly, we can hear properly, we know what to expect. And when that's shaken up it is traumatic for everyone involved.
> **—information security analyst with chronic fatigue and anxiety, age 34**

This example points to the critical need for remote work policies to be *enacted transparently, equitably, and consistently*; otherwise, they will likely be viewed as unfair. For example, during the COVID-19 pandemic, some organizations asked workers to disclose their vaccination status and then recalled vaccinated workers back to the office; this felt like a punishment to some workers who disclosed receiving the vaccine. Others left discretion to managers, which led to some departments being recalled to the office and others not.[14] Organizations should develop fair and equitable policies that align with their strategy and culture around supporting their workers, communicate those policies clearly and effectively, support managers in implementing them consistently and equitably, and hold managers accountable who are unfairly denying allowable remote work.

Intersecting marginalized identities can also lead to a preference for working from home. A recent study found that lesbian, gay, bisexual, transgender, and queer (LGBTQ) adults experienced less stress and fatigue while working at home during the pandemic compared to working in the office.[15] Further, working in the office was more detrimental to LGBTQ workers' well-being compared to non-LGBTQ workers. The researchers concluded that working at home mitigates minority stressors experienced at work.[15] Organizations should *be aware of the negative impacts their return-to-office policies have on marginalized groups*, particularly those with CHCs, and consider *retaining flexible work policies as much as is feasible*.

7.2 Management Strategies: Supervisor Support

Supervisor support is another critical job resource that reflects the extent to which employees perceive that their supervisor *generally cares about their well-being and values their contributions*.[16] If you are currently in a leadership position, you are likely well aware of the fact that effective support is helpful for all employees; it is also consistently linked to better subordinate job attitudes and performance in research studies.[17] And if you are living with a CHC, you are likely sensitive to the fact that supportive supervision is also *critical* to successful continued work for people with CHCs. Workers with CHCs are dependent upon their supervisors to *facilitate work modifications* or accommodations to help them continue working. Supervisors also *provide necessary resources and information, facilitate interpretation of corporate policies, and give general emotional support that helps workers cope*.[18] In short, supervisors are often viewed as the proverbial gatekeepers. With that in mind, an employee is more likely to disclose their CHC to a supervisor who is generally supportive and cares about them both as a person and a worker. As a reminder, such disclosures are beneficial to all parties because they open the door to problem-solving as noted in Chapters 4 and 5. Supportive supervisors are less likely to discriminate against workers with CHCs. Finally, some of the previously mentioned autonomy-related work design elements are contingent upon supervisors providing support for employees having some control at work and refraining from micro-managing them.

7.2.1 Types of Support

Social support at work is generally classified as *emotional support*, including listening, empathy, and encouragement; *instrumental support*, including tangible assistance or helpful resources; *informational support*, including provision of information that is helpful to address a challenge; and *appraisal support*, including evaluative information about the support recipient.[19]

Emotional and instrumental support are most commonly studied and are similarly linked to lower worker strain and better job attitudes and job performance.[17] In addition, "mental health supportive supervisor behaviors"[20] include the following dimensions of support that overlap with the aforementioned ones and may be applied to supporting workers with various CHCs:

- *Emotional support*: expressing care and concern for employees' health and well-being.
- *Practical support*: providing resources or services available through employee assistance programs or other sources within the organization and adjusting schedules to reduce conflicts between work and health management. This could also include ensuring access to supportive infrastructure, such as a refrigerator to store medication or food, or a private space to inject medication or rest.[21]
- *Role modeling*: leading through modeling positive health-protective behaviors; for example, taking time off for health needs (and communicating that to employees).
- *Stigma reduction*: communicating that it is typical and expected to get support for health needs.

In a study of supervisor support for workers with CHCs, researchers Dr. Candace Nelson and colleagues interviewed supervisors about their strategies to help workers stay on the job despite a CHC and associated symptom flareups.[18] The researchers found that supervisors worked to *build trust through daily interactions* so that a worker may feel comfortable coming to them when a health issue arises.[18] This included:

- overlooking minor infractions,
- ensuring workers are treated fairly,

- respecting workers' confidentiality,
- actively listening to workers' needs, and
- giving workers latitude to handle health challenges, through allowing them to leave work and seek medical care.

In our study, we heard from several participants that support from their supervisor helped them maintain their work ability.[4] These provide some helpful detail to flesh out the aforementioned research findings around helpful support. For example,

> My boss allows flexibility when I need it, he knows when I'm struggling and lets me take any time that I need to rest and recover from what's bothering me. He's perceptive and knows when I need him to not pressure me for results and demands.
> —lab manager with hypertension, age 46

> Allows me to come in late on bad pain days and whenever I have a sleepless night. Watches my station when I need to rest or reset a joint. Steps in to help me focus when I start to have an anxiety attack. Allows me to work late after my shift to finish tasks I couldn't focus on with typical restaurant chaos.
> —pastry chef with PTSD, anemia, ehlers-danlos syndrome, chronic migraines, and rheumatoid arthritis, age 44

> My employer keeps in good contact to make sure things are going okay. And they are pretty understandable if I have anything to do to take care of myself. So they watch out for my well-being.
> —high school teacher with rheumatoid arthritis and chronic pain, age 35

> I work closely with my supervisor who lets me come in later when a migraine hits and lets me make up hours in the evening or on the weekends.
> —customer service representative with chronic migraines, age 52

> My boss is very understanding. If I'm tired or hurting, I can find something to do while sitting.
> —childcare provider with spinal stenosis and arthritis, age 29

> My boss is very lenient about letting me leave for doctor's appointments, and when I'm not feeling well, he allows me to work at my own pace.
> —landscape design manager with chronic sinusitis and headaches, age 28

As these quotes illustrate, *informal support* is very important to workers with CHCs. In a year-long project to identify best practices to avoid disability, leading scholars noted that *implementing individualized solutions and supports* for workers with CHCs is critical.[22] In a separate study, researchers found that for supervisors, *having flexibility and authority in applying organizational policies and making changes to workers' schedules and duties*, was helpful in optimally supporting workers with CHCs.[18] In sum, while formal policies for accommodation are critical to ensuring access for all workers, some leeway for supervisors to problem-solve and implement informal or customized supports is also helpful in many cases.

While all of this may sound ideal, in some cases there are of course, operational challenges to work through to enable support is possible alongside meeting operational demands. To help with this, supervisors may work to *build coworker support* through *encouraging teamwork and cross-training workers* to fill in for each other when one is out sick.[18] If workers are able and willing to cover for each other, operational impacts will be lessened when a worker needs time off. It is important to promote a positive team culture where supporting each other is the norm for this to be effective.

Reflection Exercise: Supervisor Support

- If you are in a managerial position, reflect on ways that you might be able to demonstrate one or more of the forms of support discussed in this section for your employee(s) with CHCs.
- Or, if you are not currently in a managerial position but see yourself in one in the future, imagine ways you might be able to support your future subordinates who may have CHCs.
- In either scenario, which forms of support do you think will be relatively easier for you to provide? Which do you think will be more difficult to provide? Are there any that you think will come more naturally to you? Are there any that might require some practice or other resources?

7.2.2 Support Pitfalls

Importantly, support is not always perceived as helpful; some support can even be perceived as harmful by the recipient.[17,23] This includes the forms of ableism described in Chapters 2 and 4, such as:

- Referring to someone with a CHC as "inspirational" for completing simple daily tasks (i.e., "inspiration porn"),

- Making degrading or pitying comments such as "I don't know how you could live like this—I couldn't do it."
- Providing unsolicited or unhelpful advice; for instance, implying that having a positive attitude or outlook will cause the person's CHC to improve or be cured.
- Assuming someone cannot do a task and doing it for them without asking. A particularly egregious example of this is touching a person's wheelchair to move them out of the way without asking them first.

Dr. Cheryl Gray and colleagues asked employees to recall a time when they received ineffective/unhelpful support at work and to describe the incident and what made it unhelpful. The researchers found the following categories of *un*helpful workplace support that supervisors should try to avoid.[23]

- *Impractical support*: unreasonable, misinforming support
- *Partial support*: imprecise, unclear support
- *Undependable support*: the provider overpromises and underdelivers support
- *Critical of the recipient support*: support that makes the recipient feel insulted
- *Incompatible support*: support that is in conflict with how the recipient works
- *Imposing support*: support that is unwanted or forced
- *Shortsighted support*: the provider of support completes a task without teaching the recipient how to do it for themselves
- *Poorly assigned support*: the supervisor assigns an employee to help the recipient with a task, but the employee provided was unhelpful because they were not trained or skilled
- *Stress magnifying support*: support that causes the recipient to focus more on the stressor
- *Conflicting support*: when multiple sources of support provide conflicting information or advice
- *Uncomforting support*: support that is intended to be emotionally comforting but is not perceived that way by the recipient (e.g., saying "It could be worse")

7.2.3 Supportive Responses to a Health Disclosure

Although this next topic is not relevant to all workers—technically rendering it outside the realm of a primary preventive strategy—I am including it in this section because it is a critical support element for workers with CHCs. Disclosing a CHC to a supervisor is a significant event in a worker's employment—one that many times invokes stress for the worker, who may fear an unsupportive or unhelpful response, and/or potential future discrimination. It is also likely stressful for the manager, who may want to be supportive but experience fear or uncertainty about how to respond.

As noted in Chapter 4, an employee may need to disclose a CHC because they are going through a new diagnosis of a lifelong condition, and/or experiencing a flare-up of symptoms, a sudden change in the disease course or progression, or a change in treatment that necessitates job or schedule modifications. It is important for others to know that *the point at which a worker discloses a CHC may be among the most difficult, stressful times in their life*, something you may be keenly aware of if you have a CHC yourself. For example, the person disclosing may be experiencing a high level of stress due to impacts of the disease and its implications for their future, including their ability to work, financial challenges due to high costs of medical care in the US, impacts of their health challenges on family members, and possible medical trauma. Further, due to it being a time of heightened emotions, the discloser will *likely remember how others responded* to their disclosure. Therefore, those on the receiving end of a medical disclosure should do everything possible to *ensure their reactions are of comfort to the worker disclosing* and that they *provide appropriate support*.

It is easy to say that managers should react with compassion and appropriate levels of support; what this looks like in practice, however, is elusive. In my interviews of HR professionals and managers in organizations, I have found that most supervisors receive no training on these issues and there are very few written guidelines for doing so. To compound the issue, disclosure recipients tend to be unaware of how they come across to a person who discloses. In one study, researchers found that participants without a mental illness who received a disclosure were *not aware of how negatively their unsupportive behaviors and responses were perceived* by those who disclosed a mental illness.[24] On the other hand, they also did not fully appreciate how *positively their emotional support was perceived* by those who disclosed a mental illness.[24] Overall, these findings point to the need for managers and other disclosure recipients to be more attuned to their disclosure reactions.

The same researchers asked participants with depression for examples of supportive and unsupportive responses to disclosure. Supportive responses included four types of support: (1) emotional, (2) appraisal (affirmation), (3) informational (advice), and (4) instrumental (tangible assistance). On the other hand, unsupportive responses included (1) insulting behavior, (2) denial of symptoms, (3) avoidance (e.g., silence), (4) denial of assistance (dismissing requests for support), and (5) negative behavior (e.g., exclusion or termination).[24]

In an article for the Harvard Business Review, I provided several *tips for responding to CHC disclosures at work*.[25] The list below includes some of these and contains additional points to help supervisors and HR professionals guide the interaction and point the conversation toward shared problem-solving.

- *Go to a private location*, if the setting is not conducive to discussing the topic, to help preserve the confidentiality of sensitive information.
- *Display empathy*—for example, "This sounds like it may be very challenging to deal with."
- *Thank the person for sharing*—such as "I imagine that this may have been difficult for you to bring up; thank you for trusting me with this information."
- *Listen actively and carefully* to what the worker says. Try to be in the present moment, rather than thinking of what you will say next.
- *Take your time*. It is okay to not respond immediately. If you are struggling with what to say, don't be afraid to admit that.
- *Ask if they are experiencing or expect to experience any health-related challenges with meeting work responsibilities, but don't assume they are*—for example, "Is there anything I should know about how this affects or might affect your work?"
- *Ask what they need to continue working and meeting expectations for their role. In other words, do not try to immediately come up with solutions for them*—for example, "What do you need from me or the organization to help you continue to work most effectively?"
- *Point the worker to available supportive resources, benefits, and policies* (e.g., relevant employee resource groups, company-sponsored programs, employee assistance programs).

- *Tell the worker that you will follow up with them.* Make sure they know the conversation will be ongoing—and they should come to you when needed.
- *Maintain confidentiality.* Assure the worker you will not tell others the information they have shared, unless they explicitly give you permission to talk to other organizational representatives (e.g., HR) on their behalf.

In addition, there are some potential pitfalls to avoid when responding to a disclosure, including:

- *Do not violate a workers' boundaries* by asking questions about the disease, its course, or other diagnosis or health-related details. Keep the focus on work and what the person needs from you to continue doing their job effectively.
- *Do not use a disclosure as an opportunity to spotlight your own health or other life challenges*; keep the focus on the employee. It is ok to disclose your own challenges later, and this may even work to build rapport and trust with your employee. However, it is likely not beneficial to disclose your own struggles in direct response to an employee's disclosure, as it may come across as insensitive to their disclosure.
- *Do not discuss other people you may know who have the same CHC, and especially do not give worst-case scenarios* (e.g., "My friend's cousin had this disease and was disabled within a year of diagnosis"). Even a positive story (e.g., "My uncle had that disease, and he ran marathons and worked until he was 80!") can be detrimental in that it may undermine that individual worker's experience with the disease. Keep in mind that individuals' disease courses and symptoms will usually vary, even with the same disease.
- *Do not offer medical advice or alternative medicines, herbal remedies, lifestyle changes, or other therapies as possible solutions* (e.g., "I take turmeric pills to cure my fatigue"). Keep in mind that the person with the disease is likely already an expert on their condition and has considered or tried several remedies. It will likely come across as condescending to propose that you might know more than they do, and suggesting a simple solution may come across as minimizing the problem.
- *Do not overpromise on job modifications/accommodations.* You can always work with HR and come back to the employee with more information later.

7.2.4 Supervisor Training

Given the importance of supervisor support, and the lack of resources to help supervisors navigate these issues, supervisor training is clearly important as a job resource to help support workers with CHCs, as well as to help decrease stress and protect the well-being of supervisors who may be dealing with something like this for the first time. Yet supervisor trainings on supporting workers with CHCs are lacking. Such training may include building awareness of challenges workers face; building trust to facilitate disclosure; and educating managers on how to respond to disclosure, how to have difficult conversations around health and work, legal responsibilities and rights, helpful resources to refer employees to, collaborative problem-solving, and accommodations processes.

7.3 Examples of Work Design and Management Interventions

A few tangentially related trainings and other related interventions exist that I will detail in the following subsections. Beyond those described, this is an area ripe for innovation and I hope to see materials and programs developed for this purpose.

7.3.1 STAR Intervention to Increase Flexibility and Supervisor Support

Designed and evaluated by researchers at the Work, Family, and Health Network in the US, STAR is an organizational change intervention to support employees' work–life balance through increasing work scheduling autonomy and supervisor support for workers' personal lives and work performance, along with aligning organizational culture around flexibility and support for workers' families/non–work lives.[26] STAR was implemented and assessed in a large technology firm in the US, and was found to be associated with reduced employee burnout, stress, psychological distress, work–family conflict, and turnover intentions, as well as increased job satisfaction in a randomized controlled trial.[26-28] STAR was also adapted to be implemented in healthcare settings; toolkits for implementing STAR in both office and healthcare settings are in the Additional Resources section.

STAR programs are tailored to the setting (e.g., healthcare vs. office settings); for illustrative purposes I will describe the office setting STAR intervention.[29] In STAR for office settings, workers are given considerably increased amounts of flexibility in both *when* and *where* they work (i.e., flex time and flex place), and supervisors are trained to be supportive of their employees' personal lives outside of work. The program starts with communication about the intervention, followed by leadership education and manager/supervisor training, including online training with follow-up goal setting and tracking of supportive behaviors. Following this, all participating employees are educated about STAR and how it works. "Sludge eradication" focus groups are held that seek to identify and eliminate old, inflexible ways of working that focus on face time, with a goal of building a results-oriented, flexible culture. Participants then record sludge eradication efforts in their teams over the course of two weeks. Next, culture clinics are held to help solidify the new culture and ways of working, and the redesigned work structure goes live. Employees complete activities to track new ways of working and behaviors that support their coworkers or help them take better control of their time for two weeks after the program goes live. At this point, managers also have a check-in with facilitators and practice supportive behaviors, as well as set new goals and track progress toward those goals. Six weeks after the new work structure goes live, teams come together to share challenges and successes with the new work structure and culture, and facilitators provide coaching and encouragement.[29] In terms of cost, STAR was estimated to cost $340 USD per employee.[30]

Although STAR provides an excellent framework for changing culture and management support, and it has been found to be effective in promoting worker well-being and decreasing turnover intentions in several contexts, there are some important caveats to note related to its focus on family. One study of STAR in grocery stores found beneficial effects solely for workers with *high levels of family-to-work conflict*—in other words, those that had many family intrusions on their work that interfered with their work performance. Further, those with lower levels of family intrusions on work actually experienced *decrements* to their job satisfaction and physical health, as well as increased turnover intentions.[31] The researchers posited that those with low levels of family-to-work conflict resented the additional attention and leeway given to those with families. This group of people who did not benefit from a sole focus on family could possibly include workers with CHCs, who also are needing leeway and support from managers—though the researchers did not examine this in their study. Therefore, I recommend that future interventions do not default to assumptions that family is the only or primary domain outside of work that employees need support in navigating. Explicit attention should also be paid to CHCs and other nonwork challenges that employees may be facing—yet the goal should be inclusion and well-being for *all* employees.

In sum, a key takeaway from the STAR intervention studies is that leaders and those implementing interventions should acknowledge various challenging issues employees may face, including CHCs, but not solely focus on one specific set of challenges or group of employees when intervening for culture, management, and work design, as doing so may create backlash from excluded groups of employees.[32] This is another reason to focus on primary prevention efforts (i.e., ones that positively affect *all* workers) first when intervening to support workers with CHCs.

7.3.2 Interventions to Increase Support for Worker Mental Health

One example of a supervisor training to support workers with chronic mental health conditions is the Mental Health Awareness Training, or MHAT, developed by Drs. Jennifer Dimoff and Kevin Kelloway. MHAT was designed to promote mental health literacy for managers. The three-hour training includes lecture, interactive case studies, and videos, and includes information on five common mental illnesses and associated behavioral warning signs. It also provides information to managers on various resources available to employees. Further, it teaches managers how to display empathy while remaining professional and how to support employees without violating their boundaries.[33,34] Study results indicated that MHAT resulted in several important benefits, including:[33,34]

- Supervisors having increased knowledge about mental health issues;
- Supervisors having improved attitudes toward mental health issues;
- Supervisors reporting increased willingness to talk with employees about mental health in the workplace;
- Supervisors sharing more information about mental health and available resources and actively encouraging employees to use them;
- Supervisors being more supportive of employees' mental health issues;
- Employees reporting increased willingness to seek out and use available mental health resources;
- Reduced duration of short-term disability claims related to mental health problems.

Moreover, MHAT is cost-effective—estimated to range between $100 and $450 per leader, depending on how much customization is required. In general, the success of MHAT in the workplace is encouraging and points to likely benefits of implementing supervisor trainings for mental health literacy more widely. The focus on mental health specifically is beneficial, as these conditions are highly stigmatized and difficult for many to discuss. However, some of the issues—particularly around initiating discussions and pointing employees to available resources—are not specific to mental health problems, and it seems plausible to expand the training to those associated with many types of chronic physical and mental health conditions.

7.4 Secondary Work-Focused Strategies

Beyond the primary preventive strategies already discussed, secondary preventive work-focused strategies include job accommodations and reduced load work.

7.4.1 Job Modifications/Accommodations

> I am in the process of discussing possible accommodations for my position. It is extremely difficult to have no assistance in navigating the process. Employers do not have easy directions on the steps to follow, or who needs to be contacted. I have to maintain certain hours otherwise I will lose my health insurance, and I will not be able to afford my treatment. The anxiety can be overwhelming at times when trying to manage living with a chronic illness.
> —pediatric registered nurse with psoriatic arthritis and depression, age 33

Job accommodations are critical supports for workers with CHCs to help preserve work ability and well-being and prevent disability leave. Because they are typically reactive in nature and are used solely for workers with qualified disabilities, they are classified as secondary preventive strategies. As detailed in Chapter 2 job accommodations are modifications or adjustments to the work environment, job tasks, or work structure that are necessary to enable the employee to perform job functions.

Accommodations are critical to helping individuals with CHCs and other disabilities to remain employed and perform to their potential; in fact, of several factors, accommodations were most strongly related to continued employment of workers with disabilities in a recent systematic review.[35] However, they do not solely help workers—they also help managers ensure their employees are working to their optimal capacities, and they help organizations retain talented workers and reap the benefits of a diverse workforce that includes workers with disabilities. Further, the prompt implementation of accommodations helps promote a culture of diversity, equity, inclusion, and accessibility (DEIA) as discussed in Chapter 6.

In the US, employers are required by law to provide reasonable accommodations to workers with disabilities, which include most CHCs. Table 2.3 in Chapter 2 lists several examples of accommodations; one example is relocating an individual's workstation to a quieter location or allowing remote work to accommodate a worker with a CHC that causes cognitive fatigue that is worsened with distractions. Notably, principles of universal design, as discussed in Chapter 6, would have ensured access to quiet workstations for all workers, precluding the need for this accommodation.

Because many CHC-related disabilities are nonapparent or invisible to others (e.g., pain, fatigue, weakness, cognitive dysfunction, emotion dysregulation, immune-compromised status), supervisors and other workers may doubt that a worker needs a requested accommodation and think that they are malingering or taking advantage of the system. Perhaps for this reason, workers also report feeling that the employment relationship becomes more adversarial when they request formal accommodations.[36] While there may be cases of this, it is safe to say (and best to assume) the vast majority of people requesting accommodations have legitimate disabilities they need accommodations for, as noted in Chapter 4. There are a few reasons for this. First, as noted in Chapters 4 and 5, discrimination is common and many workers experience fear that disclosing their CHC to attain an accommodation will result in discrimination and lost career opportunities now or in the future. Second, medical "proof" that an accommodation is necessary is required to attain an accommodation in most cases. There are also negative consequences of failing to believe an employee needs an accommodation, including a "chilling effect" where fewer people request accommodations in the future, likely inducing reduced performance due to needs not being accommodated, along with increased turnover—not to mention potential discrimination lawsuits. It will also perpetuate a culture that is not inclusive or supportive. In sum, it is always better to *believe employees when they request accommodations and work with the employee to promptly provide reasonable accommodations* to ensure their needs are met.

There are several myths around accommodations at work that serve to perpetuate negative attitudes toward accommodations. These myths and the realities accompanying each are listed below.

- *Myth: accommodations are costly.* To the contrary, most accommodations do not cost anything or incur a one-time cost $300 USD or less.[37]

- *Myth: accommodations can be used to decrease performance expectations.* Again, this is not true—accommodated employees should still be held to the same performance standards as other employees. Employers may take appropriate action as they would for nondisabled employees, including termination if performance standards are not met with accommodations.[38]
- *Myth: job accommodations can be used to remove essential parts of an employee's job.* Accommodations may not be used to remove essential job functions—instead, they are meant to ensure the disabled employee has equal access to perform essential job functions as nondisabled employees.
- *Myth: employers must hire a worker with a disability when other qualified candidates also apply for the job.* To the contrary, under US law, employers are free to hire their choice of applicant, as long as the decision is not based on disability status.[38]
- *Myth: if a worker with a disability receives an accommodation, employers must then provide the accommodation to all workers.* In the US, formal accommodations under the ADA are made an individual basis due to the individual having a qualified disability. However, issues of fairness are a concern, as discussed in Chapter 5. Employers may not disclose the health condition of a worker with an accommodation to their coworkers, though they should stress that the accommodation is necessary, and is not special treatment but is meant to allow that person equal access to perform essential job functions.

7.4.2 Reduced-Load Work

Finding a way to encourage people with limited energy to continue to contribute without being able to work 8–10 hours a day would be a great way to utilize the real "human resources" in our nation.
—self-employed individual with multiple sclerosis, age 54

Reduced-load work refers to reduced workload and hours, with a commensurate pay cut, while remaining on a professional career track. Reduced-load work is considered a talent management strategy to retain salaried, white-collar, professional workers, particularly highly skilled or talented workers, and is implemented through customized arrangements with a manager.[39] A reduced load allows individuals to build sustainable careers, helping reduce the changes of overwork which often results in strain or turnvover.[39]

Reduced-load work has been linked to better well-being outcomes for those who use it.

Reduced-load work is typically used by women seeking to reduce work–family conflict due to childcare and/or eldercare responsibilities; as of the writing of this book, there are no published studies of reduced-load work for workers with CHCs. Nevertheless, reduced-load work is an obvious strategy that may be used to retain talented workers with CHCs. For example, a newly diagnosed worker may desire six months of reduced-load work to adjust to living with a disease, get necessary testing, or get settled on treatment while remaining on a career track. As another example, a worker with chronic fatigue from a CHC may benefit from longer-term reduced-load work to get adequate rest so that they can perform to their optimal capacity on workdays. Whereas they may drive themselves to the point of needing to leave the workforce on disability if they continued working long hours, reduced-load work may allow them to proactively better manage their health while maintaining good job performance during their reduced work hours and remaining on their desired career track.

Provision of reduced-load work is dependent upon the manager, and by extension, the employee's relationship with their manager. Studies of reduced-load work have found that managers are more supportive of and flexible with reduced-load work when they are in an organization with a supportive culture, with support from senior management, along with adaptation of HR systems to accommodate reduced-load work.[40] Further, managers are more likely to support reduced-load work when the employee is a high-performer, is flexible about the implementation of reduced-load work (e.g., willing to work more when needed), and has a job that the manager perceives to be conducive to reduced-load work (e.g., not core to the organization's functioning).[40] Therefore, reduced-load work is not a scalable, widely available strategy for all workers with CHCs, but should be a helpful option for those fortunate enough to have the optimal conditions (trusting, collaborative working relationship with a supervisor, excellent performance record, supportive organizational culture, and conducive job type). Notably, such workers (in the US) will likely need to retain their health insurance coverage for this arrangement to work for them. This likely means they need to work a certain number of hours per week to be eligible for benefits.

In sum, reduced-load work should not solely be considered for women managing work–family conflict; it is also an excellent option to help reduce work–health management interference for workers with CHCs. With the right conditions, it can be a win-win strategy, such that it allows workers sustainable careers, while helping managers retain talented workers.

7.5 Summary of Recommendations: Work-Focused Strategies

- Provide employee autonomy to the extent possible.
  - Provide autonomy in work methods and order of task completion to allow work to be done at optimal times and in optimal ways to maximize functionality.
  - Provide autonomy in taking breaks to allow self-management of symptoms as needed.
  - Think creatively about small ways you can work to increase your employees' levels of autonomy in their daily jobs.
- Facilitate shift flexibility and/or shift schedule predictability to allow workers to attend to symptom flares, self-manage their illness, and access medical care when needed.
  - Consider allowing shift swaps without managerial approval.
  - Cross-train employees so they can cover for one another.
  - Allow employees to provide input into their work schedules.
  - Provide two weeks' notice of shift schedules when possible.
  - Encourage a positive, supportive team culture.
- Allow flexible work arrangements (flex time and flex place) to the extent possible.
  - Develop fair and equitable flexible work policies, support managers in implementing them, and hold managers accountable for their appropriate use.
  - Set positive norms for using flexible work arrangements by using policies.
  - Track talent management outcomes to reduce bias against those who use them.
  - Communicate frequently with remote workers and set up virtual social events to help employees stay connected.
  - Provide appropriate equipment for individuals who work from home.
- Build supportive relationships with subordinates to encourage open communication and cooperative problem-solving for work–health challenges.
  - Look for ways to provide emotional as well as practical support to employees.
  - Role model healthy behaviors (e.g., taking time off to manage health).
  - Build trust through daily interactions that signal fairness, confidentiality, and active listening to workers.
  - Support workers' autonomy in work timing, methods, and breaks to allow self-management and to maximize functioning.
  - Implement individualized solutions, including flexible, informal, and innovative accommodations to help workers continue to work and perform to their potential.
  - Avoid support pitfalls (e.g., support that is uncomforting, imposing, undependable, short-sighted, or stress-magnifying).
- Gain skills in supportive reactions when a worker discloses a CHC.
- Promptly implement formal accommodations when requested; yet enable supervisors to consider more informal, flexible accommodations first, when possible.
- Consider implementing programs and policies described in this chapter, such as supervisor trainings to support employees with CHCs and reduced-load work policies.

Additional Resources

- Center for Supportive Leadership (includes workplace mental health support): https://www.supportiveleadership.org/
- Centre for Transformative Work Design: https://www.transformativeworkdesign.com/

- Family Supportive Supervisors Training Manual: https://workfamilyhealthnetwork.org/files/wfhn/files/fssb_training_manual10_13.pdf
- Harvard Work and Well-Being Initiative Employer Toolkit: Work Design for Health: https://workwellbeinginitiative.org/employertoolkit
- Job Accommodation Network (JAN) Workplace Accommodation Toolkit: https://askjan.org/toolkit/index.cfm
- Job Demands and Accommodation Planning Tool for Workers: https://aced.iwh.on.ca/jdapt/worker-en
- Northwest ADA Center Factsheet on Universal Design at Work: https://nwadacenter.org/factsheet/universal-design-workplace
- (US) Employers and the ADA: Myths and Facts: https://www.dol.gov/agencies/odep/publications/fact-sheets/americans-with-disabilities-act
- US Surgeon General's Report on Workplace Mental Health and Well-Being: https://www.hhs.gov/surgeongeneral/priorities/workplace-well-being/index.html

Chapter 8
Individual Worker-Focused Strategies

In the previous two chapters, I discussed organization- and work-focused strategies for supporting workers with CHCs: those that target the work environment, culture, job design, and supervision. The placement of organization- and work-focused, primary preventive strategies prior to individual worker-focused, secondary preventive strategies in this book was purposeful, as strategies targeting organizations, jobs, and supervision generally benefit not just those with CHCs, but all workers. In addition, as you likely noted, most serve to *proactively* promote well-being and prevent declines in employee work ability, rather than mitigating harms.

Yet many workers with CHCs have work–health challenges that *necessitate additional targeted secondary approaches* to prevent further decline and preserve existing work ability and well-being, alongside primary preventive approaches. This is likely something you have experienced firsthand, either as a leader in your organization, or as someone with a CHC. Challenges may emerge with new diagnoses of CHCs, changes to work roles and responsibilities, new or existing symptom flare-ups impairing work, sudden disease progression, new treatments necessitating time off or side effect management, and so on. Further, not all jobs are amenable to high levels of autonomy and flexibility; not all supervisors are willing to be supportive or are able to be given limited resources; and not all organizational cultures will value worker inclusion and well-being. Workers in those situations need strategies they can enact that are independent of the work environment and structure to help them:

- reflect and make sense of their circumstances,
- problem-solve,
- plan for their future careers,
- advocate for themselves,
- manage stress, and
- receive support from others.

As opposed to the *work-focused* secondary preventive strategy presented in Chapter 7 (job accommodations), in this chapter I focus on *individual worker-focused interventions*. Individual-focused interventions are those that address work–health challenges to promote work-related well-being and work ability by changing the individual in some way (e.g., learning, skill development, problem-solving), rather than changing the job structure, work environment, or supervisor behaviors as with organizational- and work-focused interventions.

Remember from the job demands–resources model in Chapter 4 that personal resources are helpful for workers to maintain their work ability. These individual-focused approaches work to *build their personal resources*, which better help them manage work–health challenges and therefore, help improve their work ability.[1] Workers may find this chapter helpful in advocating for themselves at work about the need for resources such as these, and managers may find this chapter helpful in build a case to leadership for why programs such as these are needed and would be helpful in supporting workers.

Individual-focused interventions in this chapter are limited to those that are both work-related and preventive—in other words, focusing on maintaining or improving work-related well-being and work ability. I therefore exclude more general health-related interventions with sole focus on health management behaviors or health metrics without a connection to work (e.g., health coaching, diabetes prevention programs, and smoking cessation programs). I also exclude more tertiary work-related interventions, such as most vocational rehabilitation programs and return-to-work programs for those already on disability leave (though these are detailed in Chapter 3).

Individual-focused individual interventions in this chapter range from being one-on-one to group-based and being focused on specific CHCs to generalized and not focused on any one CHC. Across different programs, themes include:

- learning/psychoeducational components,
- motivational/accountability components,
- problem-solving/cognitive strategizing components,
- interpersonal/social components (e.g., building communication skills, developing identity management strategies),
- stress management/coping/emotion regulation components, and
- social support components.

8.1 Individualized Programs

One-on-one, individualized approaches provide *targeted attention and focus on a worker's current specific work–health problem(s)*. Since CHCs and associated symptoms often wax and wane over the course of an illness, and how they interact with work also may vary significantly depending on the job and working conditions, it is helpful to have *flexibility and customization* built into the framework of a program addressing CHCs and work. Such flexibility to address specific work-health problems arising from the specific CHC and the job or organizational characteristics may be built into one-on-one approaches, most notably coaching—yet, at the same time, a common structure and framework may be used across individuals. Further, a common set of anticipated challenges may be used to educate coaches and/or prepare foundational educational materials (as described in Chapter 4). One-on-one programs are also helpful in that they can be *applied to many different types of CHCs* and are not limited in terms of their applicability to specific CHCs. This means these programs will inherently be able to help a greater number of workers than programs targeted to a specific disease or condition. Not surprisingly, researchers have found that organizations generally prefer programs and resources that are more general and *not* specific to certain CHCs.[2]

8.1.1 Coaching

I led a study of coaching for workers with CHCs with colleagues Rosalind Joffe and Dr. Joy Beatty; this first-hand experience informs my detailed discussion of coaching in this chapter. Rosalind, who is an International Coach Federation–certified coach and has been coaching workers with CHCs for 20 years, worked with Joy and I to standardize and evaluate a coaching program. The program included six one-hour, phone-based, one-on-one coaching sessions over 12 weeks.[1] Importantly, this was *not* a health coaching program to increase motivation for health-related behaviors, such as diet or exercise. Instead, it addressed client-selected challenges and goals related to working with CHCs to improve well-being and work ability and decrease work-related burnout. The first session focused on clarifying challenges and identifying a goal for coaching; subsequent sessions included brief mindfulness exercises, motivational interviewing/powerful questioning from the coach, discussing goal progress, and homework between sessions.[1] Importantly, the coach provided confidential support and empathy; she also has personal lived experience with CHCs that she shared with clients as appropriate. Many participants voiced that they found this to be helpful, as they felt that their issues were often invisible, underappreciated, or misunderstood.

In line with the job demands–resources model explained in Chapter 4, we proposed that coaching would help build individuals' personal resources to effectively manage work-related physical, social, and emotional challenges associated with CHCs, leading to improvements to work ability and work-related well-being and decreased burnout. We tested our hypotheses using a randomized control trial design with 59 individuals working full-time with various CHCs in the US. We found that compared to scores from a waitlisted control group over the same timeframe, participants in the intervention group had higher levels of work ability, mental resources, resilience, and core-self evaluations, along with lower levels of exhaustion burnout after coaching versus at baseline.[1] Further, these positive effects were stable at a three-month post-coaching assessment, suggesting the benefits of coaching last at least three months.[1] Our positive findings for coaching are consistent with findings from meta-analyses that demonstrate coaching's effectiveness in organizations more generally.[3,4]

However, we did not find evidence that coaching benefited participants' work disengagement or job satisfaction.[1] This may be because coaching is an individual-focused intervention that does not directly address work-related factors. It is feasible that coaching may work to affect working conditions through improvements to clients' confidence, ability to self-advocate, and improve their social relationships at work over a longer time period, leading to better downstream job satisfaction—yet we were unable to test this with our short follow-up timeframe. Future studies should follow participants for longer time periods to determine possible delayed effects on work satisfaction and engagement.

We also analyzed exit interviews from coaching participants to further evaluate coaching. Acknowledging that CHCs can be threatening to existing notions of the self and disrupt professional and work identities, as detailed in Chapter 4,[5] we sought to understand whether and how coaching may help with work or professional identity disruptions from CHCs.[6] As illustrated by quotes from participants below, we found that coaching facilitated both internal (self) and external (social) work identity issues.

Internal identity work included understanding illness dynamics and how they affect work and establishing realistic expectations and goals for work.[6]

> [I'm] scheduling time to rest in the day and working on gently and easily going through instead of just pushing through and pushing myself to my limit so that I'll be very productive for a couple days and then I'll crash for a couple days. I mean I still do that, I'm aware of it, and I try to do it less.
> —writer with erythropoietic protoporphyria, age 37

Internal work also included developing confidence and realizing one's value as an employee.[6]

> [Coaching] helped me to see that . . . I was discounting my contribution . . . I came away with a stronger reserve of inner strength from the coaching, that was a huge thing for me. As well as techniques for giving myself a break and not beating myself up about it. I tended to push through stuff, I tended to assume that if I let myself slack off this day because I'm not feeling particularly well it might become a habit . . . It's just not really in me to do that and I wasn't seeing that in myself.
> —**electronic document specialist with chronic inflammatory demyelinating polyneuropathy and lupus, age 44**

In addition, internal work included adopting needed assistive devices, including medication.[6]

> Accepting that sometimes you do need to take medication. I was beating myself up for needing to take medication sometimes to function. Whereas now I have my threshold and once I hit this point I am going to take medicine—that's better for me than waiting until it to get above that and go okay, oh my God I need medicine.
> —**security analyst with psoriatic arthritis, aortic valve disease, and anxiety, age 30**

External identity work included working through how and what to ask for regarding an accommodation or other support.[6]

> Last week I was put on new medications and I was having serious reactions and I wasn't telling anybody. I was just doing my best to hold off without saying anything at work. One day I just walked into my boss's office and said you know I might not be in at the same time every morning I'm dealing with this medication reaction and I'm really, really tired. I'm getting my work done but it's hard for me to get out of bed physically in the morning so please just bear with me and it should be out of my system soon and I will be back to normal but I just need a little slack this week. And I was surprised she just said do whatever you need to do. I wasn't expecting that. But the fact that I could even walk in there and say that . . . I might not have done that before.
> —**electronic document specialist with chronic inflammatory demyelinating polyneuropathy and lupus, age 44**

External work also included improving communication skills and developing impression management strategies.[6]

> I'm more willing to talk to people about the chronic illness and make jokes about it than I had been . . . I try not to talk about it too much (that is never a good idea) but I can talk about it, I can joke about it, and I can advocate for myself a little easier . . .

And [the coach] also gave me a few tips about how to feel, or appear in control, so that it doesn't appear that chronic illness is all that I am to my coworkers (which had been one of my concerns).
—engineering draftsperson with mold sensitivity and chronic migraines, age 27

I think [before coaching] I would have agonized a bit more over what to say to [my boss] and how to say it to him and how much... I think the thing [the coach] helped me with the most was figuring out how to communicate what outcome do I want? And how much does someone need to hear to get to that outcome.
—college professor with inner ear disorder, chronic migraines, and a blood clotting disorder, age 40

Finally, we analyzed transcripts of individual coaching sessions to understand common topics and issues related to working with CHCs that were discussed during coaching sessions. Coaches, HR professionals, and managers should be aware of these common topics, as they are likely to be prevalent issues workers with CHCs face and need assistance with. Further, based on the large proportion of people living with CHCs, it is likely that CHC-related issues may present during coaching sessions, even for clients who engage with coaching for other reasons (e.g., executive coaching, health coaching, life coaching). The most frequent CHC-related topics discussed during coaching sessions, in descending order, were as follows:[7]

- *Illness management*: Discussion of medical appointments, medications, treatments, side-effects, doctors, hospitals, alternative medicine, self-treatments (e.g., sleep, eating certain foods), and managing symptoms.
- *Work–health related*: Discussion and problem-solving related to, for example, work health management interference, informal or formal accommodations, applicable US disability law, experiences of discrimination, meeting work expectations, and need for time off.
- *Symptoms*: Discussion of CHC-related symptoms, such as headaches, pain, fatigue, brain fog, and depressive symptoms.
- *Communication and impression management*: Discussion of communication strategies, such as how to approach conversations.
- *Stress*: Discussion of work and/or CHC-related stress.
- *Work ability and/or job performance*: Discussion of maintaining work ability or job performance (and strategies for doing so), along with declines in work ability or job performance due to health issues.
- *Identity issues*: Discussion of the CHC as it affects the client's personal identity, sense of self, or professional identity.

- *Disclosure of CHC*: Discussion of when, where, to whom, and how to reveal one's illness to others, including how much information to reveal when disclosing.
- *Accommodations*: Discussion of job accommodations, such as flexible work arrangements or getting certain days off for treatment.
- *Diagnosis issues*: Discussion of CHC diagnosis (e.g., how it was diagnosed, the length of time it took to get a diagnosis, when it was diagnosed).
- *Sick days*: Discussion of the need to be away from work due to illness.

Coaching is the most expensive of the programs in this chapter. Costs vary widely, based on the level of the client and the coach's background. For nonexecutives, a six-session program may cost an estimated $1,500 USD, including the coach's preassessment work and paperwork. To date, this type of coaching has been typically paid for by individuals who are seeking assistance outside of their organizations. The cost means that coaching is out of reach of many workers who could benefit from it.

Organizations cannot feasibly provide coaching to everyone who wants it; however, they may consider *contracting with coaches who are well-versed in work–health issues to provide services at partially subsidized or discounted rates* through their EAP, or a limited number of sessions, after which the employee would pay to continue. Alternatively, they may consider *offering it to all employees above a certain level in the organization*, to assist with retaining highly talented workers and maximize return on investment. Notably, offering such coaching services sends a strong signal of organizational support for worker well-being, along with recognition of the challenges that workers with CHCs face. Implemented alongside recommendations in Chapter 6, it can help promote a culture that supports inclusion and well-being. If organizations are unable to financially sponsor coaching, they may refer employees to some of the free online tools in the next section, and/or consider a mentoring program, discussed in the next section.

One of the biggest benefits of coaching, compared to most other interventions in this chapter, is that it allows workers to participate discreetly and confidentially. Like other EAP services, supervisors do not need to know their workers are accessing coaching. This means it can be implemented in a variety of workplaces and is not dependent upon a supportive culture to prevent backlash from disclosing a CHC to access the program. For this reason, I recommend *using external, contracted coaches* rather than in-house coaches.

It is important to recognize, though, that access to coaching may be limited due to lack of providers. Finding coaches trained in work–health issues may be difficult; very few coaches advertise this as part of their portfolios. One way to increase access is to *have EAPs train their counselors and coaches on these issues*. Box 8.1 contains tips for coaches looking to work with employees with CHCs. Similar to supervisor trainings mentioned in Chapter 7, this is an area ripe for opportunity. An effective, evidence-based training program for managers, HR professionals, and coaches/counselors on supporting workers with CHCs is sorely needed. Additionally, I noted earlier that many participants in our study mentioned they appreciated the coach's firsthand experience with chronic illness. While it is typically helpful for a coach to have personal experience with CHCs, coaches without CHCs can still successfully coach clients with CHCs by displaying empathy and sensitivity and using effective questioning and problem-solving. Research demonstrates that the development of a *healthy social relationship* and *high-quality working alliance* are key drivers of coaching success across different industries and contexts.[4,8]

As a caveat, it is important to recognize that coaching is not psychotherapy and should not be used as a substitute for psychological or psychiatric services. Many CHCs are mental health-related, and many physical CHCs involve comorbid mental health problems; therefore, some clients may need mental health services in addition to coaching. Coaches are responsible for making this clear to clients, and if they are not being adequately treated, referring them out to mental health services to be used instead of, or in conjunction with, coaching.

In sum, coaching is an effective strategy to support workers with a variety of CHCs in managing work–health challenges and working through identity-related issues. Compared to other programs, it is more developmental in nature and has the benefit of allowing the worker to access it without disclosing a CHC at work. However, coaching does not address more systemic issues as noted in Chapters 6 and 7; further, coaches with training on these issues may be difficult to find. Coaching is relatively expensive compared to other programs; yet organizations that choose to sponsor coaching in some capacity (e.g., through their EAP) will signal to workers with CHCs that their needs are acknowledged, and they are being supported.

Box 8.1 Tips for Coaching Workers with CHCs

- Be aware of common challenges and topics related to work and health.
- Use effective questioning.
- Leverage shared experiences with health issues to build credit and rapport.
- Maintain sensitivity with difficult, private topics.
- Work to develop good working relationships with clients.

- Understand the limitations of coaching if used in the absence of commensurate changes to work design, supervision, or culture.
- Make it convenient—for example, offer virtual coaching when desired.
- Allow workers to maintain confidentiality—use external coaches and do not require disclosure to HR or supervisors.
- Evaluate its effectiveness and measure longer-term effects (up to a year post-coaching).

8.1.2 Mentoring Programs

Not all organizations are able or willing to pay for coaching; certainly not all workers can afford to self-pay for coaching. Further, it may be difficult to find coaches with this specialty. Mentoring programs, the focus of this section, may also be helpful and cost very little for organizations to implement. Mentoring does not allow for the deep developmental work that coaching affords—in addition, mentoring on work–health issues in organizations is limited to those who are willing to disclose a CHC. However, mentoring can be beneficial in ways coaching cannot, including development of supportive relationships within the organization and getting advice and support from someone with firsthand knowledge of the organization. Although there are currently no published studies on mentoring programs for workers with CHCs, I provide information and guidance for implementing such programs from the general research on workplace mentoring.

Mentoring may be established informally, as mentor-protégé relationships may naturally form at work, or formally, through programs. Mentoring programs in organizations generally focus on helping advance careers of protégés through socialization; mentors also provide emotional support for protégés and act as role models.[9] Mentoring programs for workers with CHCs may provide emotional support and help with career advice and problem-solving around work–health challenges, such as navigating career paths or communicating about health issues.

Mentor-protégé dyads should be matched to the extent possible based on work roles—typically a mentor is at a higher level in the organization than the protégé, but within a similar function or department. However, a mentor at a similar organizational level may be relevant for protégés looking for mentoring more exclusively around CHC-related challenges rather than career advancement. One way to help identify mentors and facilitate pairings is by *running mentoring programs through related Employee Resource Groups (ERGs) in organizations.*

Nestlé's THRIVE Network ERG program (described in Chapter 6) includes a mentoring program. As part of the ERG, employees may connect with peers who have personally experienced relevant challenges, including various CHCs, and who offer one-on-one support and listening with empathy. Peer-to-peer engagement can help support employees and destigmatize the full use of the suite of benefits and services the company offers. While peers do not provide any kind of medical advice or HR assistance, THRIVE mentors work to support through shared experience and having walked the path the employee is currently walking.

Research on mentoring in organizations reveals consistent positive, but small effects of mentoring on protégés' career outcomes, including compensation and promotion; larger positive effects of mentoring are observed on protégés' job satisfaction, job performance, work motivation, self-efficacy, career satisfaction, and career commitment.[9,10] However, mentoring's benefits are not limited to protégés—mentoring is also beneficial for mentors, in that mentors often find mentoring meaningful. Research also shows that mentors experience higher levels of job satisfaction, commitment to the organization, and career success than nonmentors.[11]

How can organizations help ensure that mentoring is successful? The most positive mentoring experiences and outcomes emerge when relationship quality is high, and when protégés perceive high levels of both psychosocial support and instrumental support (i.e., support that facilitates career outcomes, such as task assistance or sponsorship).[9] Relationship length and frequency of interaction both affect provision of support and relationship quality, as does similarity in experience between mentor and protégé, such as educational background, department, or functional area in the organization. Similarity between the mentor and protégé in terms of attitudes, values, beliefs, and personality is also a strong predictor of relationship quality and support for the protégé.[9]

All of this means that when implementing mentoring programs, organizations should be mindful of creating *frequent opportunities for interaction between mentors and protégés.* Hybrid or remote work arrangements may pose challenges for connection, yet can still be beneficial by creating opportunities to speak one-on-one via Zoom with predetermined discussion questions, for example.[12] Organizations should also be *mindful when matching mentors and protégés*—looking at experience and backgrounds when doing so, and possibly allowing mentors to select their protégés. Organizations may also *provide opportunities for informal mentoring relationships to develop* outside of formal programs, such as through CHC/disability-related ERG meetings, speakers, and social events.

In sum, mentoring programs cost little to nothing to implement in organizations and can benefit both protégés and mentors alike. However, they do require support from the organization to be successful as noted. There is potential for protégés to get bad advice and for poor pairings to happen—therefore, some mentor screening and oversight should be included. Mentoring programs should not be implemented in unsupportive organizational cultures because they require CHC disclosure. To avoid potential discrimination or other repercussions from disclosure, the *organization's culture and leadership support for the program should be assessed before implementation.*

8.1.3 Vocational Counseling Programs

Vocational counseling programs are typically offered to individuals after a job loss due to a CHC or other disability has occurred. However, in response to calls for more preventive programs, Dr. Saralynn Allaire and colleagues in the US tested a preventive vocational rehabilitation intervention aimed at preventing subsequent disability in workers with rheumatic diseases. The content of this program was delivered by rehabilitation counselors over two 90-minute in-person, one-on-one sessions. Counselors traveled to meet participants at times and locations convenient to them (e.g., their homes, public libraries).[13] Content included identification of work challenges and solutions, education, and vocational guidance, including alternative job options if the current job was unable to meet the participant's needs.[13] Study results supported the effectiveness of the intervention; specifically, time to job loss was greater and incidence of job loss was lesser for an intervention group compared to a control group.[13] The researchers noted that the program would likely be helpful beyond rheumatic diseases, as the program content was not specific to rheumatic diseases.

The content of this program overlaps somewhat with the coaching intervention described above—yet is different in a few notable ways. One is that the coaching program was more time-intensive, involving six hours of contact with the coach as opposed to three hours of contact with the vocational counselor. More time allows the coach and client to achieve greater depth of discussion and problem-solving. More time may also allow more of a trusting relationship to develop between the coach and the client. Second, coaching tends to be more developmental, whereas vocational rehabilitation is more educational, and problem focused. It is also important to recognize that the term "vocational rehabilitation" may carry stigma for some workers with CHCs who may not see themselves as needing rehabilitation services but desire the opportunity to get recognition and support for and work through their unique work–health issues with an understanding coach. The term "coaching" is more commonly used in professional spaces to imply a growth-oriented change process that is likely more attractive to employees than a rehabilitation focus, which implies something is broken or in need of fixing.

With less direct contact and less expensive labor costs, the vocational rehabilitation program costs substantially less than coaching. The program was tested several years ago, so costs are undoubtedly underestimated in today's market—however, counselors at that time were paid $75 USD per hour, and the market value of the program was estimated at $300 per person[14]. However, because the program assists with alternative job placement, organizations may not anticipate an associated favorable return on investment. Therefore, I don't recommend organizational sponsorship of vocational rehabilitation—yet managers and HR professionals should be aware that more preventive vocational programs exist and refer employees to them as appropriate.

8.2 Online Programs

Online programs have an advantage of scope—they can reach more people and are less expensive than one-on-one programs, particularly when many workers need access to services. Online programs, similar to individual programs, also allow workers to be discreet about their participation, in contrast to group programs described below. Despite their potential benefits, few online programs exist to support workers with CHCs. Most online resources provide information (e.g., videos, webpage, or podcast) without interactivity needed to help users apply information to their specific work–health challenges (e.g., workbook or online course).[15] Below are some examples of the few existing online programs or interactive websites that address work–health challenges for workers with CHCs.

8.2.1 Pain at Work Toolkit (PAW)

The Pain at Work (PAW) toolkit, developed by Dr. Holly Blake and colleagues in the UK, is the first online self-management program for workers with chronic pain. The PAW toolkit includes five sections with information on chronic pain, UK laws related to work disability, how to get help with workplace discrimination and harassment, self-management of stress and pain, and additional resources.[16] As of the time this book was written, the PAW toolkit was taken down from the website to be evaluated for effectiveness, and no data was available yet.[17] Overall, the PAW toolkit appears to be a promising online tool. Its lack of interactive discussion with a coach or counselor will limit its potential to be developmental for users; however, pending the results of its evaluation, managers and HR professionals should be aware of it as a resource for employees.

8.2.2 Job Demands and Accommodation Planning Tool (JDAPT)

The Job Demands and Accommodation Planning Tool (JDAPT) is not a program, but a tool that workers can use for self-help with identifying appropriate accommodations. JDAPT is an online, publicly accessible tool developed by the Institute for Work and Health in Canada that guides workers to specific work strategies and accommodations based on the physical, cognitive, and social job demands of their jobs in combination with their health-related limitations.[18] Workers identify their job demands and report their difficulties meeting those job demands, and are presented with individual strategies they can enact to help them better meet those demands, and work accommodations they may decide to request to change the nature of their job or working environment to help them perform better at work. The tool takes about 15 minutes to use, and users can download and save a PDF of their results.[18] The JDAPT costs nothing to use and is an excellent tool for its intended purpose, though it is inherently limited in what it can offer to users compared to more interactive, individualized approaches. Therefore, it is best used as an adjunct to other approaches. Coaches, HR professionals, and managers should be aware of JDAPT and refer employees to it as appropriate.

8.3 Group Programs

Like the individual programs discussed above, group programs also may be generalized across different conditions. Importantly, participation in a group program inherently involves disclosure of a CHC to other group members. For this reason, *success of these programs is likely limited to organizations* with supportive cultures in which employees feel comfortable participating (i.e., disclosing). If program meetings are held during work time, they also require understanding supervisors who support their subordinates' participation during work hours. Group programs are framed using varying terms such as "empowering" or "cognitive-behavioral"—but most share commonalities, involving motivational, educational, stress management and coping, interpersonal, and/or problem-solving components.

8.3.1 Manage at Work Program

The Manage at Work worksite self-management program was developed by Dr. William Shaw and colleagues in the US to improve self-efficacy for managing work-related challenges of CHCs.[19] The in-person group program was one of the first employer-sponsored, group-based, in-person, onsite programs delivered to support workers with CHCs in the US. Program facilitators were licensed psychologists or social workers trained on the program (some of whom were already providing services through the organizations' EAPs), and groups ranged in size from three to 10 workers.[19] Sessions were generally one hour each for 10 sessions, but were modified to fit organizational preferences (e.g., five two-hour sessions). Sessions were held after work hours or during breaks.

The evidence-based program included education on pain and fatigue (session 1), individual problem-solving and strategies related to pacing work and using work flexibility (session 2), effective communication about illness and illness disclosure (session 3), coping strategies, mindfulness, and social support (session 4), and goal-setting, group problem-solving, and role play (session 5).[20] To provide a bit more context, the communication module promoted assertive communication about health needs, but facilitators balanced this with realities around work relationships and work expectations. The intervention also emphasized *informal*, rather than formal, job accommodations when possible.[19]

In testing the program's effectiveness, the researchers found that at six month follow-up, program participants showed improvement in work engagement and reduced intent to turnover; however, no significant reductions in work functional limitations were observed.[19] Further, while trends toward improved job satisfaction, self-efficacy, and work fatigue were observed, these improvements were not statistically significant and therefore cannot be deemed reliable.[19] Costs of the program include meetings with management to address questions, trainings for facilitators, labor costs for training and intervention delivery, and food/beverage and materials costs, summing to a total estimated cost per participant between $500 and $1,000 USD.

Overall, Manage at Work is an evidence-based group program with demonstrated success that costs slightly less per employee than one-on-one coaching. Its pragmatic nature focuses on helping employees with CHCs meet their health needs within the bounds of work culture, relationships, and expectations. Further, it is generalized across many types of CHCs and therefore can reach a larger audience. However, because it involves disclosure by virtue of participating and teaches participants to self-advocate to get support for health issues at work, it is only recommended in workplaces with cultures that can support its success. If implemented in an unsupportive culture, employees would likely choose not to participate for fear of backlash, and those who did participate may experience backlash for participating or using recommended self-advocacy techniques.

8.3.2 Chronic Disease Self-Management Program

The Chronic Disease Self-Management Program (CDSMP), developed by Dr. Kate Lorig and colleagues in the US, is a six-week peer-led small group program that was developed for adults age 50+ with various CHCs to improve symptom management and self-efficacy. Program topics include coping with health problems, solving health-related problems, action planning, goal setting, focusing on nutrition and physical activity, assessing new treatments, and communicating with healthcare providers.[21] The CDSMP has been tested in multiple studies, and found to be effective at improving self-efficacy, self-management behaviors, and physical and mental health of participants, as well as decreasing healthcare utilization.[22,23] There are several adaptations of the CDSMP to specific conditions (e.g., diabetes, chronic pain, cancer, and HIV), modalities (virtual and in-person) and contexts (community and workplace).[24]

The worksite-tailored CDSMP, the Live Healthy, Work Healthy program, also known as Workplace CDSMP or wCDSMP, is a version of the CDSMP that was modified slightly by Dr. Matthew Smith and colleagues in the US to be delivered in the workplace. Changes were made to the program delivery (twice a week for 50 minutes over an eight weeks instead of once a week for 2.5 hours over six weeks), targeted ages (age 40+ instead of 50+) and content (added information about work–life balance, added work-related examples and focused more communication content on supervisors and coworkers and less on physicians)—yet 75% of the content mirrored the CDSMP.[21,25] Live Healthy, Work Healthy program facilitators completed a four-day CDSMP training, plus a four-hour bridge training for the Live Healthy, Work Healthy program. The program was delivered in groups of no more than 16 employees, and each group had two facilitators.

A recent study found that Live Healthy, Work Healthy program participants reported lower levels of burnout, as well as improved perceptions of organizational support, and increased levels of work engagement, work ability, and organizational commitment.[25] Notably, researchers found that the benefits to organizationally relevant outcomes were due to organizations offering the program to employees on work time.[25] This provides evidence that organizations should consider not only financially sponsoring such programs, but also *allowing workers to participate on work time* in order to yield the full range of possible benefits from the program. Again, this program is only recommended in organizations with supportive cultures to avoid potential backlash from supervisors and other workers.

One 2015 estimate of CDSMP costs is $350 USD per employee participant to cover personnel, training, licensure, and marketing costs.[26] However, this estimate does not include lost wages from employee time spent in workshops, for organizations that offer this benefit. Because some costs of group programs are fixed (training, licensure, materials, marketing), group-based programs are likely more cost-effective than individual programs when a large number of employees are expected to participate. A CDSMP cost calculator is linked in the Additional Resources section.

When implementing this and other similar programs, I recommend that organizations open programs to employees of all ages and *not target or restrict participation based on age*. Although CDSMP targets participants aged 50+ and the Live Healthy, Work Healthy program targets those who are 40+, there are an increasing number of younger workers with CHCs that need support. Further, these workers likely need the most support early in their diagnosis, which may be at younger ages. Managers should be aware that younger workers may benefit from programs such as these, and refer employees when workers disclose or report a work–health issue, regardless of age.

In sum, the Live Healthy, Work Healthy program's rigorous design and extensive testing is commendable, and no other program can match its evidence base, especially when considering its CDSMP roots. Further, it is one of the least expensive programs in this chapter to implement, and many resources for implementation are available online. Considering this, the *Live Healthy, Work Healthy program is currently the best option for organizations looking to implement a group program to support workers with CHCs.* However, as noted, because participation requires disclosure of a CHC, I only recommend implementing it if the organizational culture is supportive. Further, allowing workers to participate on work time signals support for workers and has been found to confer additional benefits to worker outcomes. Yet if supervisors are not fully on board with the program, it is best to only offer sessions outside of work hours to avoid backlash to participants.

8.3.3 Other Group Programs

There are a few other types of group programs to briefly describe; each of these originated outside of the US. First, Dr. Inge Varekamp and colleagues in the Netherlands designed and tested a group-based *empowerment training program* for workers with various CHCs. The program was designed to help workers with CHCs solve work-related problems; like the aforementioned programs, it was also designed to improve workers' self-efficacy through education, problem-solving, and skill-building. Workers attended three-hour group sessions every two weeks for six weeks, and a seventh session two months after the sixth session.[27] In addition, workers received three sessions of individual counseling. Each session included identification and clarification of work-related problems, insight into thoughts related to CHCs, communication at work, legislation around disabilities, goal-setting, plans for problem-solving, and follow-up.[27] Results of a randomized controlled trial to test the program's effectiveness indicated that at a two-year post-program follow-up, program participants' levels of self-efficacy and fatigue improved; however, there were no significant improvements to job satisfaction or job retention compared to the control group.[27] Notably, the program was not sponsored by the organization and was not held onsite at work during work hours.

Second, Dr. Steven Linton and colleagues in Sweden tested and compared the results of cognitive-behavioral therapy, physical therapy, and minimal treatment programs for work disability prevention for workers with chronic neck or back pain. The program was run outside of participants' workplaces.[28] The cognitive behavioral therapy program included six, two-hour group sessions with six to 10 people per group. Sessions were run by trained therapists, and included education, problem-solving with case studies, and skills training, including coping skills, problem-solving skills, and stress management skills.[28] Participants developed their own coping programs based on their learnings and assessment of what would work best for them.

The researchers found that compared to a minimal treatment control group, the cognitive behavioral therapy group and a group with physical therapy plus cognitive behavioral therapy had a five-fold decreased risk of future disability compared to the minimal treatment control group.[28] Interestingly, they found no differences between the cognitive behavioral therapy group and the cognitive behavioral therapy plus physical therapy group, suggesting that the cognitive behavioral therapy program was particularly helpful for helping avoid future disability.[28] Combined with the results from other studies,[29] evidence suggests that exercise and physical therapy programs are not effective on their own, and that organizations should address psychological, social, and behavioral issues in any program they adopt to support workers with CHCs.

8.4 Summary and Recommendations

While primary preventive organizational- and work-focused strategies for supporting workers with CHCs should be prioritized, secondary preventive work- and individual-focused strategies are critical, targeted supports that help workers identify, manage, and resolve various work–health challenges, gain perspective on the value they add to their organizations, and learn to effectively and judiciously advocate for their health-related needs so that they can maximize their work ability and maintain well-being. Such programs help organizations retain needed talent and maximize the potential of valued employees.

A first step for leaders looking to support their employees with programs such as these is to *take stock of existing programs*, such as through an EAP, to see which may be used as-is or tweaked to support workers with CHCs. If such programs exist, *promote them widely and encourage employees' use of them*. When considering new programs, I offer the following suggestions. First, because many challenges are common across different types of CHCs, to maximize program reach and potential return on investment, I recommend *offering programs that may be applied to many different CHCs*, instead of limiting programs to one or more specific CHCs. In addition, because work–health challenges are dynamic—shifting with changes in symptoms, illness progression, work roles, treatment, and other factors, I also recommend that *programs should be interactive and flexible*, such that participants may get assistance with and apply content specifically to their current most pressing challenges. Further, any program must be led by *well-trained, knowledgeable facilitators* who are understanding of and sensitive to CHC-related challenges. Sessions should be *convenient to participants* in terms of scheduling and location, and participants' *privacy and confidentiality should be prioritized*.

The decision of whether to offer an individualized program, a group program, or both will depend on available resources and the culture of your organization. I recommend taking an honest assessment of your company's present culture—not the aspirational culture, but the actual current culture and appetite for investing resources in this area. *If the organization has a supportive culture that values worker inclusion and well-being and is willing to invest resources, I recommend either implementing coaching or an onsite group program such as the Live Healthy, Work Healthy program*. Because some workers will likely still not feel free to participate in a group program, and others will have challenges that are uniquely sensitive or outside the scope of a group program protocol, I recommend supplementing a group program with one-on-one coaching.

On the other hand, *if the organization is unwilling or unable to invest financial resources, yet the culture is supportive of worker well-being and inclusion, I recommend implementing a mentoring program through an associated ERG, combined with a compilation of free online resources* linked from the organization's EAP site or a webpage for the ERG. These resources should be widely communicated (e.g., recommended by supervisors, linked from benefits pages, included in company communications).

Conversely, *if the culture is currently weak, I suggest starting with strategies in Chapter 6 to build up the culture* before implementing any downstream programs that involve disclosure. As noted, I do not recommend implementing mentoring or group programs in companies with a current weak culture of support for worker well-being and inclusion, as workers in those environments will likely be hesitant to out themselves as facing work–health issues in order to access support. Further, if supervisors are not on board, workers may face backlash for participating. In those situations, offering *one-on-one, telephonic coaching* as a benefit through an EAP would still be beneficial, as it allows workers to discreetly participate without disclosing a CHC. Publicly available online resources may also be linked from the organization's EAP site.

Regardless of the offering(s), *programs and resources should be well-advertised* across the organization to maximize their use. *Supervisors should be be made aware of available programs* so they can refer employees to them when appropriate.

Reflection Exercise: Individual-Focused Programs

Reflecting upon the individual worker-focused programs presented in this chapter, and considering your organization's culture, which one(s) do you think would work best in your organization, and why? What resources would be needed to help with their implementation in your organization? Who could assist you with attaining needed resources for implementation? Take a few minutes to write down your responses.

_____

_____

_____

_____

8.5 Takeaways and Recommendations

- Take stock of existing programs that may be leveraged or tweaked to support workers with CHCs and disseminate these widely, encouraging their use.
  - Educate supervisors on existing programs and encourage them to refer their employees.
  - Include them in company communications and link to them from your company's benefits site, EAP site, and/or associated ERG web pages.
- Take stock of your organization's culture when considering program options.
  - Do not attempt to implement programs that require disclosure of a CHC (group programs) in an unsupportive culture. Instead, first work on the culture (Chapter 6) while offering confidential programs that protect worker privacy (e.g., coaching with an external coach).
- Implement programs that will be optimally effective:
  - Generalized programs that help with common challenges across *various CHCs*, instead of condition-specific programs, and
  - Interactive programs that are *customizable* to address workers' specific, current work–health challenges.
- Inform supervisors about implemented program(s) and build their support for workers' participation; encourage supervisors to share the program as a resource to employees.
- Consider allowing workers to participate in the program *during work hours* if supervisors are on board and supportive.
- Ensure program facilitators are skilled in effective questioning, sensitive to difficult topics, empathetic, and well-trained on common challenges.
- Protect the privacy of program participants by not disclosing participation and requiring confidentiality of what is said during sessions.

- Ensure sessions are convenient for workers to participate.
- Evaluate your program's effectiveness and measure effects over the long term if possible (up to a year or more after the program ends).
- Remember that individual worker-focused programs are inherently limited in that they *do not change the job or work environment*. These programs are most effective when used in a supportive culture where *communication and collaboration between supervisors and subordinates is common and encouraged*, and *workers are afforded autonomy to implement strategies* they learn to help preserve their work ability.

Additional Resources

- Cancer and Work Site for Employers and Cancer Survivors: https://www.cancerandwork.ca/
- Epilepsy @ Work Site (Training and information on supporting workers with epilepsy in the workplace): http://www.epilepsyatwork.com/en
- Job Demands and Accommodation Planning Tool for Workers: https://aced.iwh.on.ca/jdapt/worker-en
- Rosalind Joffe's coaching site: https://cicoach.com/ and blog "Working with Chronic Illness: https://cicoach.com/blog/
- Open Access article on coaching and professional identities:[6] https://radar.brookes.ac.uk/radar/items/10de2fa4-dcb6-4f8a-98a0-faf1013f6ac3/1/
- Workplace Chronic Disease Self-Management Program (wCD SMP)/LHWH Program: https://selfmanagementresource.com/programs/small-group/workplace-chronic-disease-self-management-small-group/
- CDSMP Cost Calculator: https://www.ncoa.org/article/chronic-disease-self-management-program-cost-calculator
- Workplace Strategies for Mental Health: https://www.workplacestrategiesformentalhealth.com/

Chapter 9
Implementing and Evaluating an Integrated Approach

Now that you have learned about strategies to support workers with CHCs at the levels of the organization (Chapter 6), the job and management (Chapter 7), and the individual worker (Chapter 8), I will tie these together, providing a framework for, and steps to achieve, an integrated approach. I first make a business case for doing so, recapping the shared characteristics of CHCs that often lead to overlooked work–health challenges, and describing why common organizational practices addressing CHCs in the workplace are insufficient for addressing them. I then advance a rationale for more proactive supportive strategies and recommend an integrated approach that includes supportive strategies at organizational, job, and individual worker levels. Finally, I provide steps for how to develop integrated approaches, along with guidance on how to evaluate cost savings (i.e., return on investment as well as broader returns, i.e., value of investment).

9.1 Making a Business Case

CHCs and their associated challenges in the workplace are not going away. Projections have consistently pointed to increasing prevalence of CHCs over time—even prior to the COVID-19 pandemic and concurrent explosion in cases of long COVID. Current reactive approaches that address disability once it occurs (i.e., return-to-work programs) and health promotion/wellness programs that may help prevent a subset of diseases (e.g., diabetes prevention programs) are not sufficient for the 50% or more of the workforce currently managing work–health challenges. Put another way, if you hold a leadership role, you likely already have at least one employee who is managing a work–health challenge, even if you are unaware of it. And the likelihood of your employees facing such challenges will only increase with time. With that in mind, more proactively addressing threats to inclusion, work ability, and well-being of workers with CHCs is therefore not just the right thing to do—it is also an opportunity to gain competitive advantage for those organizations ahead of the curve on these issues.

The shared CHC characteristics that lead to work–health challenges, and that set many CHCs apart from other disabilities and diversity categories in organizations include the following:

1. CHCs and associated symptoms may lead to *declines in work ability and well-being*, and subsequent disability leave or early workforce departure, if not addressed.
2. CHCs and associated symptoms are often *variable (and sometimes unpredictable) in their impacts on work function over time*, necessitating associated changes in needed supports over time.
3. CHCs *require ongoing management*, which may conflict with work expectations around schedules and attendance.
4. CHCs *have differing and changing courses or trajectories of health and functionality*—and those with progressive disease courses may need to plan job or career contingencies for when functionality declines.
5. Many CHCs, particularly mental illnesses and other nonapparent conditions are *highly stigmatized at work*, which can lead to social isolation, along with denial of needed accommodations and other forms of discrimination.
6. Most CHCs are *nonapparent* or invisible to others. This can lead coworkers and supervisors to not believe the person needs support, puts a burden on individuals to "prove" their disabilities, and necessitates decision-making around disclosure.
7. Most CHCs are acquired, not congenital, requiring *adjustment, integration with work identity, and acceptance of needed medications, assistive devices, and so on.*

You may identify with some of these challenges if you have a CHC. And if you are managing employees with CHCs, you may recognize by this point in the book that you can support your employees experiencing the first four challenges on this list with *dynamic, flexible accommodations* and/or *autonomy to self-accommodate* when needed, along with *collaborative working relationships with and support from you and other supervisors and coworkers*. You may also recognize that the next three challenges on this list can be addressed through *culture interventions and supervisor training on challenges and available resources to point employees to as appropriate, as well as coaching or another individualized program to help workers build confidence and manage challenges*. As I have stated throughout this book, all these supports are made possible by and bolstered by an organizational culture that is inclusive and supports worker well-being.

Reactive programs, including disability policies to provide partial pay for those on sick leave and return-to-work programs, are undoubtedly important—yet they do not proactively help workers manage these challenges and prevent declines in work ability and well-being before they require temporary or permanent disability leave. On the other hand, proactive strategies to promote inclusion, accessibility, work ability, and well-being will help support workers in addressing work–health challenges, ideally *before* they lead to costly disability claims, turnover, grievances, or litigation. And notably, many of the organization- and job-focused recommendations in this book contribute to a healthy, equitable, inclusive, accessible, and supportive work environment, promoting the morale and well-being of *all* workers, and not just those with CHCs.

In sum, in addition to offering reactive programs as is customary, I argue that *it is important and beneficial for organizations to critically examine factors contributing to lack of inclusion and accessibility, and declining work ability at the organizational, job, and individual worker levels and address them through proactive interventions.* I describe some suggestions for such an examination later in this chapter; in short, input from employees is essential, such as through focus groups and confidential surveys. As noted in Chapter 6, a good start to this process would be to add a disability status question to existing employee engagement surveys (e.g., "Do you have an apparent or nonapparent disability? Yes/No/Prefer not to say"), and ensure such surveys include relevant questions about culture, inclusion, accessibility, support, and work ability (examples of surveys measures are in Box 9.1). Discrepancies in perceptions of work ability and support by disability status could indicate an issue, for example, and data could be further probed to illuminate driving factors for your organization to address.

Similarly, *health/wellness promotion programs* may help promote healthy behaviors and prevent some diseases, but do not address the more complex work–health challenges noted. In addition, it is important to note that while lifestyle changes and health behavior adoption may be helpful in preventing and altering the disease courses of some CHCs such as diabetes and cardiovascular diseases, they are of more limited value to other CHCs, including some autoimmune diseases, some neurological diseases, and some cancers. To help manage work–health challenges detailed earlier in this chapter and in Chapters 4 and 5, such challenges need to be *acknowledged* (i.e., beyond the illness itself, acknowledge that the intersection of illness and work can create difficulties that are currently underappreciated) and *supports need to be allocated at the organizational, job, and individual worker levels* as described in Chapters 6–8.

This is, of course, not to say that health/wellness programs are not beneficial—they can have many positive effects, especially when integrated with supportive structural, organization- and job-level changes.[1] Benefits are not only realized to worker well-being, but also the bottom line:

- Companies that won the C. Everett Koop National Health Award for workplace health promotion programs outperformed the S&P 500—their stock values appreciated by 325% compared to the market average of 105% over 14 years.[2]
- Companies applying for the Corporate Health Achievement Award that scored well on health and/or safety outperformed the S&P 500 average, ranging from 204% to 333%, compared to the 105% average over a 14-year period.[3]
- Of companies using the Health Enhancement Research Organization (HERO) Employee Health Management Best Practices Scorecard, those that scored well enjoyed a 235% appreciation in stock value versus 159% over a six-year period.[4]

Considering that a growing number of companies report adopting health/wellness programs to reduce disability claims, sick days, and presenteeism, and increase employee job satisfaction, morale, and retention,[5] it is an obvious next step to integrate more proactive strategies to support their many workers with CHCs. Proactive strategies supporting work–health challenges for workers with CHCs are currently outside the scope of most companies' health and safety promotion/wellness strategies—yet they may be *built onto existing programs* to improve the reach and beneficial effects of those programs. In sum, if your company's current offerings exclude or do not maximize integrated proactive factors for inclusion, work ability, and work-related well-being for their workers with CHCs, you are missing opportunities to move the needle on these outcomes for a significant percentage of your workforce, while positively benefitting all workers with cultural, policy-based, management-focused, and work design improvements to support worker health and well-being.

9.2 An Integrated Approach

I provided a framework in Chapter 6 for recommended supportive strategies, adapting an intervention framework from public health that includes primary- and secondary-preventive strategies at the levels of the organization, the job/work, and individual worker (see Figure 9.1).

Each level in this framework is important to address, and the best support strategies will layer supports from different levels. It may be tempting for organizational leaders to solely implement individual worker-focused programs, which are less expensive and time-consuming than systemic approaches. Changing work design, training managers, changing culture, and introducing new policies and benefits take much more time and effort, and their cost benefits are less easily determined. Yet they are the foundation upon which more targeted individual approaches will have the most benefit. To be clear, when more primary preventive/systemic changes are not possible, it is better to implement individual worker-focused approaches than nothing at all. But individual worker-focused approaches will only have limited effectiveness on their own. With an integrated approach, systemic supports, including culture, policies, benefits, and work design provide conditions in which the greatest number of employees will benefit in terms of improved inclusion and well-being, and in which individually targeted approaches for workers with CHCs may have maximal benefit (e.g., a worker with a CHC can freely implement learned strategies for preserving their work ability because they have autonomy, a supportive supervisor, and understanding coworkers).

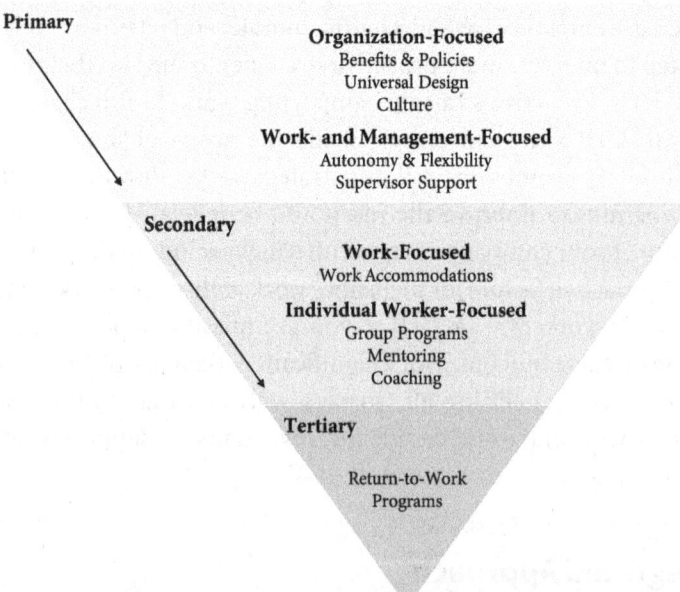

Figure 9.1 Hierarchy of support strategies to promote inclusion, well-being, and work ability for workers with chronic health conditions

Stated plainly, organizations cannot expect meaningful individual change to address work–health strategies in the absence of any supports at higher levels. This puts too much pressure and onus on frontline managers and the employees they manage. As noted, workers cannot enact strategies they use to maintain their work ability in the face of illness symptoms, such as frequent stretching or walking breaks, without autonomy built into their jobs to do so. Managers cannot adequately support their employees by giving them grace when they experience flare-ups if their own leaders do not grant them the latitude or resources to do so. If you are managing employees yourself, you may have at times found yourself constrained by your organization's culture and lack of support from leaders above you in terms of what you can do to support your employees. You may therefore find yourself advocating for more systemic change by "managing up" and presenting a case to your organization's leaders for some of the more primary preventive approaches in Chapters 6 and 7.

An integrated approach can support the health and well-being of all workers, while simultaneously specifically supporting workers with CHCs. An integrated approach is one that is comprehensive, shaped by input and participation from employees at all levels of the organization, supported by top management, and driven and evaluated with data.[1] Targets of such an approach would be determined by stakeholders, including employees, and will vary based on an assessment of the organization, but may include strengthening alignment with values of DEIA and worker well-being, as detailed in Chapter 6.

An example of an integrated approach for worker health, safety, and well-being, is one advocated by the Total Worker Health® program at the National Institute for Occupational Safety and Health (NIOSH). Total Worker Health collectively addresses all aspects of work to protect and promote worker health, safety, and well-being.[6] Links to additional guidance on integrated intervention development and evaluation, including Total Worker Health, are listed in the Additional Resources section.

Integrated approaches may be developed, implemented, and evaluated using the following theory- and evidence-based steps.[1,7,8] Importantly, at every stage, it is critical to take a *participatory approach*—that is, meaningfully involve employees at all levels.[8] Employees are experts on their jobs and work environments, and their voices are critical to ensuring the intervention is optimally designed and executed. Further, participatory approaches help maximize fairness and promote a sense of empowerment for employees.[8]

1. Preparation and Initiation[8]
   a. A steering committee is set and the roles of those involved, including employees, managers, external consultants, and leaders, are initially defined (though they may change during the process).
   b. Readiness for change is assessed. Buy-in from senior managers, or lack thereof, has a trickle-down effect on mid-level managers. Without manager support, the intervention is likely to fail, as time and other resources will not be allocated to ensure its success, and employees will receive signals that their participation will not be recognized as a valuable use of time.
   c. A communication strategy is developed, including communication on why the change is needed, what the timeframe is, how the change is progressing, and so on. Effective, timely, transparent communication is critical to the approach's success. However, the committee must be careful not to overpromise, as doing so will generate cynicism. Communication should also be two-way; in addition to communication about intervention efforts to employees, employee feedback should also be taken into consideration by the steering committee at all stages of the process.
   d. Ethical boundaries are determined—for example, how anonymity or confidentiality of data will be approached.
2. Identification of problem areas[8]
   a. Data is gathered to help determine problem areas for potential intervention. This typically includes data from employee focus groups, interviews, and/or surveys. Interviews and/or focus groups could be used to get an initial take on problematic areas, and a company-wide survey could be developed based on those results to home in on specific identified problem areas. To ensure accuracy of results, it is important to use measures that are psychometrically validated and reliable. I include a table with possible targets/outcomes and suggested measures in Box 9.1; measures may be found using the associated citations in the References section. In addition, existing systems (e.g., benefits, policies, and programs) may be audited to optimize use of existing resources and reduce redundancies. Additional measures may be helpful to supplement subjective employee data in determining problem areas and building a case for the intervention; examples of these are in Box 9.2.
   b. Results of data gathering and analysis are shared with employees.

3. Action Planning[8]
   a. A clear Action Plan is created to address identified problem areas, considering available resources and other constraints. Initiatives, targets of initiatives, roles of responsible parties, resources required, and timelines are identified. Primary preventive strategies, such as those in Chapters 6 and 7, should be prioritized, followed by secondary preventive strategies (Chapter 8), and then tertiary strategies (Chapter 3).
   b. To assist with evaluation, desired outcomes of the intervention, timing of data collection, and operationalization of outcomes, including targets identified in Step 2, are determined. Also, any additional needed baseline data to assist with evaluation should be collected at this stage.
   c. The Action Plan is communicated to employees, feedback from employees is considered, and revisions are made to the Action Plan as needed.
4. Implementation of Action Plan[8]
   a. Mid-level managers are heavily involved in the implementation, encouraging their employees' involvement in the intervention.
   b. Implementation efforts are communicated to employees, and feedback from employees is considered throughout the process.
   c. The steering committee monitors and adjusts intervention activities as needed.
5. Evaluation[7]
   a. Evaluation is critical to determine the effectiveness of the integrated intervention efforts. Did intervention efforts have the intended effects as determined in Steps 2 and 3?
   b. Data is gathered at the predetermined intervals. Data are likely gathered from another survey of employees and/or focus groups, as used in Step 2, but may also include any other sources of data examined in Step 2 and 3, such as those in Box 9.1.
   c. A best practice evaluation recommendation is to evaluate change at various levels, ranging from the individual/micro level (e.g., employee attitudes) to the team or department level (e.g., team climate), to the organizational/macro level (e.g., organizational culture or practices).[7] This comprehensive framework for evaluating the effects of integrated interventions is detailed in the Model for Evaluating Organization-Level Interventions link in the Additional Resources section.

d. A prepost analysis is conducted using data gathered in Steps 2 and 3 as baseline data and data gathered after the intervention ends as follow-up data.
e. Evaluation may include a return-on-investment (ROI) and/or value of investment (VOI) analysis, as detailed in the next section.

Box 9.1 Possible Outcomes and Suggested Self-Report Measures for Program Design and Evaluation

Outcome	Sample Validated Measure
Individual Self-Reported Outcomes	
Perceived Work Ability	Abbreviated versions of the Work Ability Index[9,10]
Burnout	Oldenburg Burnout Inventory (OLBI)[11]
Engagement	Utrecht Work Engagement Scale (UWES-9)[12]
Job Satisfaction	Single-item measure of global job satisfaction[13]
Job-related Well-Being	Job-related Affective Well-Being Scale (JAWS-20)[14]
Organizational Commitment	Klein Unidimensional, Target-free Scale (KUT)[15]
Turnover Intentions	Turnover Intentions Scale[16]
Presenteeism	Stanford Presenteeism Scale (SPS-6)[17]
Work–Health Conflict	Work–Health Management Interference Scale[18]
Work Stress	Stress in General Survey[19]
Self-Efficacy	New General Self-Efficacy Scale[20]
Work- and Supervisor-Focused Self-Reported Outcomes	
Autonomy	Factual Autonomy Scale[21] or the Work Design Questionnaire[22]
Flexibility	Work Boundary Flexibility Scale[23]
Shift Flexibility	Shift Flextime Scale[24]
Workload	Quantitative Workload Inventory[25]
Supervisor Support	Perceived Supervisor Support Scale[26]
Work Discrimination	Anticipated Work Discrimination Scale[27]
Department and Organization-focused Self-Reported Outcomes	
Organizational Support	Survey of Perceived Organizational Support-10[28]
Autonomy Climate	Organizational Climate Measure (Autonomy Subscale)[29]
Diversity Climate	Marginalized-Group-Focused Diversity Climate Scale (MGF-DCS)[30]
Health Climate	Multi-faceted Organizational Health Climate Assessment (MOHCA)[31]

Note: In addition to these recommendations, many relevant validated single-item measures may be found in Matthews et al.[32] and Fisher et al.[13]

Box 9.2 Examples of Additional Possible Measures for Program Development and Evaluation

- Exit interview data (coded for themes)
- Results of employee engagement surveys, broken down by disability status (see Chapter 6)
- Employee posts on websites such as Glassdoor.com (coded into themes)
- Absenteeism and turnover rates, overall and by disability status
- Trends in numbers of disability claims filed
- Trends in percentage of workforce with disclosed disabilities overall, also broken out by job type or management/leadership status
- Compensation audit results by disability status
- EEOC claims (in the US), or other legal claims or grievances related to unfair treatment/discrimination based on disability or CHC status
- Employee injury rates (e.g., worker's compensation claims or other organizational records)

9.3 Assessing Return on Investment and Value of Investment

In addition to the evaluation efforts noted above, organizations may desire an ROI analysis to determine cost savings achieved by implementing a program. In contrast to the comprehensive evaluation approach for integrated approaches described above, ROI analysis is more readily used for *discrete programs* (e.g., employee assistance programs, or EAPs and wellness programs). ROI analysis typically focuses specifically on a few discrete monetary outcomes, such as health care cost savings. There are multiple ways to estimate ROI; two online tools for assessing ROI are included below in Additional Resources. One method for estimating ROI for EAPs from Dr. Mark Attridge may be used to estimate cost savings from decreased work absenteeism and presenteeism as a result of EAP implementation; a simplified version of these steps include:[33]

1. *Assign a dollar amount to an hour of work* (compensation rate), including any dollar value of benefits paid by the organization. This involves estimating an average hourly wage of employees and adding in the dollar value of any associated company benefits (e.g., one default is to add 25% of the paid wage rate to account for benefits).

2. *Assign a dollar value to work productivity.* One approach is to use a revenue capacity factor—a mathematical multiplier that reflects the revenue generation capacity an employee has for the organization. A default of 2.0 times the compensation rate is considered a conservative estimate.
3. *Assign a dollar value to work absence or presenteeism* using the productivity dollar value estimate in #2 plus the compensation rate in #1 if the time off is paid. Presenteeism may be estimated as a percentage of the workday's productivity—for example, 50% of a day's shift.
4. *EAP ROI* is the ratio of money saved:money spent. The financial value of avoided absence or presenteeism per employee (estimated by pre-EAP/post-EAP comparison) is the numerator, including (compensation rate x hours missed) and (work productivity rate x hours missed) and the amount of money spent per employee on the program is the denominator. ROI of 1:1 indicates the program broke even in terms of its costs and benefits.

Other ROI estimation methods include additional indirect costs, including costs to replace workers who are absent (e.g., hiring temporary staff or paying overtime for hourly workers and line managers' time in dealing with consequences of absent staff.)[34] Notably with this approach, because the absence of more senior employees is not typically covered/replaced for short-term absences, but more junior staff are covered/replaced due to operational demands, the indirect cost estimates of absence are *higher* for more junior staff.[34] Some argue this method overestimates costs;[34] certainly, costs vary by job type, structure, and employee specialization, among other factors.

While informative, it may be clear to you that limiting measured outcomes to cost savings from health care utilization, absenteeism, and presenteeism does not allow a comprehensive view of the benefits that interventions, particularly integrated interventions, can achieve. Other benefits not measured by an ROI analysis include aligning practices with organizational values, enacting corporate social responsibility, reducing turnover, reducing disability claims, reducing grievances and/or legal claims, and increasing desirability as a place to work and the organization's ability to recruit and retain top talent. Some researchers have noted these and other criticisms of ROI analysis, including:[35]

- ROI places too much emphasis on dollar savings, and presumes a program fails if it does not produce positive ROI.

- ROI estimates confer a "false sense of precision and certainty"[35]—in reality, there is much imprecision in estimates (e.g., defaults) used in ROI analysis.
- An emphasis on ROI incentivizes the smallest possible monetary investment in programs (ratio denominator) in efforts to maximize ROI. This could mean an intervention fails or is not as successful as it could be, due to lack of investment.

Partly in response to criticisms of an exclusive focus on ROI, and partly due to desire for more holistic assessment, organizations are increasingly taking a value of/on investment (VOI) approach in addition to, or in the place of, ROI analysis. VOI is a broader assessment of value that goes beyond narrow measures of cost savings and is flexible enough to accommodate all types and combinations of programs. VOI uses conventions from cost effectiveness analysis, and its principles include:[35]

- *Considering all valued outcomes*, such as increased employee retention, improved employee productivity and performance, increased employee job satisfaction and engagement, improved recruiting ability, decreased disability claims, decreased sick days, improved employee work ability, and improved employee well-being.
- *Deciding which outcomes are most important.* Rather than being constrained to typical, more easily quantifiable ROI outcomes such as health care cost savings or sick time reductions, VOI involves prioritizing outcomes that fit the organization at the outset (e.g., those mentioned in the integrated intervention process described above and in Boxes 9.1 and 9.2).
- *Including all associated costs*, including those that are indirect or not obvious—for example, employee time, data tracking and reporting, and legal review.
- *Deciding which calculations are credible and necessary to evaluate the program*, rather than defaulting to typical or default measurement methods that may include untenable assumptions that lead to inaccurate results. This also involves evaluating the rigor with which monetized outcomes are measured and potentially discounting those that are likely to be inaccurate for the context.

More detailed information on how to operationalize a cost effectiveness analysis within a VOI analysis, with examples, are in the HERO/Population Health Alliance Report,[35] linked in the Additional Resources section.

9.4 Conclusion

CHCs have unique, shared characteristics that often lead to overlooked work–health challenges. Organizational practices supporting workers with CHCs are typically reactive in nature, applied when work ability is already decreased (e.g., disability policies; return-to-work programs) and/or focused solely on wellness/health promotion while ignoring the intersection of work (e.g., smoking cessation programs; diabetes prevention programs). As such, typical practices and programs do not adequately address work–health challenges for workers with CHCs, and more proactive supportive strategies are needed. By expanding existing health promotion activities to include integrated supportive strategies at organizational, job, and individual worker levels detailed in Chapters 6–8, organizations can help promote sustainable work and preserve work ability and well-being for all workers, including workers with CHCs. In turn, they may expect to grow their cost savings (ROI) and other returns (VOI) from such programs. Particularly in a post-COVID world, CHCs and their associated challenges for individuals and organizations alike are not going away anytime soon—and they deserve recognition and support.

9.5 Takeaways and Recommendations

- Shared CHC characteristics that lead to work–health challenges include:
  - CHCs and associated symptoms may lead to declines in work ability,
  - CHCs and associated symptoms are often variable (and sometimes unpredictable) in their impacts on work function over time,
  - CHCs require ongoing management,
  - CHCs have changing courses or trajectories of health and functionality,
  - Many CHCs are highly stigmatized at work,
  - Most CHCs are nonapparent or invisible to others, and
  - Most CHCs require adjustment, integration with work identity.
- Reactive programs (disability leave and RTW programs) and wellness programs are limited in that they do not proactively help workers manage work–health challenges and prevent work ability declines and disability leave.
- To help manage work–health challenges, work–health challenges need to be acknowledged and supports need to be allocated at the organizational, job, and individual worker levels as described in Chapters 6–8.
- An integrated approach is one that is comprehensive, participatory (shaped by input and participation from employees at all levels of the organization), supported by top management, and driven and evaluated with data.

- Steps to an integrated approach include:
  - Preparation and initiation
  - Identification of problem areas
  - Action planning
  - Implementation of action plan
  - Evaluation
- It is helpful to evaluate beyond ROI and use a VOI approach that considers and evaluates all valued outcomes, for example, employee retention, work ability, inclusion, and well-being.

Additional Resources

- Fundamentals of Total Worker Health® Approaches:
  https://www.cdc.gov/niosh/docs/2017-112/
- Guidelines for Implementing an Integrated Approach to Worker Health, Safety, and Well-Being:
  https://centerforworkhealth.sph.harvard.edu/resources/guidelines-implementing-integrated-approach
- Making the Business Case for *Total Worker Health*®, from CDC/NIOSH:
  https://www.cdc.gov/niosh/twh/business-case/index.html
- Model for Evaluating Organization-Level Interventions (Open Access Article):
  https://www.tandfonline.com/doi/full/10.1080/1359432X.2012.690556
- ROI Calculator for EAPs, from Curalink healthcare in the US:
  https://curalinc.com/dashboard
- ROI tool for EAPs, from the Institute for Employment Studies in the UK:
  https://www.employment-studies.co.uk/resource/designing-and-testing-return-investment-tool-eaps
- VOI Principles and Framework, from HERO and Population Health Alliance:
  https://hero-health.org/wp-content/uploads/2015/02/HERO-PHA-Metrics-Guide-FINAL.pdf

Glossary

ableism: devaluation of and prejudice and discrimination toward those with CHCs and other disabilities.

ally: an individual who works to end oppression through support of and advocacy for an oppressed group.

autonomy: the degree to which a worker has discretion or control over their work schedule (i.e., when they work), their work methods (i.e., how they complete tasks, the order in which they complete work tasks, and when they take breaks), and their work decision-making (i.e., using their judgment in completing work).

bridge employment: paid work after retiring from one's career before exiting the workforce.

burnout: a state of exhaustion from work that stems from experiences of depletion; also includes distancing one's self from work, which has been alternately framed as cynicism or disengagement.

chronic health conditions (CHCs): long-term, ongoing physical and mental health conditions, illnesses, diseases, and symptoms, such as chronic pain or fatigue, that require ongoing management and/or limit activities.

cognitive-behavioral therapy: a form of psychotherapy that focuses on changing people's thoughts, and thus their behaviors and emotional reactions to their thoughts.

conservation of resources theory: theory that proposes that individuals strive to attain and maintain resources, and threats to or actual loss of resources causes stress.

corporate social responsibility (CSR) reports: documents in which organizations communicate their social and sustainability performance to stakeholders.

cost effectiveness analysis (CEA): a method of cost analysis that compares the relative cost and effectiveness of two or more interventions or programs.

DEIA: acronym for diversity, equity, inclusion, and accessibility.

disability: a physical or mental impairment that substantially limits one or more life activities.

emotional labor: the regulation of emotion and associated expressions of emotion as required by one's job.

employee assistance programs (EAPs): organizationally sponsored programs designed to help employees resolve personal problems that affect their work.

employee resource groups (ERGs): groups of employees with shared characteristics (e.g., disabilities) that work to provide support and advocacy around those shared characteristics.

engagement: a positive state characterized by vigor (energy and willingness to exert energy in work), dedication to work, and absorption in work.

essential job function: fundamental or core duties of a job that an employee must be able to perform with or without an accommodation.

flexible spending account (FSA): spending accounts employees can contribute to with pretax payroll deductions to cover out-of-pocket medical expenses (e.g., copays, deductibles, medical equipment).

flexible work arrangements: autonomy or flexibility in when work is done (flex time or flexible scheduling) and when work is done (flex time).

identity management: strategies workers use to manage others' perceptions of them, such as concealing a CHC or downplaying a CHC.

inspiration porn: stories or memes of disabled people achieving goals or tasks ranging from the mundane to the extraordinary, intended to provoke a positive emotional response but commodifies disabled people.

job control: autonomy related to work methods, order of task completion, breaks, and work decision-making.

job demands: job conditions that require ongoing exertion of effort to manage, and are therefore depleting and can lead to burnout, particularly in the face of inadequate job or personal resources.

job demands–resources model: theoretical framework linking job demands and job and personal resources to worker burnout and engagement.

job resources: job conditions that aid a worker in achieving goals, promote their growth and development, and/or mitigate high levels of job demands—and subsequently lead to work engagement.

medical model of disability: disability framework that states that disability is a characteristic of the individual person and is based on the trauma, health condition, or other medical factor that caused the limitation.

meta-analysis: a research study that aggregates research findings across multiple independent studies on the same topic.

overt discrimination: unfair treatment at work, such as in hiring, promotion, or termination, harassment, or failure to accommodate.

participatory approach: an approach to workplace intervention design that meaningfully involves employees at all levels at each stage of intervention design and implementation.

presenteeism: attending work when feeling impaired—such as from illness, stress, or work–family conflict.

primary prevention: strategies applied to all workers to promote worker health and well-being and prevent illness and injury.

quality of life: an individual's subjective perception of their well-being and position in life relative to their expectations and goals.

reasonable accommodation (also called job accommodation or work accommocation): modifications or adjustments to the work environment, job tasks, or work structure to allow a worker with a disability to interview for a job or fulfill work role responsibilities.

reduced-load work: reduced workload and hours, with a commensurate pay cut, while remaining on a professional career track.

return-on-investment (ROI): an estimate of the financial profitability of an investment that considers the costs of the investment and the financial gains from the investment.

return-to-work programs: programs designed to assist workers who are on disability leave with successful returning to, and staying at, work.

secondary prevention: strategies applied to workers with CHCs who are at risk of work ability declines (e.g., job accommodations).

social model of disability: disability framework that states that disability is a product of social, cultural, and physical structures that interact with individuals' impairments.

socioeconomic status: social and economic standing of an individual that includes education level, income, and occupation.

spoon theory: a metaphor for explaining the physical and mental energy scarcity many who live with CHCs experience by using spoons.

stigma: social devaluation of a characteristic or identity in a given context.

subtle discrimination: social exclusionary behaviors (e.g., lack of verbal contact, gossiping), lowered assumptions of capability, or other low-level discriminatory treatment.

supervisor support: the extent to which a supervisor generally cares about their employees' well-being and values their contributions.

tertiary prevention: return-to-work programs and stay-at-work programs for workers with CHCs who have left work on disability leave.

universal design: design that allows for maximum accessibility for all individuals, regardless of age, ability, or size.

value of investment (VOI): a broad assessment of the value an investment that goes beyond financial returns to employee well-being, satisfaction, retention, and the like.

wellness programs: programs designed to promote healthy diets, physical exercise, stress management, smoking cessation, immunizations, early detection, and other individual behaviors that help prevent diseases.

work ability: workers' assessments of their ability to continue working in their current job.

work design: how work is structured and organized in terms of activities, tasks, and relationships.

work–health challenges: work-related challenges are common across different types of CHCs and are unique to people with CHCs, as described in Chapter 4.

work–health management interference: experience of time and energy conflicts between work and health management for workers with CHCs.

References

Chapter 1

1. CDC. About chronic diseases [internet]. CDC. 2022 [cited 2022 May 23]. Available from: https://www.cdc.gov/chronic-disease/about/
2. Bernell S, Howard SW. Use your words carefully: what is a chronic disease? Front Public Health [internet]. 2016 Aug 2 [cited 2022 May 23];4. doi: 10.3389/fpubh.2016.00159
3. Buttorff C, Ruder T, Bauman M. Multiple chronic conditions in the United States [internet]. RAND Corporation; 2017 May [cited 2022 May 23]. Available from: https://www.rand.org/pubs/tools/TL221.html
4. Non communicable diseases [internet]. [cited 2022 May 23]. Available from: https://www.who.int/news-room/fact-sheets/detail/noncommunicable-diseases
5. Song Z, Baicker K. Health and economic outcomes up to three years after a workplace wellness program: a randomized controlled trial. Health Aff. 2021 Jun 1;40(6):951–60. doi:10.1377/hlthaff.2020.01808
6. Boersma P. Prevalence of multiple chronic conditions among US adults, 2018. Prev Chronic Dis [internet]. 2020 [cited 2023 Jun 21];17. Available from: https://www.cdc.gov/pcd/issues/2020/20_0130.htm
7. Ansah JP, Chiu CT. Projecting the chronic disease burden among the adult population in the United States using a multi-state population model. Front Public Health. 2023 Jan 13;10:1082183. doi:10.3389/fpubh.2022.1082183
8. Raghupathi W, Raghupathi V. An empirical study of chronic diseases in the United States: a visual analytics approach to public health. Int J Environ Res Public Health. 2018 Mar 1;15(3):431. doi:10.3390/ijerph15030431
9. CDC. Health and economic costs of chronic diseases [internet]. CDC. 2022 [cited 2022 May 23]. Available from: https://www.cdc.gov/chronicdisease/about/costs/index.htm
10. Milken Institute. Chronic disease costs in the U.S. Milken Institute Report [internet]. [cited 2022 May 24]. Available from: https://milkeninstitute.org/report/costs-chronic-disease-us
11. Asay GRB, Roy K, Lang JE, Payne RL, Howard DH. Absenteeism and employer costs associated with chronic diseases and health risk factors in the US workforce. Prev Chronic Dis. 2016 Oct 6;13:150503. doi:10.5888/pcd13.150503
12. Theis KA, Roblin DW, Helmick CG, Luo R. Prevalence and causes of work disability among working-age U.S. adults, 2011–2013, NHIS. Disabil Health J. 2018 Jan;11(1):108–15. doi:10.1016/j.dhjo.2017.04.010
13. McGonagle AK, Fisher GG, Barnes-Farrell JL, Grosch JW. Individual and work factors related to perceived work ability and labor force outcomes. J Appl Psychol. 2015;100(2):376–98. doi:10.1037/a0037974
14. KFF. 2022 employer health benefits survey—section 12: health screening and health promotion and wellness programs [internet]. KFF; 2022 [cited 2023 Jun 20]. Available from: https://www.kff.org/report-section/ehbs-2022-section-12-health-screening-and-health-promotion-and-wellness-programs/

15. Goetzel RZ, Roemer EC, Kent KB, McCleary K. Integration of workplace prevention programs and organizational effectiveness. In: Hudson HL, Nigam JAS, Sauter SL, Chosewood LC, Schill AL, Howard J, editors. Total worker health [internet]. Washington, DC: American Psychological Association; 2019 [cited 2023 Jun 20]. p. 279–94. Available from: http://content.apa.org/books/16125-017
16. Swenor BK. Including disability in all health equity efforts: an urgent call to action. Lancet Public Health. 2021 Jun;6(6):e359–60. doi:10.1016/S2468-2667(21)00115-8.
17. Baldridge D, Beatty J, Böhm SA, Kulkarni M, Moore ME. Persons with (dis)abilities. In: Colella AJ, King EB, editors. Oxford handbook of workplace discrimination [internet]. New York: Oxford University Press; 2015 [cited 2022 May 24]. Available from: http://oxfordhandbooks.com/view/10.1093/oxfordhb/9780199363643.001.0001/oxfordhb-9780199363643-e-9
18. Gignac MAM, Bowring J, Jetha A, Beaton DE, Breslin FC, Franche RL, et al. Disclosure, privacy and workplace accommodation of episodic disabilities: organizational perspectives on disability communication-support processes to sustain employment. J Occup Rehabil. 2021 Mar;31(1):153–65. doi:10.1007/s10926-020-09901-2
19. O'Brien KK, Davis AM, Strike C, Young NL, Bayoumi AM. Putting episodic disability into context: a qualitative study exploring factors that influence disability experienced by adults living with HIV/AIDS. J Int AIDS Soc. 2009 Feb;12(1):30–30. doi:10.1186/1758-2652-12-30
20. McGonagle A, Schmidt S, Speights SL. Work–health management interference for workers with chronic health conditions: construct development and scale validation. Occup Health Sci. 2020 Dec;4(4):445–70. doi:10.1007/s41542-020-00073-2
21. Beatty JE. Career barriers experienced by people with chronic illness: a U.S. study. Employ Respons Rights J. 2012 Jun;24(2):91–110. doi:10.1007/s10672-011-9177-z
22. McGonagle A, Roebuck A, Diebel H, Aqwa J, Fragoso Z, Stoddart S. Anticipated work discrimination scale: a chronic illness application. J Manag Psychol. 2016 Feb 8;31(1):61–78. doi:10.1108/JMP-01-2014-0009
23. Barth SE, Wessel JL. Mental illness disclosure in organizations: defining and predicting (un)supportive responses. J Bus Psychol. 2022 Apr;37(2):407–28. doi: 10.1007/s10869-021-09753-4
24. Beatty JE, McGonagle A. Coaching employees with chronic illness: Supporting professional identities through biographical work. Int J Evid Based Coach Mentor. 2016;14(1):1–15.
25. Shaw WS, Feuerstein M, Haufler AJ, Berkowitz SM, Lopez MS. Working with low back pain: problem-solving orientation and function. Pain. 2001 Aug;93(2):129–37. doi: 10.1016/S0304-3959(01)00304-9
26. Miller OC Frederick W. Autoimmunity has reached epidemic levels. we need urgent action to address it [internet]. Scientific American. [cited 2024 Mar 5]. Available from: https://www.scientificamerican.com/article/autoimmunity-has-reached-epidemic-levels-we-need-urgent-action-to-address-it/
27. Chung Y. Chronic health conditions and economic outcomes. The Society of Labor Economists. 2013 Oct. Available from: https://www.sole-jole.org/assets/docs/14225.pdf
28. Watson KB. Chronic conditions among adults aged 18–34 years—United States, 2019. MMWR Morb Mortal Wkly Rep [internet]. 2022 [cited 2023 Jun 25];71. Available from: https://www.cdc.gov/mmwr/volumes/71/wr/mm7130a3.htm
29. Blue Cross Blue Shield. The health of millennials [internet]. Blue Cross Blue Shield. [cited 2023 Jun 25]. Available from: https://www.bcbs.com/the-health-of-america/reports/the-health-of-millennials

30. Rashmi R, Mohanty SK. Examining chronic disease onset across varying age groups of Indian adults using competing risk analysis. Sci Rep. 2023 Apr 10;13(1):5848. doi: 10.1038/s41598-023-32861-5
31. Conrad N, Misra S, Verbakel JY, Verbeke G, Molenberghs G, Taylor PN, et al. Incidence, prevalence, and co-occurrence of autoimmune disorders over time and by age, sex, and socioeconomic status: a population-based cohort study of 22 million individuals in the UK. The Lancet. 2023 Jun;401(10391):1878–90. doi: 10.1016/S0140-6736(23)00457-9
32. Harris ML, Egan N, Forder PM, Loxton D. Increased chronic disease prevalence among the younger generation: Findings from a population-based data linkage study to inform chronic disease ascertainment among reproductive-aged Australian women. Orueta JF, editor. PLoS ONE. 2021 Aug 18;16(8):e0254668. Available from: https://journals.plos.org/plosone/article?id=10.1371/journal.pone.0254668
33. Dinse GE, Parks CG, Weinberg CR, Co CA, Wilkerson J, Zeldin DC, et al. Increasing Prevalence of Antinuclear Antibodies in the United States. Arthritis Rheumatol. 2022 Dec;74(12):2032–41. doi: 10.1002/art.41214
34. McCarthy M. The "gender gap" in autoimmune disease. The Lancet. 2000 Sep;356(9235):1088. doi: 10.1016/S0140-6736(05)74535-9
35. Schwartzman-Morris J, Putterman C. Gender differences in the pathogenesis and outcome of lupus and of lupus nephritis. J. Immunol. Res.. 2012 May 29;2012:e604892. doi: 10.1155/2012/604892
36. Case A, Paxson C. Sex differences in morbidity and mortality. Demography. 2005 May 1;42(2):189–214. doi: 10.1353/dem.2005.0011
37. Ballering AV, Bonvanie IJ, Olde Hartman TC, Monden R, Rosmalen JGM. Gender and sex independently associate with common somatic symptoms and lifetime prevalence of chronic disease. Soc Sci Med. 2020 May;253:112968. doi: 10.1016/j.socscimed.2020.112968
38. Merone L, Tsey K, Russell D, Daltry A, Nagle C. Self-reported time to diagnosis and proportions of rediagnosis in female patients with chronic conditions in Australia: a cross-sectional survey. Womens Health Rep (New Rochelle). 2022;3(1):749–58. doi: 10.1089/whr.2022.0040
39. Din NU, Ukoumunne OC, Rubin G, Hamilton W, Carter B, Stapley S, et al. Age and gender variations in cancer diagnostic intervals in 15 cancers: analysis of data from the UK clinical practice research datalink. PLoS One. 2015;10(5):e0127717. doi: 10.1371/journal.pone.0127717
40. Samulowitz A, Gremyr I, Eriksson E, Hensing G. "Brave men" and "emotional women": a theory-guided literature review on gender bias in health care and gendered norms towards patients with chronic pain. Pain Res Manag. 2018 Feb 25; 2018:6358624. doi: 10.1155/2018/6358624
41. Claréus B, Renström EA. Physicians' gender bias in the diagnostic assessment of medically unexplained symptoms and its effect on patient–physician relations. Scand J Psychol. 2019 Aug;60(4):338–47. doi: 10.1111/sjop.12545
42. Chen EH, Shofer FS, Dean AJ, Hollander JE, Baxt WG, Robey JL, et al. Gender disparity in analgesic treatment of emergency department patients with acute abdominal pain. Acad Emerg Med. 2008 May;15(5):414–18. doi: 10.1111/j.1553-2712.2008.00100.x
43. Davis J, Penha J, Mbowe O, Taira DA. Prevalence of single and multiple leading causes of death by race/ethnicity among US adults aged 60 to 79 years. Prev Chronic Dis. 2017 Oct 19;14:E101. doi: 10.5888/pcd14.160241
44. Hill L, Ndugga N, Published SA. Key data on health and health care by race and ethnicity [internet]. KFF. 2023 [cited 2023 Nov 17]. Available from: https://www.

kff.org/racial-equity-and-health-policy/report/key-data-on-health-and-health-care-by-race-and-ethnicity/

45. Williams DR, Mohammed SA, Leavell J, Collins C. Race, socioeconomic status, and health: complexities, ongoing challenges, and research opportunities: Race, SES, and health. Ann NY Acad Sci. 2010 Feb;1186(1):69–101. doi: 10.1111/j.1749-6632.2009.05339.x

46. Splan ED, Magerman AB, Forbes CE. Associations of regional racial attitudes with chronic illness in the United States. Soc Sci Med. 2021 Jul;281:114077. doi: 10.1016/j.socscimed.2021.114077

47. Sternthal MJ, Slopen N, Williams DR. Racial disparities in health: how much does stress really matter? Du Bois Rev. 2011;8(1):95–113. doi: 10.1017/S1742058X11000087

48. Bor J, Cohen GH, Galea S. Population health in an era of rising income inequality: USA, 1980-2015. The Lancet. 2017 Apr;389(10077):1475–90. doi: 10.1016/S0140-6736(17)30571-8

49. Hajat C, Stein E. The global burden of multiple chronic conditions: a narrative review. Prev Med Rep. 2018 Dec 1;12:284–93. doi: 10.1016/j.pmedr.2018.10.008

50. Nahin RL. Estimates of pain prevalence and severity in adults: United States, 2012. J Pain. 2015 Aug;16(8):769–80. doi: 10.1016/j.jpain.2015.05.002

51. Pitcher MH, Korff MV, Bushnell MC, Porter L. Prevalence and profile of high-impact chronic pain in the United States. J Pain. 2019 Feb 1;20(2):146–60. doi: 10.1016/j.jpain.2018.07.006

52. Yong RJ, Mullins PM, Bhattacharyya N. Prevalence of chronic pain among adults in the United States. Pain. 2022 Feb;163(2):e328–32. doi: 10.1097/j.pain.0000000000002291

53. Chen C, Haupert SR, Zimmermann L, Shi X, Fritsche LG, Mukherjee B. Global prevalence of post COVID-19 condition or long COVID: a meta-analysis and systematic review. J Infect Dis. 2022 Apr 16;226(9):1593-1607. doi: 10.1093/infdis/jiac136

54. Cutler DM. The economic cost of long COVID: an update [internet]. 2023 [cited 2023 Jun 22]. Available from: https://www.hks.harvard.edu/centers/mrcbg/programs/growthpolicy/economic-cost-long-covid-update-david-cutler

55. Pomeroy C. A tsunami of disability is coming as a result of long COVID [internet]. Scientific American. [cited 2022 May 23]. Available from: https://www.scientificamerican.com/article/a-tsunami-of-disability-is-coming-as-a-result-of-lsquo-long-covid-rsquo/

56. Benjamin EJ, Virani SS, Callaway CW, Chamberlain AM, Chang AR, Cheng S, et al. Heart disease and stroke statistics—2018 update: a report from the American Heart Association. Circulation [internet]. 2018 Mar [cited 2022 May 24]; Available from: https://www.ahajournals.org/doi/abs/10.1161/cir.0000000000000558

57. Cutler DM. The costs of long COVID. JAMA Health Forum. 2022 May 12;3(5):e221809. doi: 10.1001/jamahealthforum.2022.1809

58. Gaskin DJ, Richard P. The economic costs of pain in the United States [internet]. Relieving pain in America: a blueprint for transforming prevention, care, education, and research. National Academies Press (US); 2011 [cited 2022 May 24]. Available from: https://www.ncbi.nlm.nih.gov/books/NBK92521/

59. Hargrave GE, Hiatt D, Alexander R, Shaffer IA. EAP treatment impact on presenteeism and absenteeism: implications for return on investment. J Workplace Behav Health. 2008 Aug 25;23(3):283–93. doi: 10.1080/15555240802242999

60. McGregor A, Sharma R, Magee C, Caputi P, Iverson D. Explaining variations in the findings of presenteeism research: a meta-analytic investigation into the moderating effects of construct operationalizations and chronic health. J Occup Health Psychol. 2018 Oct;23(4):584–601. doi: 10.1037/ocp0000099

61. Wang M, Lu C, Lu L. The positive potential of presenteeism: an exploration of how presenteeism leads to good performance evaluation. J Organ Behavior. 2023 Jul;44(6):920–935. doi: 10.1002/job.2604
62. Karanika-Murray M, Biron C. The health-performance framework of presenteeism: towards understanding an adaptive behaviour. Hum Relat. 2020 Feb;73(2):242–61. doi: 10.1177/0018726719827081
63. Cavaiola TS, Pettus JH. Management Of type 2 diabetes: selecting amongst available pharmacological agents. In: Feingold KR, Anawalt B, Boyce A, Chrousos G, de Herder WW, Dhatariya K, et al., editors. Endotext [internet]. South Dartmouth (MA): MDText.com, Inc.; 2000 [cited 2022 May 27]. Available from: http://www.ncbi.nlm.nih.gov/books/NBK425702/
64. Bach K. Is 'long Covid' worsening the labor shortage? [internet]. Brookings. 2022 [cited 2022 May 24]. Available from: https://www.brookings.edu/research/is-long-covid-worsening-the-labor-shortage/
65. Peterson CL, Murphy G. Transition from the labor market: older workers and retirement. Int J Health Serv. 2010 Oct;40(4):609–27. doi: 10.2190/HS.40.4.c
66. Schofield DJ, Shrestha RN, Percival R, Passey ME, Callander EJ, Kelly SJ. The personal and national costs of mental health conditions: impacts on income, taxes, government support payments due to lost labour force participation. BMC Psychiatry. 2011 Dec;11(1):72. doi: 10.1186/1471-244X-11-72
67. Clarke DM, Currie KC. Depression, anxiety and their relationship with chronic diseases: a review of the epidemiology, risk and treatment evidence. Med J Aust [internet]. 2009 Apr [cited 2022 May 25];190(S7). doi: 10.5694/j.1326-5377.2009.tb02471.x
68. Li H, Ge S, Greene B, Dunbar-Jacob J. Depression in the context of chronic diseases in the United States and China. Int J Nurs Sci. 2019 Jan;6(1):117–22. doi: 10.1016/j.ijnss.2018.11.007
69. Miller VJ, Nahar S, Praetorius R, Rivedal J. The art of living with chronic health conditions. Illness, Crisis & Loss. 2022 Jan;30(1):51–67. doi: 10.1177/1054137319857088
70. Wilson C, Stock J. The impact of living with long-term conditions in young adulthood on mental health and identity: what can help? Health Expect. 2019 Oct;22(5):1111–21. doi: 10.1111/hex.12944
71. Sharpe L, Michalowski M, Richmond B, Menzies RE, Shaw J. Fear of progression in chronic illnesses other than cancer: a systematic review and meta-analysis of a transdiagnostic construct. Health Psychol Rev. 2022 Feb 18;17(2), 301–20.
72. Strunin L, Boden LI. Family consequences of chronic back pain. Soc Sci Med. 2004 Apr;58(7):1385–93. doi: 10.1016/S0277-9536(03)00333-2

Chapter 2

1. World Health Organization. Disability [internet]. [cited 2022 Jun 1]. Available from: https://www.who.int/health-topics/disability
2. CDC. Disability impacts all of us infographic [internet]. CDC. 2019 [cited 2022 Jun 17]. Available from: https://www.cdc.gov/ncbddd/disabilityandhealth/infographic-disability-impacts-all.html
3. Andrews EE, Powell RM, Ayers K. The evolution of disability language: choosing terms to describe disability. Disabil Health J. 2022 Apr;101328. doi: 10.1016/j.dhjo.2022.101328
4. Sharif A. Disability Terminology Project [internet]. Disability Terminology Project. [cited 2024 Mar 6]. Available from: https://disabilityterminology.athersharif.com/#/#ageGroup

5. CDN. icfbeginnersguide.pdf [internet]. [cited 2022 Jun 3]. Available from: https://cdn.who.int/media/docs/default-source/classification/icf/icfbeginnersguide.pdf
6. Office of Developmental Primary Care. Medical and social models of disability [internet]. [cited 2022 Jun 3]. Available from: https://odpc.ucsf.edu/clinical/patient-centered-care/medical-and-social-models-of-disability
7. Liddiard K. Liking for like's sake: the commodification of disability on Facebook. J Dev Disabil. 2014;20(3):94–101.
8. Santuzzi AM, Waltz PR. Disability in the workplace: a unique and variable identity. J Manage. 2016 Jul;42(5):1111–35. doi: 10.1177/0149206315626269
9. ADA. Introduction to the ADA [internet]. [cited 2022 Jun 6]. Available from: https://www.ada.gov/ada_intro.htm
10. US Department of Labor. ADA Amendments Act of 2008 frequently asked questions [internet]. [cited 2022 Jun 7]. Available from: https://www.dol.gov/agencies/ofccp/faqs/americans-with-disabilities-act-amendments
11. US Bureau of Labor Statistics. Persons with a disability: labor force characteristics summary—2021 A01 results [internet]. [cited 2022 Jun 7]. Available from: https://www.bls.gov/news.release/disabl.nr0.htm
12. US Department of Labor. Voluntary self-identification of disability form [internet]. DOL. [cited 2023 Jun 26]. Available from: http://www.dol.gov/agencies/ofccp/self-id-forms
13. EEOC. The EEO status of workers with disabilities in the federal sector [internet]. EEOC. [cited 2022 Jul 18]. Available from: https://www.eeoc.gov/federal-sector/reports/eeo-status-workers-disabilities-federal-sector
14. Rutigliano P, O'Connell M. The State of Disability 2022 Employee Engagement Intersectionality. Mercer in partnership with Global Disability Inclusion. 2022 Feb.
15. ADA. A guide to disability rights laws [internet]. [cited 2022 Jun 7]. Available from: https://www.ada.gov/cguide.htm#anchor62335
16. EEOC. The Americans with Disabilities Act Amendments Act of 2008 [internet]. EEOC. [cited 2022 Jun 7]. Available from: https://www.eeoc.gov/statutes/americans-disabilities-act-amendments-act-2008
17. EEOC. Fact sheet on the EEOC's final regulations implementing the ADAAA [internet]. EEOC. [cited 2022 Jun 7]. Available from: https://www.eeoc.gov/laws/guidance/fact-sheet-eeocs-final-regulations-implementing-adaaa
18. US Department of Health and Human Services. Civil Rights: Guidance on "long COVID" as a disability under the ADA, Section 504, and Section 1557 [internet]. HHS. 2021 [cited 2022 Jun 8]. Available from: https://www.hhs.gov/civil-rights/for-providers/civil-rights-covid19/guidance-long-covid-disability/index.html
19. EEOC. The ADA: your responsibilities as an employer [internet]. EEOC. [cited 2023 Jun 26]. Available from: https://www.eeoc.gov/publications/ada-your-responsibilities-employer
20. EEOC. S&C Electric Company to pay $315,000 to settle EEOC disability discrimination lawsuit [internet]. EEOC. [cited 2022 Jul 5]. Available from: https://www.eeoc.gov/newsroom/sc-electric-company-pay-315000-settle-eeoc-disability-discrimination-lawsuit
21. EEOC V. Ranew's Management Company, Inc., Ranew's Truck & Equipment Company, LLC, Ranew's Fleet Service, LLC, Ranew's Outdoor Equipment, Inc., Ranew's Companies, LLC, And Ranew's (2021), States News Service. (US District Court for the Middle District of Georgia December 20, 2021).
22. EEOC. Mine Rite Technologies to pay $75,000 to settle EEOC disability suit [internet]. EEOC. [cited 2022 Jul 7]. Available from: https://www.eeoc.gov/newsroom/mine-rite-technologies-pay-75000-settle-eeoc-disability-suit

23. EEOC V. Mine Rite Technologies LLC (2017), States News Service. (US District Court for the District of Wyoming March 31, 2017).
24. Americans with Disabilities Act of 1990, AS AMENDED with ADA Amendments Act of 2008 [internet]. [cited 2022 Jun 7]. Available from: https://www.ada.gov/pubs/adastatute08.htm#subchapterI
25. 12.6 ADA—ability to perform essential functions—factors. Model jury instructions [internet]. [cited 2023 Jun 26]. Available from: https://www.ce9.uscourts.gov/jury-instructions/node/216
26. EEOC. Enforcement guidance on reasonable accommodation and undue hardship under the ADA [internet]. EEOC. [cited 2022 Jun 7]. Available from: https://www.eeoc.gov/laws/guidance/enforcement-guidance-reasonable-accommodation-and-undue-hardship-under-ada
27. Job Accommodation Network. Costs and benefits of accommodation [internet]. [cited 2024 May 22]. Available from: https://askjan.org/topics/costs.cfm
28. Porter NB. A new look at the ADA's undue hardship defense. Missouri Law Review. 2019;84:57.
29. EEOC. Work at home/telework as a reasonable accommodation [internet]. EEOC. 2003 [cited 2023 Jun 26]. Available from: https://www.eeoc.gov/laws/guidance/work-hometelework-reasonable-accommodation
30. EEOC. What you should know about COVID-19 and the ADA, the Rehabilitation Act, and other EEO laws [internet]. EEOC. [cited 2023 Jun 26]. Available from: https://www.eeoc.gov/wysk/what-you-should-know-about-covid-19-and-ada-rehabilitation-act-and-other-eeo-laws
31. EARN. Recruit. Hire. Retain. Advance. Section 501 Info Center [internet]. [cited 2022 Jul 5]. Available from: https://askearn.org/page/section-501-info-center
32. US Department of Labor. Section 503 regulations frequently asked questions [internet]. US DOL [cited 2022 Jul 5]. Available from: https://www.dol.gov/agencies/ofccp/faqs/section-503
33. US Department of Labor. FMLA frequently asked questions [internet]. DOL [cited 2022 Jul 5]. Available from: https://www.dol.gov/agencies/whd/fmla/faq#1
34. CDC. Health Insurance Portability and Accountability Act of 1996 (HIPAA) [internet]. CDC. 2022 [cited 2022 Jul 5]. Available from: https://www.cdc.gov/phlp/publications/topic/hipaa.html
35. US Department of Health and Human Services. Employers and health information in the workplace [internet]. HHS. 2008 [cited 2022 Jul 5]. Available from: https://www.hhs.gov/hipaa/for-individuals/employers-health-information-workplace/index.html
36. Alder S. Does HIPAA apply to employers? [internet]. HIPAA Journal. 2021 [cited 2022 Jul 5]. Available from: https://www.hipaajournal.com/does-hipaa-apply-to-employers/
37. US Department of Health and Human Services. Affairs (ASPA) AS for P. 3028—If my employer requires proof of my COVID-19 vaccination status, does that violate my rights under HIPAA? [internet]. HHS. 2021 [cited 2022 Jul 5]. Available from: https://www.hhs.gov/answers/if-my-employer-requires-proof-of-my-covid-19-vaccination-status/index.html

Chapter 3

1. Tetrick LE, Campbell Quick J. Overview of occupational health psychology: public health in occupational settings. In: Handbook of occupational health psychology. American Psychological Association; 2011. p. 3–20.

2. Moen P, Kelly EL, Fan W, Lee SR, Almeida D, Kossek EE, et al. Does a flexibility/support organizational initiative improve high-tech employees' well-being? evidence from the work, family, and health network. Am Sociol Rev. 2016;81(1):134–64. doi: 10.1177/0003122415622391
3. McGonagle AK, Bardwell T, Flinchum J, Kavanagh K. Perceived work ability: a constant comparative analysis of workers' perspectives. Occup Health Sci. 2022;6(2):207–46. doi: 10.1007/s41542-022-00116-w
4. KFF. Section 12: Health screening and health promotion and wellness programs [internet]. KFF. 2023. Available from: https://www.kff.org/report-section/ehbs-2022-section-12-health-screening-and-health-promotion-and-wellness-programs/
5. Song Z, Baicker K. Health and economic outcomes up to three years after a workplace wellness program: a randomized controlled trial: study examines the health and economic outcomes of a workplace wellness program. Health Aff. 2021;40(6):951–60. doi: 10.1377/hlthaff.2020.01808
6. Jones D, Molitor D, Reif J. What do workplace wellness programs do? evidence from the Illinois workplace wellness study. Q. J. Econ. 2019;134(4):1747–91. doi: 10.1093/qje/qjz023
7. SHRM. Do corporate wellness programs work? [internet]. SHRM. 2021 [cited 2022 Jul 21]. Available from: https://www.shrm.org/hr-today/news/hr-magazine/spring2021/pages/do-corporate-wellness-programs-work.aspx
8. Mattke S, Liu H, Caloyeras J, Huang C, Van Busum K, Khodyakov D, et al. Workplace wellness programs study: final report [internet]. RAND Corporation; 2013 [cited 2022 Jul 21]. Available from: https://www.rand.org/pubs/research_reports/RR254.html
9. Goetzel RZ, Fabius R, Fabius D, Roemer EC, Thornton N, Kelly RK, et al. The stock performance of C. Everett Koop award winners compared with the Standard & Poor's 500 index. J Occup Environ Med. 2016;58(1):9–15. doi: 10.1097/JOM.0000000000000632
10. Grossmeier J, Fabius R, Flynn JP, Noeldner SP, Fabius D, Goetzel RZ, et al. Linking workplace health promotion best practices and organizational financial performance: Tracking market performance of companies with highest scores on the HERO scorecard. J Occup Environ Med. 2016;58(1):16–23. doi: 10.1097/JOM.0000000000000631
11. Fabius R, Loeppke RR, Hohn T, Fabius D, Eisenberg B, Konicki DL, et al. Tracking the market performance of companies that integrate a culture of health and safety: an assessment of corporate health achievement award applicants. J Occup Environ Med. 2016;58(1):3–8. doi: 10.1097/JOM.0000000000000638
12. Beatty JE. Career barriers experienced by people with chronic illness: A U.S. study. Employ Respons Rights J. 2012;24(2):91–110. doi: 10.1007/s10672-011-9177-z
13. The Hopkinton Conference Working Group on Workplace Disability Prevention, Pransky GS, Fassier JB, Besen E, Blanck P, Ekberg K, et al. Sustaining work participation across the life course. J Occup Rehabil. 2016;26(4):465–79. doi: 10.1007/s10926-016-9670-1
14. McGonagle AK, Beatty JE, Joffe R. Coaching for workers with chronic illness: evaluating an intervention. J Occup Health Psychol. 2014;19(3):385–98. doi: 10.1037/a0036601
15. Stay-at-work/Return-to-work: key facts, critical information gaps, and current practices and proposals [internet]. Mathematica. [cited 2022 Jul 15]. Available from: https://www.mathematica.org/publications/stay-at-work-return-to-work-key-facts-critical-information-gaps-and-current-practices-and-proposals
16. Ben-Shalom Y, Burak H. The case for public investment in stay-at-work/return-to-work programs [internet]. Mathematica. [cited 2022 Jul 16]. Available from: https://www.mathematica.org/publications/the-case-for-public-investment-in-stayatworkreturntowork-programs

17. Lecours A, Durand MJ, Coutu MF, Groleau C, Bédard-Mercier R. Stay at work after a period of disability due to an occupational injury: a complex process marked by social exchanges. J Occup Rehabil. 2022;32(2):319–28. doi: 10.1007/s10926-021-10008-5
18. Promoting retention or reemployment of workers after a significant injury or illness [internet]. Mathematica. [cited 2022 Jul 16]. Available from: https://www.mathematica.org/publications/promoting-retention-or-reemployment-of-workers-after-a-significant-injury-or-illness
19. Blalock AC, Stephen Mcdaniel J, Farber EW. Effect of employment on quality of life and psychological functioning in patients with HIV/AIDS. Psychosomatics. 2002;43(5):400–4. doi: 10.1176/appi.psy.43.5.400
20. Miller A, Dishon S. Health-related quality of life in multiple sclerosis: the impact of disability, gender and employment etatus. Qual Life Res. 2006;15(2):259–71. doi: 10.1007/s11136-005-0891-6
21. Barišin A, Benjak T, Vuletić G. Health-related quality of life of women with disabilities in relation to their employment status. Croat Med J. 2011;52(4):550–56. doi: 10.3325/cmj.2011.52.550
22. Ra YA, Kim WH. Impact of employment and age on quality of life of individuals with disabilities: a multilevel analysis. Rehabil Couns Bull. 2016;59(2):112–20. doi: 10.1177/0034355215573538
23. Nielsen K, Yarker J, Munir F, Bültmann U. IGLOO: an integrated framework for sustainable return to work in workers with common mental disorders. Work Stress. 2018 2;32(4):400–17. doi: 10.1080/02678373.2018.1438536
24. Munir F, Yarker J, Hicks B, Donaldson-Feilder E. Returning employees back to work: developing a measure for supervisors to support return to work (SSRW). J Occup Rehabil. 2012;22(2):196–208. doi: 10.1007/s10926-011-9331-3
25. Nielsen K, Yarker J. What can I do for you? line managers' behaviors to support return to work for workers with common mental disorders. JMP. 2023;38(1):34–46. doi: 10.1108/JMP-09-2021-0500
26. Klevanger NE, Aasdahl L, By Rise M. Work as an arena for health—supervisors' experiences with attending to employees' sick leave and return-to-work process. Olorunlana A, editor. PLoS ONE. 2023;18(4):e0284369. doi: 10.1371/journal.pone.0284369
27. Costa-Black KM. Core components of return-to-work interventions. In: Loisel P, Anema JR, editors. Handbook of work disability [internet]. New York: Springer New York; 2013 [cited 2022 Jul 25]. p. 427–40. Available from: http://link.springer.com/10.1007/978-1-4614-6214-9_26
28. van Oostrom SH, Boot CRL. Workplace interventions. In: Loisel P, Anema JR, editors. Handbook of work disability [internet]. New York: Springer New York; 2013 [cited 2022 Jul 25]. p. 335–55. Available from: http://link.springer.com/10.1007/978-1-4614-6214-9_21
29. Epstein Z, Wood M, Grosz M, Prenovitz S, Nichols A. Synthesis of stay-at-work/return-to-work (SAW/RTW) programs, models, efforts, and definitions [internet]. US Department of Labor (DOL). 2020. Available from: https://www.dol.gov/resource-library/synthesis-stay-workreturn-work-sawrtw-programs-models-efforts-and-definitions
30. Dibben P, Wood G, O'Hara R. Do return to work interventions for workers with disabilities and health conditions achieve employment outcomes and are they cost effective? a systematic narrative review. Empl Relat. 2018;40(6):999–1014. doi: 10.1108/ER-01-2017-0023
31. Nichols A, Geyer J, Grosz M, Epstein Z, Wood M. Synthesis of evidence about stay-at-work/ return-to-work (SAW/RTW) and related programs [internet]. 2020. Available from: https://www.dol.gov/sites/dolgov/files/OASP/evaluation/pdf/SAW-RTW_Deliverable-2-2_SynthesisofEvidence_508c.pdf

32. Gensby U, Labriola M, Irvin E, Amick BC, Lund T. A classification of components of workplace disability management programs: results from a systematic review. J Occup Rehabil. 2014;24(2):220–41. doi: 10.1007/s10926-013-9437-x
33. van Vilsteren M, van Oostrom SH, de Vet HC, Franche RL, Boot CR, Anema JR. Workplace interventions to prevent work disability in workers on sick leave. Cochrane Work Group, editor. Cochrane Database of Systematic Reviews [internet]. 2015 Oct 5 [cited 2022 Jul 28];2015(10). Available from: http://doi.wiley.com/10.1002/14651858.CD006955.pub3
34. Schandelmaier S, Ebrahim S, Burkhardt SCA, de Boer WEL, Zumbrunn T, Guyatt GH, et al. Return to work coordination programmes for work disability: a meta-analysis of randomised controlled trials. Fehlings M, editor. PLoS ONE. 2012;7(11):e49760. doi: 10.1371/journal.pone.0049760
35. Mikkelsen MB, Rosholm M. Systematic review and meta-analysis of interventions aimed at enhancing return to work for sick-listed workers with common mental disorders, stress-related disorders, somatoform disorders and personality disorders. Occup Environ Med. 2018;75(9):675–86. doi: 10.1136/oemed-2018-105073
36. Franche RL, Cullen K, Clarke J, Irvin E, Sinclair S, Frank J, et al. Workplace-based return-to-work interventions: a systematic review of the quantitative literature. J Occup Rehabil. 2005;15(4):607–31. doi: 10.1007/s10926-005-8038-8
37. Dol M, Varatharajan S, Neiterman E, McKnight E, Crouch M, McDonald E, et al. Systematic review of the impact on return to work of return-to-work coordinators. J Occup Rehabil. 2021;31(4):675–98. doi: 10.1007/s10926-021-09975-6
38. Cancelliere C, Donovan J, Stochkendahl MJ, Biscardi M, Ammendolia C, Myburgh C, et al. Factors affecting return to work after injury or illness: best evidence synthesis of systematic reviews. Chiropr Man Therap. 2016;24(1):32. doi: 10.1186/s12998-016-0113-z
39. Main CJ, Shaw WS, Nicholas MK, Linton SJ. System-level efforts to address pain-related workplace challenges. Pain. 2022;163(8):1425–31. doi: 10.1097/j.pain.0000000000002548
40. The Hopkinton Conference Working Group on Workplace Disability Prevention, Main CJ, Shaw WS. Employer policies and practices to manage and prevent disability: conclusion to the special issue. J Occup Rehabil. 2016;26(4):490–98. doi: 10.1007/s10926-016-9655-0

Chapter 4

1. Demerouti E, Bakker AB, Nachreiner F, Schaufeli WB. The job demands–resources model of burnout. J Appl Psychol. 2001;86(3):499–512.
2. Lesener T, Gusy B, Wolter C. The job demands–resources model: a meta-analytic review of longitudinal studies. Work Stress. 2019 Jan 2;33(1):76–103. doi: 10.1080/02678373.2018.1529065
3. Demerouti E, Mostert K, Bakker AB. Burnout and work engagement: a thorough investigation of the independency of both constructs. J Occup Health Psychol. 2010 Jul;15(3):209–22. doi: 10.1037/a0019408
4. Kahn WA. Psychological conditions of personal engagement and disengagement at work. AMJ. 1990 Dec 1;33(4):692–724. doi: 10.2307/256287
5. Rich BL, Lepine JA, Crawford ER. Job engagement: antecedents and effects on job performance. AMJ. 2010 Jun;53(3):617–35. doi: 10.5465/AMJ.2010.51468988
6. Bakker AB, Demerouti E. Job demands–resources theory: taking stock and looking forward. J Occup Health Psychol. 2017 Jul;22(3):273–85. doi: 10.1037/ocp0000056
7. Brady GM, Truxillo DM, Cadiz DM, Rineer JR, Caughlin DE, Bodner T. Opening the black box: examining the nomological network of work ability and its role in organizational research. J Appl Psychol. 2020 Jun;105(6):637–70. doi: 10.1037/apl0000454

8. McGonagle AK, Fisher GG, Barnes-Farrell JL, Grosch JW. Individual and work factors related to perceived work ability and labor force outcomes. J Appl Psychol. 2015;100(2):376–98. doi: 10.1037/a0037974
9. McGonagle AK, Bardwell T, Flinchum J, Kavanagh K. Perceived work ability: a constant comparative analysis of workers' perspectives. Occup Health Sci. 2022 Jun;6(2):207–46. doi: 10.1007/s41542-022-00116-w
10. Ahlstrom L, Grimby-Ekman A, Hagberg M, Dellve L. The work ability index and single-item question: associations with sick leave, symptoms, and health: a prospective study of women on long-term sick leave. Scand J Work Environ Health. 2010 Apr 7;36(5):404–12. doi: 10.5271/sjweh.2917
11. Sell L. Predicting long-term sickness absence and early retirement pension from self-reported work ability. Int Arch Occup Environ Health. 2009 Oct;82(9):1133–38. doi: 10.1007/s00420-009-0417-6
12. von Bonsdorff MB, Seitsamo J, Ilmarinen J, Nygard CH, von Bonsdorff ME, Rantanen T. Work ability in midlife as a predictor of mortality and disability in later life: a 28-year prospective follow-up study. Can Med Assoc J. 2011 Mar 8;183(4):E235–42. doi: 10.1503/cmaj.100713
13. McGonagle AK, Barnes-Farrell JL, Di Milia L, Fischer FM, Hobbs BBB, Iskra-Golec I, et al. Demands, resources, and work ability: a cross-national examination of health care workers. Eur J Work Organ Psychol. 2014 Nov 2;23(6):830–46. doi: 10.1080/1359432X.2013.819158
14. Pak K, Kooij Dtam, De Lange AH, Heuvel S, Van Veldhoven MJPM. The influence of human resource practices on perceived work ability and the preferred retirement age: a latent growth modelling approach. Hum Resour Manag J. 2021 Jan;31(1):311–25. doi: 10.1111/1748-8583.12304
15. The Spoon Theory written by Christine Miserandino [internet]. But you don't look sick? support for those with invisible illness or chronic illness. 2013 [cited 2022 Nov 7]. Available from: https://butyoudontlooksick.com/articles/written-by-christine/the-spoon-theory/
16. Winders S, Lyon DE, Stechmiller JK, Kelly DL. Biomarkers of sleep disturbance in adults with chronic illness: A scoping review. Chronic Illness. 2022 Feb 18;174239532110736. doi: 10.1177/17423953211073697
17. Azzolino D, Cesari M. Fatigue in the COVID-19 pandemic. Lancet Healthy Longev. 2022 Mar;3(3):e128–9.
18. McGonagle A, Schmidt S, Speights SL. Work–health management interference for workers with chronic health conditions: construct development and scale validation. Occup Health Sci. 2020 Dec;4(4):445–70. doi: 10.1007/s41542-020-00073-2
19. Alarcia R, Ara JR, Martín J, Bertol V, Bestué M. Importance and factors related to chronic fatigue in multiple sclerosis. Neurologia. 2005 Mar;20(2):77–84.
20. Finan PH, Goodin BR, Smith MT. The association of sleep and pain: an update and a path forward. J Pain. 2013 Dec;14(12):1539–52. doi: 10.1016/j.jpain.2013.08.007
21. Reed, BN, McGonagle, AK. Ups and downs: workers with fluctuations in chronic pain and work–health management interference. Int J Stress Manag. 2024;31(3):279–291. doi:10.1037/str0000332
22. Tveito TH, Shaw WS, Huang YH, Nicholas M, Wagner G. Managing pain in the workplace: a focus group study of challenges, strategies and what matters most to workers with low back pain. Disabil Rehabil. 2010 Jan;32(24):2035–45. doi: 10.3109/09638281003797398
23. Fragoso ZL, McGonagle AK. Chronic pain in the workplace: a diary study of pain interference at work and worker strain. Stress Health. 2018 Aug;34(3):416–24. doi: 10.1002/smi.2801

24. Fifield J, Mcquillan J, Armeli S, Tennen H, Reisine S, Affleck G. Chronic strain, daily work stress and pain among workers with rheumatoid arthritis: does job stress make a bad day worse? Work Stress. 2004 Oct;18(4):275–91. doi: 10.1080/02678370412331324996
25. Gignac MAM, Bowring J, Jetha A, Beaton DE, Breslin FC, Franche RL, et al. Disclosure, privacy and workplace accommodation of episodic disabilities: organizational perspectives on disability communication-support processes to sustain employment. J Occup Rehabil. 2021 Mar;31(1):153–65. doi: 10.1007/s10926-020-09901-2
26. Prince MJ. Persons with invisible disabilities and workplace accommodation: findings from a scoping literature review. JVR. 2017 Jan 25;46(1):75–86. doi: 10.3233/JVR-160844
27. The Hopkinton Conference Working Group on Workplace Disability Prevention, Pransky GS, Fassier JB, Besen E, Blanck P, Ekberg K, et al. Sustaining work participation across the life course. J Occup Rehabil. 2016 Dec;26(4):465–79. 10.1007/s10926-016-9670-1
28. Taylor SR. The body is not an apology: the power of radical self-love. 2nd ed. Oakland, CA: Berrett-Koehler Publishers, Inc; 2021. 159 p.
29. Warren MA, Warren MT. The EThIC model of virtue-based allyship development: a new approach to equity and inclusion in organizations. J Bus Ethics. 2023 Jan;182(3):783–803. doi: 10.1007/s10551-021-05002-z
30. Kaye HS, Jans LH, Jones EC. Why don't employers hire and retain workers with disabilities? J Occup Rehabil. 2011 Dec;21(4):526–36. doi: 10.1007/s10926-011-9302-8
31. Hebl M, Cheng SK, Ng LC. Modern discrimination in organizations. Annu Rev Organ Psychol Organ Behav. 2020 Jan 21;7(1):257–82. doi: 10.1146/annurev-orgpsych-012119-044948
32. McGonagle AK, Hamblin LE. Proactive responding to anticipated discrimination based on chronic illness: double-edged sword? J Bus Psychol. 2014 Sep;29(3):427–42. doi: 10.1007/s10869-013-9324-7
33. Bergman ME, Palmieri PA, Drasgow F, Ormerod AJ. Racial/ethnic harassment and discrimination, its antecedents, and its effect on job-related outcomes. J Occup Health Psychol. 2012 Jan;17(1):65–78. doi: 10.1037/a0026430
34. Pascoe EA, Smart Richman L. Perceived discrimination and health: a meta-analytic review. Psychol Bull. 2009;135(4):531–54. doi: 10.1037/a0016059
35. Hinze SW, Lin J, Andersson TE. Can we capture the intersections? older Black women, education, and health. Women's Health Issues. 2012 Jan;22(1):e91–8. doi: 10.1016/j.whi.2011.08.002
36. Berdahl JL, Moore C. Workplace harassment: double jeopardy for minority women. J Appl Psychol. 2006 Mar;91(2):426–36. doi: 10.1037/0021-9010.91.2.426
37. Kulshreshtha A, Alonso A, McClure LA, Hajjar I, Manly JJ, Judd S. Association of stress with cognitive function among older Black and white US adults. JAMA Netw Open. 2023 Mar 1;6(3):e231860. doi: 10.1001/jamanetworkopen.2023.1860
38. Byron K, Khazanchi S, Nazarian D. The relationship between stressors and creativity: a meta-analysis examining competing theoretical models. J Appl Psychol. 2010 Jan;95(1):201–12. doi: 10.1037/a0017868
39. Santuzzi AM, Keating RT, Martinez JJ, Finkelstein LM, Rupp DE, Strah N. Identity management strategies for workers with concealable disabilities: antecedents and consequences. J Soc Issues. 2019 Sep;75(3):847–80. doi: 10.1111/josi.12320
40. Santuzzi AM, Waltz PR, Finkelstein LM, Rupp DE. Invisible disabilities: unique challenges for employees and organizations. Ind Organ Psychol. 2014 Jun;7(2):204–19. doi: 10.1111/iops.12134
41. Chaudoir SR, Quinn DM. Revealing concealable stigmatized identities: the impact of disclosure motivations and positive first-disclosure experiences on fear of disclosure and well-being: revealing concealable stigmatized identities. J Soc Issues. 2010 Sep 2;66(3):570–84. doi: 10.1111/j.1540-4560.2010.01663.x

42. Ragins BR. Disclosure disconnects: antecedents and consequences of disclosing invisible stigmas across life domains. AMR. 2008 Jan;33(1):194–215. doi: 10.2307/20159383
43. Smart L, Wegner DM. Covering up what can't be seen: concealable stigma and mental control. J Pers Soc Psychol. 1999;77(3):474–86. doi: 10.1037//0022-3514.77.3.474
44. Beatty JE, Kirby SL. Beyond the legal environment: how stigma influences invisible identity groups in the workplace. Employ Respons Rights J. 2006 Mar;18(1):29–44. doi: 10.1007/s10672-005-9003-6
45. Clair JA, Beatty JE, Maclean TL. Out of sight but not out of mind: managing invisible social odentities in the workplace. AMR. 2005 Jan;30(1):78–95. doi: 10.2307/20159096
46. Lyons BJ, Martinez LR, Ruggs EN, Hebl MR, Ryan AM, O'Brien KR, et al. To say or not to say: different strategies of acknowledging a visible disability. J Manage. 2018 May;44(5):1980–2007. doi: 10.1177/0149206316638160
47. Grandey AA. Emotional regulation in the workplace: a new way to conceptualize emotional labor. J Occup Health Psychol. 2000;5(1):95–110. doi: 10.1037//1076-8998.5.1.95
48. Grandey AA, Melloy RC. The state of the heart: emotional labor as emotion regulation reviewed and revised. J Occup Health Psychol. 2017 Jul;22(3):407–22. doi: 10.1037/ocp0000067
49. Grandey A, Foo SC, Groth M, Goodwin RE. Free to be you and me: a climate of authenticity alleviates burnout from emotional labor. J Occup Health Psychol. 2012 Jan;17(1):1–14. doi: 10.1037/a0025102
50. Jones KP, King EB. Managing concealable stigmas at work: a review and multilevel model. J Manage. 2014 Jul;40(5):1466–94. doi: 10.1177/0149206313515518
51. Beatty JE, Joffe R. An overlooked dimension of diversity: Organ Dyn. 2006 Jan;35(2):182–95. doi: 10.1016/j.orgdyn.2006.03.006
52. Reeve J, Lloyd-Williams M, Payne S, Dowrick C. Revisiting biographical disruption: exploring individual embodied illness experience in people with terminal cancer. Health (London). 2010 Mar;14(2):178–95. doi: 10.1177/1363459309353298
53. Beatty J, McGonagle AK. Chronic health conditions and Work Identity from a Lifespan Development Frame. In: Werth S, Brownlow C, editors. Work and Identity [internet]. Cham: Springer International Publishing; 2018 [cited 2023 Apr 16]. p. 9–22. Available from: http://link.springer.com/10.1007/978-3-319-73936-6
54. Beatty JE. Career barriers experienced by people with chronic illness: a U.S. study. Employ Respons Rights J. 2012 Jun;24(2):91–110. doi: 10.1007/s10672-011-9177-z

Chapter 5

1. Braun V, Clarke V. Using thematic analysis in psychology. Qual Res Psychol. 2006 Jan;3(2):77–101. doi: 10.1191/1478088706qp063oa
2. Bosma AR, Boot CRL, Snippen NC, Schaafsma FG, Anema JR. Supporting employees with chronic conditions to stay at work: perspectives of occupational health professionals and organizational representatives. BMC Public Health. 2021 Dec;21(1):592. doi: 10.1186/s12889-021-10633-y
3. Blake H, Somerset S, Greaves S. The pain at work toolkit for employees with chronic or persistent pain: a collaborative-participatory study. Healthcare. 2021 Dec 29;10(1):56. doi: 10.3390/healthcare10010056
4. Werth S. Managerial attitudes: influences on workforce outcomes for working women with chronic illness. Econ Labour Relat Rev. 2015 Jun;26(2):296–313. doi: 10.1177/1035304615571244
5. Feldman DB, Crandall CS. Dimensions of mental illness stigma: what about mental illness causes social rejection? J Soc Clin Psychol. 2007 Feb;26(2):137–54. doi: 10.1521/jscp.2007.26.2.137

6. Beatty JE, Joffe R. An overlooked dimension of diversity. Organ Dyn. 2006 Jan;35(2):182–95. 10.1016/j.orgdyn.2006.03.006
7. Santuzzi AM, Waltz PR, Finkelstein LM, Rupp DE. Invisible disabilities: unique challenges for employees and organizations. Ind Organ Psychol. 2014 Jun;7(2):204–19. 10.1111/iops.12134
8. Kaye HS, Jans LH, Jones EC. Why don't employers hire and retain workers with disabilities? J Occup Rehabil. 2011 Dec;21(4):526–36. doi: 10.1007/s10926-011-9302-8
9. Haafkens JA, Kopnina H, Meerman MG, van Dijk FJ. Facilitating job retention for chronically ill employees: perspectives of line managers and human resource managers. BMC Health Serv Res. 2011 Dec;11(1):104. doi: 10.1186/1472-6963-11-104
10. Schneider B, Ehrhart MG, Macey WH. Perspectives on organizational climate and culture. In: Zedeck S, editor. APA handbook of industrial and organizational psychology, Vol 1: Building and developing the organization [internet]. Washington, DC: American Psychological Association; 2011 [cited 2023 Feb 7]. p. 373–414. Available from: http://content.apa.org/books/12169-012
11. Gignac MAM, Bowring J, Jetha A, Beaton DE, Breslin FC, Franche RL, et al. Disclosure, privacy and workplace accommodation of episodic disabilities: organizational perspectives on disability communication-support processes to sustain employment. J Occup Rehabil. 2021 Mar;31(1):153–65. doi: 10.1007/s10926-020-09901-2
12. Galinsky AD. When you're in charge, your whisper may feel like a shout (published 2015) [internet]. 2015 [cited 2023 Feb 7]. Available from: https://www.nytimes.com/2015/08/16/jobs/when-youre-in-charge-your-whisper-may-feel-like-a-shout.html
13. Schutte KJ, Eaton SC. Sloan Network encyclopedia entry. Sloan Work and Family Research Network Encyclopedia [internet]. 2004; Available from: https://wfrn.org/wp-content/uploads/2018/09/Perceived_Usability_of_Policies-encyclopedia.pdf
14. Nelson CC, Shaw W, Robertson M. Supervisors and presenteeism: how do supervisors accommodate and support skilled workers with chronic health concerns? Employ Respons Rights J. 2016 Dec;28(4):209–23. doi: 10.1007/s10672-015-9275-4

Chapter 6

1. McGonagle AK, Bardwell T, Flinchum J, Kavanagh K. Perceived work ability: a constant comparative analysis of workers' perspectives . Occup Health Sci. 2022 Jun;6(2):207–46. doi: 10.1007/s41542-022-00116-w
2. KFF. Health Insurance Coverage of the Total Population [internet]. KFF. 2022 [cited 2023 Feb 19]. Available from: https://www.kff.org/other/state-indicator/total-population/
3. Rosso RJ, Bryan, SL. U.S. health care coverage and spending.Congressional Research Service. 2024 Dec. Available from: https://sgp.fas.org/crs/misc/IF10830.pdf
4. Commonwealth Fund. Mirror, mirror 2021: reflecting poorly [internet]. 2021 [cited 2023 May 15]. Available from: https://www.commonwealthfund.org/publications/fund-reports/2021/aug/mirror-mirror-2021-reflecting-poorly
5. Goldman DP, Cohen BG, Ho JY, McFadden DL, Ryan MS, Tysinger B. Improved survival for individuals with common chronic conditions in the Medicare population. Health Econ. 2021 Nov;30(S1):80–91. doi: 10.1002/hec.4168
6. KFF. 2023 employer health benefits survey [internet]. KFF. 2023 [cited 2024 May 27]. Available from: https://www.kff.org/health-costs/report/2023-employer-health-benefits-survey/
7. Jiang DH, Mundell BF, Shah ND, McCoy RG. Impact of high deductible health plans on diabetes care quality and outcomes: systematic review. Endocr Pract. 2021 Nov;27(11):1156–64. doi: 10.1016/j.eprac.2021.07.001

References

8. SHRM. 2022 employee benefits survey [internet]. [cited 2024 May 27]. Available from: https://www.shrm.org/about/press-room/shrm-releases-2022-employee-benefits-survey
9. Scott D. Who thought flexible spending accounts were a good idea? [internet]. Vox. 2023 [cited 2024 May 27]. Available from: https://www.vox.com/policy/23892823/healthcare-flexible-spending-account-fsa-hsa-wageworks
10. MHE. The rise in formulary exclusions. MHE [internet]. 2021 May 19 [cited 2023 Feb 21];31(5). Available from: https://www.managedhealthcareexecutive.com/view/the-rise-in-formulary-exclusions
11. Armstrong D, Rucker P, Miller M. UnitedHealthcare tried to deny coverage to a chronically ill patient. he fought back, exposing the insurer's inner workings. [internet]. ProPublica. 2023 [cited 2023 Feb 21]. Available from: https://www.propublica.org/article/unitedhealth-healthcare-insurance-denial-ulcerative-colitis
12. Patient Advocate Foundation [internet]. Home. [cited 2023 Feb 21]. Available from: https://www.patientadvocate.org/
13. KFF. 2022 employer health benefits survey—summary of findings [internet]. KFF. 2022 [cited 2023 May 16]. Available from: https://www.kff.org/report-section/ehbs-2022-summary-of-findings/
14. Life Happens. What happens if I'm denied life insurance? [internet]. Life Happens. [cited 2023 Feb 21]. Available from: https://lifehappens.org/life-insurance-101/what-happens-if-im-denied-life-insurance/
15. Annuity Expert Advice. What disqualifies you from long-term care insurance? (2023) [internet]. 2022 [cited 2023 Feb 21]. Available from: https://www.annuityexpertadvice.com/what-disqualifies-from-long-term-care-insurance/
16. Lent AB, Garrido CO, Baird EH, Viela R, Harris RB. Racial/ethnic disparities in health and life insurance denial due to cancer among cancer survivors. Int J Environ Res Public Health. 2022 Feb 15;19(4):2166. doi: 10.3390/ijerph19042166
17. Insurance Information Institute. Should I buy long-term care insurance? | III [internet]. [cited 2023 May 16]. Available from: https://www.iii.org/article/should-i-buy-long-term-care-insurance
18. Namely. Namely HR data report reveals that high-performers take more vacation time [internet]. [cited 2023 Feb 21]. Available from: https://www.prnewswire.com/news-releases/namely-hr-data-report-reveals-that-high-performers-take-more-vacation-time-300476454.html
19. Money. Unlimited vacation is hot right now. but is it actually a good job perk? [internet]. Money. [cited 2023 Feb 21]. Available from: https://money.com/unlimited-pto-vacation-pros-cons/
20. De Bloom J, Kompier M, Geurts S, De Weerth C, Taris T, Sonnentag S. Do we recover from vacation? meta-analysis of vacation effects on health and well-being. J Occup Health. 2009 Jan;51(1):13–25. doi: 10.1539/joh.k8004
21. Attridge M. Employee assistance programs: evidence and current trends. In: Gatchel RJ, Schultz IZ, editors. Handbook of pccupational health and wellness [internet]. Boston: Springer US; 2012 [cited 2023 May 8]. p. 441–67. Available from: https://link.springer.com/10.1007/978-1-4614-4839-6_21
22. SHRM. What is an employee assistance program (EAP)? [internet]. SHRM. 2021 [cited 2023 May 8]. Available from: https://www.shrm.org/resourcesandtools/tools-and-samples/hr-qa/pages/whatisaneap.aspx
23. Hargrave GE, Hiatt D, Alexander R, Shaffer IA. EAP treatment impact on presenteeism and absenteeism: implications for return on investment. J Workplace Behav Health. 2008 Aug 25;23(3):283–93. doi: 10.1080/15555240802242999
24. Joseph B, Walker A, Fuller-Tyszkiewicz M. Evaluating the effectiveness of employee assistance programmes: a systematic review. Eur J Work Organ Psychol. 2018 Jan 2;27(1):1–15. doi: 10.1080/1359432X.2017.1374245

25. Musser G. Fixing the hated open-design office [internet]. Scientific American. [cited 2023 May 22]. Available from: https://www.scientificamerican.com/article/fixing-the-hated-open-design-office/
26. James O, Delfabbro P, King DL. A comparison of psychological and work outcomes in open-plan and cellular office designs: a systematic review. SAGE Open. 2021 Jan;11(1):215824402098886. doi: 10.1177/2158244020988869
27. Bernstein ES, Turban S. The impact of the "open" workspace on human collaboration. Phil Trans R Soc B. 2018 Aug 19;373(1753):20170239. doi: 10.1098/rstb.2017.0239
28. Northwest ADA Center. Universal Design in the Workplace [internet]. [cited 2023 Mar 1]. Available from: https://nwadacenter.org/factsheet/universal-design-workplace
29. Sheppard-Jones K, Goldstein P, Leslie M, Singleton P, Gooden C, Rumrill P, et al. Reframing workplace inclusion through the lens of universal design: considerations for vocational rehabilitation professionals in the wake of COVID-19. JVR. 2021 Jan 29;54(1):71–79. doi: 10.3233/JVR-201119
30. Gould R, Harris SP, Mullin C, Jones R. Disability, diversity, and corporate social responsibility: learning from recognized leaders in inclusion. JVR. 2020 Feb 7;52(1):29–42. doi: 10.3233/JVR-191058
31. Schneider B, Ehrhart MG, Macey WH. Perspectives on organizational climate and culture. In: Zedeck S, editor. APA handbook of industrial and organizational psychology, Vol 1: Building and developing the organization [internet]. Washington, DC: American Psychological Association; 2011 [cited 2023 Feb 7]. p. 373–414. Available from: http://content.apa.org/books/12169-012
32. Gould R, Mullin C, Parker Harris S, Jones R. Building, sustaining and growing: disability inclusion in business. EDI. 2022 Apr 20;41(3):418–34. doi: 10.1108/EDI-06-2020-0156
33. Colella A, Hebl M, King E. One hundred years of discrimination research in the Journal of Applied Psychology: a sobering synopsis. J Appl Psychol. 2017;102(3):500–13. doi: 10.1037/apl0000084
34. Verbit.ai. The "A" in DEIA: why corporate leaders must include accessibility [internet]. [cited 2023 May 18]. Available from: https://www.accessibility.com/blog/the-a-in-deia-why-corporate-leaders-must-include-accessibility
35. Global Disability Inclusion. The state of employee disability engagement. Whitepaper download [internet]. Global Disability In. [cited 2022 Jul 18]. Available from: https://www.globaldisabilityinclusion.com/disability-employee-engagement
36. SHRM. How to build a strong organizational culture. [Internet]. SHRM Toolkit. [cited 2024 Dec 21]. Available from https://www.shrm.org/topics-tools/tools/toolkits/understanding-developing-organizational-culture
37. Goetzel RZ, Fabius R, Fabius D, Roemer EC, Thornton N, Kelly RK, et al. The stock performance of C. Everett Koop award winners compared with the Standard & Poor's 500 Index. J Occup Environ Med. 2016 Jan;58(1):9–15. doi: 10.1097/JOM.0000000000000632
38. Johnson & Johnson. Our Credo [internet]. Content Lab U.S. [cited 2023 Jun 13]. Available from: https://www.jnj.com/credo/
39. Northrop Grumman. Northrop Grumman named a 2022 best place to work for disability inclusion [internet]. Northrop Grumman Newsroom. [cited 2023 May 22]. Available from: https://news.northropgrumman.com/news/releases/northrop-grumman-named-a-2022-best-place-to-work-for-disability-inclusion
40. Brodey D. 62% of employees want leadership to speak openly about mental health [internet]. Forbes. [cited 2023 Mar 5]. Available from: https://www.forbes.com/sites/denisebrodey/2019/10/15/62-of-employees-want-leadership-to-speak-openly-about-mental-health/
41. Helm B. A debilitating mental health crisis almost ended his life. now he wants to save others [internet]. Inc.com. 2020 [cited 2023 Mar 5]. Available from: https://www.inc.com/burt-helm/made-of-millions-mental-health.html

42. Kaye HS, Jans LH, Jones EC. Why don't employers hire and retain workers with disabilities? J Occup Rehabil. 2011 Dec;21(4):526–36. doi: 10.1007/s10926-011-9302-8
43. Schloemer-Jarvis A, Bader B, Böhm SA. The role of human resource practices for including persons with disabilities in the workforce: a systematic literature review. Int J Hum Resour Manag. 2022 Jan 2;33(1):45–98. doi: 10.1080/09585192.2021.1996433
44. Reed BN, McGonagle AK, Gil-Rivas VG, Khan F. Navigating diabetes at work: An inductive exploration of workers' journeys. Southern Management Association Conference; 2024 Nov; San Antonio.
45. Rutigliano P, O'Connell M. The State of Disability 2022 Employee Engagement Intersectionality. Mercer in partnership with Global Disability Inclusion. 2022 Feb.
46. Deloitte. Equitable workforce outcomes [internet]. [cited 2023 May 22]. Available from: https://www.deloitte.com/global/en/our-thinking/insights/topics/talent/human-capital-trends/2023/diversity-equity-inclusion-belonging.html
47. Nović S. The harmful ableist language you unknowingly use [internet]. [cited 2023 May 22]. Available from: https://www.bbc.com/worklife/article/20210330-the-harmful-ableist-language-you-unknowingly-use
48. Beller L. Inspiration porn: how "feel-good" imagery demeans the disabled community… [internet]. Medium. 2022 [cited 2023 May 22]. Available from: https://medium.com/age-of-awareness/inspiration-porn-c08b419d35c9
49. Bezrukova K, Spell CS, Perry JL, Jehn KA. A meta-analytical integration of over 40 years of research on diversity training evaluation. Psychol Bull. 2016 Nov;142(11):1227–74. doi: 10.1037/bul0000067
50. Ruggs EN, McGonagle AK. Can brief video trainings reduce bias and improve knowledge and attitudes toward applicants with disabilities? J Bus Psychol. 2023 Apr;38(2):305–26. doi: 10.1007/s10869-022-09857-5
51. Devine PG, Ash TL. Diversity training goals, limitations, and promise: a review of the multidisciplinary literature. Annu Rev Psychol. 2022 Jan 4;73(1):403–29. doi: 10.1146/annurev-psych-060221-122215
52. Kalinoski ZT, Steele-Johnson D, Peyton EJ, Leas KA, Steinke J, Bowling NA. A meta-analytic evaluation of diversity training outcomes: diversity training. J Organiz Behav. 2013 Nov;34(8):1076–104. doi: 10.1002/job.1839
53. Sanchez JI, Medkik N. The effects of diversity awareness training on differential treatment. Group Organ Manag. 2004 Aug;29(4):517–36. doi: 10.1177/1059601103257426

Chapter 7

1. Parker SK. Beyond motivation: job and work design for development, health, ambidexterity, and more. Annu Rev Psychol. 2014 Jan 3;65(1):661–91. doi: 10.1146/annurev-psych-010213-115208
2. Deci EL, Olafsen AH, Ryan RM. Self-determination theory in work organizations: the state of a science. Annu Rev Organ Psychol Organ Behav. 2017 Mar 21;4(1):19–43. doi: 10.1146/annurev-orgpsych-032516-113108
3. Morgeson FP, Humphrey SE. The Work Design Questionnaire (WDQ): developing and validating a comprehensive measure for assessing job design and the nature of work. J Appl Psychol. 2006;91(6):1321–39. doi: 10.1037/0021-9010.91.6.1321
4. McGonagle AK, Bardwell T, Flinchum J, Kavanagh K. Perceived work ability: a constant comparative analysis of workers' perspectives. Occup Health Sci. 2022 Jun;6(2):207–46. doi: 10.1007/s41542-022-00116-w
5. Wheatley D. Autonomy in paid work and employee subjective well-being. Work Occup. 2017 Aug;44(3):296–328. doi: 10.1177/0730888417697232

6. Tveito TH, Shaw WS, Huang YH, Nicholas M, Wagner G. Managing pain in the workplace: a focus group study of challenges, strategies and what matters most to workers with low back pain. Disabil Rehabil. 2010 Jan;32(24):2035–45. doi: 10.3109/09638281003797398
7. Global Disability Inclusion. The state of employee disability engagement. Whitepaper download [internet]. Global Disability In. [cited 2022 Jul 18]. Available from: https://www.globaldisabilityinclusion.com/disability-employee-engagement
8. Shifrin NV, Michel JS. Flexible work arrangements and employee health: a meta-analytic review. Work Stress. 2022 Jan 2;36(1):60–85. doi: 10.1080/02678373.2021.1936287
9. French KA, Agars MD, Arvan ML. The shift flextime scale: a measure of flextime availability, use, and consequences for shift workers. J Bus Psychol [internet]. 2023 Mar 25 [cited 2023 May 28]. doi: 10.1007/s10869-023-09879-7
10. Harknett K, Schneider D, Irwin V. Improving health and economic security by reducing work schedule uncertainty. Proc Natl Acad Sci USA. 2021 Oct 19;118(42):e2107828118. doi: 10.1073/pnas.2107828118
11. Henly JR, Lambert SJ. Unpredictable work timing in retail jobs: implications for employee work–life conflict. ILR Review. 2014 Jul;67(3):986–1016. doi: 10.1177/0019793914537458
12. Shockley KM, Allen TD, Dodd H, Waiwood AM. Rapid transition to remote work during COVID-19: [internet]. National Science Foundation; [cited 2023 Mar 2]. Available from: https://428ebe77-6430-4a0a-92fe-b51111a62291.filesusr.com/ugd/0ab1e4_1d7c3f55b39b4bf4ad47ce9621716b50.pdf
13. Shockley KM. Telecommuting [internet]. Scientific Affairs Committee of the Society for Industrial and Organizational Psychology; [cited 2023 Mar 2] p. 1–11. (SIOP White Paper Series). Available from: https://www.siop.org/Portals/84/docs/White%20Papers/ScientificAffairs/telecommuting.pdf
14. Abril D. For some workers, office mandates aren't just a pain. They're harmful. [internet]. Washington Post. 2022 [cited 2023 Mar 2]. Available from: https://www.washingtonpost.com/technology/2022/06/30/return-to-office-inequity/
15. Amerikaner L, Yan HX, Sayer LC, Doan L, Fish JN, Drotning KJ, et al. Blurred border or safe harbor? emotional well-being among sexual and gender minority adults working from home during COVID-19. Soc Sci Med. 2023 Apr;323:115850. doi: 10.1016/j.socscimed.2023.115850
16. Kottke JL, Sharafinski CE. Measuring perceived supervisory and organizational support. Educ Psychol Meas. 1988 Dec;48(4):1075–79. doi: 10.1177/0013164488484024
17. Mathieu M, Eschleman KJ, Cheng D. Meta-analytic and multiwave comparison of emotional support and instrumental support in the workplace. J Occup Health Psychol. 2019 Jun;24(3):387–409. doi: 10.1037/ocp0000135
18. Nelson CC, Shaw W, Robertson M. Supervisors and presenteeism: how do supervisors accommodate and support skilled workers with chronic health concerns? Employ Respons Rights J. 2016 Dec;28(4):209–23. doi: 10.1007/s10672-015-9275-4
19. House JS. Work stress and social support. Reading, MA: Addison-Wesley Pub. Co; 1981. 156 p.
20. Hammer LB, Dimoff J, Mohr CD, Allen SJ. A framework for protecting and promoting employee mental health through supervisor supportive behaviors. Occup Health Sci [internet]. 2024 Jan 30 [cited 2024 May 28]. doi: 10.1007/s41542-023-00171-x
21. Reed BN, McGonagle AK, Gil-Rivas VG. Navigating diabetes at work: an inductive exploration of workers' journeys. Working paper. 2024.
22. The Hopkinton Conference Working Group on Workplace Disability Prevention, Pransky GS, Fassier JB, Besen E, Blanck P, Ekberg K, et al. Sustaining work participation across the life course. J Occup Rehabil. 2016 Dec;26(4):465–79. doi: 10.1007/s10926-016-9670-1

23. Gray CE, Spector PE, Lacey KN, Young BG, Jacobsen ST, Taylor MR. Helping may be harming: unintended negative consequences of providing social support. Work Stress. 2020 Oct 1;34(4):359–85. doi: 10.1080/02678373.2019.1695294
24. Barth SE, Wessel JL. Mental illness disclosure in organizations: defining and predicting (un)supportive responses. J Bus Psychol. 2022 Apr;37(2):407–28. doi: 10.1007/s10869-021-09753-4
25. McGonagle A. How organizations can support employees with chronic health conditions. Harv Bus Rev [internet]. 2021 Jan 19 [cited 2023 Mar 4]; Available from: https://hbr.org/2021/01/how-organizations-can-support-employees-with-chronic-health-conditions
26. Moen P, Kelly EL, Fan W, Lee SR, Almeida D, Kossek EE, et al. Does a flexibility/support organizational initiative improve high-tech employees' well-being? evidence from the Work, Family, and Health Network, Am Sociol Rev. 2016 Feb;81(1):134–64. doi: 10.1177/0003122415622391
27. Moen P, Kelly EL, Lee SR, Oakes JM, Fan W, Bray J, et al. Can a flexibility/support initiative reduce turnover intentions and exits? results from the Work, Family, and Health Network, Soc Probl. 2017 Feb;64(1):53–85. doi: 10.1093/socpro/spw033
28. Kelly EL, Moen P, Oakes JM, Fan W, Okechukwu C, Davis KD, et al. Changing work and work–family conflict: evidence from the Work, Family, and Health Network, Am Sociol Rev. 2014 Jun;79(3):485–516. doi: 10.1177/0003122414531435
29. Work Family Health Network. STAR: Office [internet]. [cited 2023 Mar 5]. Available from: https://workfamilyhealthnetwork.org/star
30. Barbosa C, Bray JW, Brockwood K, Reeves D. Costs of a work–family intervention: evidence from the Work, Family, and Health Network, Am J Health Promot. 2014 Mar;28(4):209–17. doi: 10.4278/ajhp.121108-QUAN-542
31. Hammer LB, Kossek EE, Anger WK, Bodner T, Zimmerman KL. Clarifying work–family intervention processes: the roles of work–family conflict and family-supportive supervisor behaviors. J Appl Psychol. 2011;96(1):134–50. doi: 10.1037/a0020927
32. Schloemer-Jarvis A, Bader B, Böhm SA. The role of human resource practices for including persons with disabilities in the workforce: a systematic literature review. Int J Hum Resour Manag. 2022 Jan 2;33(1):45–98. doi: 10.1080/09585192.2021.1996433
33. Dimoff JK, Kelloway EK, Burnstein MD. Mental health awareness training (MHAT): the development and evaluation of an intervention for workplace leaders. Int J Stress Manag. 2016 May;23(2):167–89. doi: 10.1037/a0039479
34. Dimoff JK, Kelloway EK. With a little help from my boss: the impact of workplace mental health training on leader behaviors and employee resource utilization. J Occup Health Psychol. 2019 Feb;24(1):4–19. doi: 10.1037/ocp0000126
35. Jansen J, van Ooijen R, Koning PWC, Boot CRL, Brouwer S. The role of the employer in supporting work participation of workers with disabilities: a systematic literature review using an interdisciplinary approach. J Occup Rehabil. 2021 Dec;31(4):916–49. doi: 10.1007/s10926-021-09978-3
36. Beatty JE. Career barriers experienced by people with chronic illness: a U.S. study. Employ Respons Rights J. 2012 Jun;24(2):91–110. doi: 10.1007/s10672-011-9177-z
37. Job Accommodation Network. Costs and benefits of accommodation [internet]. [cited 2024 May 22]. Available from: https://askjan.org/topics/costs.cfm?csSearch=2546498_1
38. US Department of Labor. Employers and the ADA: myths and facts [internet]. DOL. [cited 2023 May 30]. Available from: http://www.dol.gov/agencies/odep/publications/fact-sheets/americans-with-disabilities-act
39. Kossek EE, Ollier-Malaterre A. Desperately seeking sustainable careers: redesigning professional jobs for the collaborative crafting of reduced-load work. J Vocat Behav. 2020 Mar;117:103315. doi: 10.1016/j.jvb.2019.06.003

40. Kossek EE, Ollier-Malaterre A, Lee MD, Pichler S, Hall DT. Line managers' rationales for professionals' reduced-load work in embracing and ambivalent organizations. Hum Resour Manage. 2016 Jan;55(1):143–71. doi: 10.1002/hrm.21722

Chapter 8

1. McGonagle AK, Beatty JE, Joffe R. Coaching for workers with chronic illness: evaluating an intervention. J Occup Health Psychol. 2014;19(3):385–98. doi: 10.1037/a0036601
2. Gignac MAM, Bowring J, Jetha A, Beaton DE, Breslin FC, Franche RL, et al. Disclosure, privacy and workplace accommodation of episodic disabilities: organizational perspectives on disability communication-support processes to sustain employment. J Occup Rehabil. 2021 Mar;31(1):153–65. doi: 10.1007/s10926-020-09901-2
3. Theeboom T, Beersma B, Vianen AEM van. Does coaching work? a meta-analysis on the effects of coaching on individual level outcomes in an organizational context. J Posit Psychol [internet]. 2013 Dec 4 [cited 2023 May 2]; Available from: https://www.tandfonline.com/doi/abs/10.1080/17439760.2013.837499
4. Sonesh SC, Coultas CW, Lacerenza CN, Marlow SL, Benishek LE, Salas E. The power of coaching: a meta-analytic investigation. Coaching-Int J Theor [internet]. 2015 Aug 25 [cited 2023 May 2]; Available from: https://www.tandfonline.com/doi/abs/10.1080/17521882.2015.1071418
5. Beatty J, McGonagle AK. Chronic health conditions and work identity from a lifespan development frame. In: Werth S, Brownlow C, editors. Work and identity [internet]. Cham: Springer International Publishing; 2018 [cited 2023 Apr 16]. p. 9–22. Available from: http://link.springer.com/10.1007/978-3-319-73936-6
6. Beatty JE, McGonagle A. Coaching employees with chronic illness: supporting professional identities through biographical work. Int J Evid Based Coach Mentor. 2016;14(1):1–15.
7. McGonagle AK, McMillan A. Coaching workers with chronic health conditions: Common challenges. Coaching in Leadership & Healthcare Conference; 2017 Oct; Boston.
8. Graßmann C, Schölmerich F, Schermuly CC. The relationship between working alliance and client outcomes in coaching: a meta-analysis. Hum Relat. 2020 Jan;73(1):35–58. doi: 10.1177/0018726718819725
9. Eby LT de T, Allen TD, Hoffman BJ, Baranik LE, Sauer JB, Baldwin S, et al. An interdisciplinary meta-analysis of the potential antecedents, correlates, and consequences of protégé perceptions of mentoring. Psychol Bull. 2013 Mar;139(2):441–76. doi: 10.1037/a0029279
10. Allen TD, Eby LT, Poteet ML, Lentz E, Lima L. Career benefits associated with mentoring for proteges: a meta-analysis. J Appl Psychol. 2004;89(1):127–36. doi: 10.1037/0021-9010.89.1.127
11. Ghosh R, Reio TG. Career benefits associated with mentoring for mentors: a meta-analysis. J Vocat Behav. 2013 Aug;83(1):106–16. doi: 10.1016/j.jvb.2013.03.011
12. Tu M, Li M. What great mentorship looks like in a hybrid workplace [internet]. Harv Bus Rev. 2021 [cited 2023 May 3]. Available from: https://hbr.org/2021/05/what-great-mentorship-looks-like-in-a-hybrid-workplace
13. Allaire SH, Jingbo Niu, LaValley MP. Employment and satisfaction outcomes from a job retention intervention delivered to persons with chronic diseases. Rehabil Couns Bull. 2005 Jan;48(2):100–9. doi: 10.1177/00343552050480020401
14. Allaire SJ, Niu J, Zhu Y, Brett B. Providing effective early intervention vocational rehabilitation at the community level. Rehabil Couns Bull. 2011 Apr;54(3):154–63. doi: 10.1177/0034355210392242

15. Van Eerd D, Bowring J, Jetha A, Breslin FC, Gignac MAM. Online resources supporting workers with chronic episodic disabilities: an environmental scan. Int J Workplace Health Manag. 2020 Dec 18;14(2):129–48. doi: 10.1108/IJWHM-08-2020-0137
16. Blake H, Somerset S, Greaves S. The pain at work toolkit for employees with chronic or persistent pain: a collaborative-participatory study. Healthcare. 2021 Dec 29;10(1):56. doi: 10.3390/healthcare10010056
17. Pain at Work Toolkit. A toolkit for people with chronic or persistent pain at work [internet]. [cited 2023 May 7]. Available from: https://xerte.nottingham.ac.uk/play_24452&page=4#page1
18. ACED. JDAPT for workers [internet]. [cited 2023 May 7]. Available from: https://aced.iwh.on.ca/jdapt/worker-en/access
19. Shaw WS, McLellan RK, Besen E, Namazi S, Nicholas MK, Dugan AG, et al. A worksite self-management program for workers with chronic health conditions improves worker engagement and retention, but not workplace function. J Occup Rehabil. 2022 Mar;32(1):77–86. doi: 10.1007/s10926-021-09983-6
20. Shaw WS, Besen E, Pransky G, Boot CR, Nicholas MK, McLellan RK, et al. Manage at work: a randomized, controlled trial of a self-management group intervention to overcome workplace challenges associated with chronic physical health conditions. BMC Public Health. 2014 Dec;14(1):515. doi: 10.1186/1471-2458-14-515
21. Smith M, Wilson M, Robertson M, Padilla H, Zuercher H, Vandenberg R, et al. Impact of a translated disease self-management program on employee health and productivity: six-month findings from a randomized controlled trial. Int J Environ Res Public Health. 2018 Apr 25;15(5):851. doi: 10.3390/ijerph15050851
22. Lorig KR, Sobel DS, Stewart AL, Brown BW, Bandura A, Ritter P, et al. Evidence suggesting that a chronic disease self-management program can improve health status while reducing hospitalization: a randomized trial. Med Care. 1999 Jan;37(1):5–14. doi: 10.1097/00005650-199901000-00003
23. Lorig KR, Ritter P, Stewart AL, Sobel DS, William Brown B, Bandura A, et al. Chronic disease self-management program: 2-year health status and health care utilization outcomes. Med Care. 2001 Nov;39(11):1217–23. doi: 10.1097/00005650-200111000-00008
24. Self Management Resource Center. Programs [internet]. SMRC. [cited 2023 May 6]. Available from: https://selfmanagementresource.com/programs/
25. Haynes NJ, Vandenberg RJ, Wilson MG, DeJoy DM, Padilla HM, Smith ML. Evaluating the impact of the live healthy, work healthy program on organizational outcomes: a randomized field experiment. J Appl Psychol. 2022 Oct;107(10):1758–80. doi: 10.1037/apl0000977
26. NCOA. Chronic disease self-management program cost calculator [internet]. NCOA. [cited 2023 May 11]. Available from: https://www.ncoa.org/article/chronic-disease-self-management-program-cost-calculator
27. Varekamp I, Verbeek JH, de Boer A, van Dijk FJ. Effect of job maintenance training program for employees with chronic disease: a randomized controlled trial on self-efficacy, job satisfaction, and fatigue. Scand J Work Environ Health. 2011 Jul;37(4):288–97. doi: 10.5271/sjweh.3149
28. Linton SJ, Boersma K, Jansson M, Svärd L, Botvalde M. The effects of cognitive-behavioral and physical therapy preventive interventions on pain-related sick leave: a randomized controlled trial. Clin J Pain. 2005 Mar;21(2):109–19. doi: 10.1097/00002508-200503000-00001
29. Friedrich M, Gittler G, Arendasy M, Friedrich KM. Long-term effect of a combined exercise and motivational program on the level of disability of patients with chronic low back pain: Spine. 2005 May;30(9):995–1000. doi: 10.1097/01.brs.0000160844.71551.af

Chapter 9

1. Center for Work, Health, & Well-Being. Guidelines for implementing an integrated approach [internet]. [cited 2023 Jun 15]. Available from: https://centerforworkhealth.sph.harvard.edu/resources/guidelines-implementing-integrated-approach
2. Goetzel RZ, Fabius R, Fabius D, Roemer EC, Thornton N, Kelly RK, et al. The stock performance of C. Everett Koop award winners compared with the Standard & Poor's 500 Index. J Occup Environ Med. 2016 Jan;58(1):9–15. doi: 10.1097/JOM.0000000000000632
3. Fabius R, Loeppke RR, Hohn T, Fabius D, Eisenberg B, Konicki DL, et al. Tracking the market performance of companies that integrate a culture of health and safety: an assessment of corporate health achievement award applicants. J Occup Environ Med. 2016 Jan;58(1):3–8. doi: 10.1097/JOM.0000000000000638
4. Grossmeier J, Fabius R, Flynn JP, Noeldner SP, Fabius D, Goetzel RZ, et al. Linking workplace health promotion best practices and organizational financial performance: tracking market performance of companies with highest scores on the HERO scorecard. J Occup Environ Med. 2016 Jan;58(1):16–23. doi: 10.1097/JOM.0000000000000631
5. Ozminkowski RJ, Serxner S, Marlo K, Kichlu R, Ratelis E, Van de Meulebroecke J. Beyond ROI: Using value of investment to measure employee health and wellness. Population Health Management. 2016 Aug;19(4):227–29. doi: 10.1089/pop.2015.0160
6. CDC. Total Worker Health [internet]. CDC. 2023 [cited 2023 Jun 19]. Available from: https://www.cdc.gov/niosh/twh/default.html
7. Nielsen K, Abildgaard JS. Organizational interventions: a research-based framework for the evaluation of both process and effects. Work Stress. 2013 Jul;27(3):278–97. doi: 10.1080/02678373.2013.812358
8. Nielsen K, Randall R, Holten AL, González ER. Conducting organizational-level occupational health interventions: what works? Work Stress. 2010 Jul;24(3):234–59. doi: 10.1080/02678373.2010.515393
9. Ahlstrom L, Grimby-Ekman A, Hagberg M, Dellve L. The work ability index and single-item question: associations with sick leave, symptoms, and health: a prospective study of women on long-term sick leave. Scand J Work Environ Health. 2010 Apr 7;36(5):404–12. doi: 10.5271/sjweh.2917
10. McGonagle AK, Fisher GG, Barnes-Farrell JL, Grosch JW. Individual and work factors related to perceived work ability and labor force outcomes. J Appl Psychol. 2015;100(2):376–98. doi: 10.1037/a0037974
11. Demerouti E, Bakker AB, Nachreiner F, Schaufeli WB. The job demands–resources model of burnout. J Appl Psychol. 2001;86(3):499–512.
12. Schaufeli WB, Bakker AB, Salanova M. The measurement of work engagement with a short questionnaire: a cross-national study. Educ Psychol Meas 2006 Aug;66(4):701–16. doi: 10.1177/0013164405282471
13. Fisher GG, Matthews RA, Gibbons AM. Developing and investigating the use of single-item measures in organizational research. J Occup Health Psychol. 2016 Jan;21(1):3–23. doi: 10.1037/a0039139
14. Van Katwyk PT, Fox S, Spector PE, Kelloway EK. Using the job-related affective well-being scale (JAWS) to investigate affective responses to work stressors. J Occup Health Psychol. 2000;5(2):219–30. doi: 10.1037//1076-8998.5.2.219
15. Klein HJ, Cooper JT, Molloy JC, Swanson JA. The assessment of commitment: advantages of a unidimensional, target-free approach. J Appl Psychol. 2014;99(2):222–38. doi: 10.1037/a0034751
16. Michaels CE, Spector PE. Causes of employee turnover: a test of the Mobley, Griffeth, Hand, and Meglino model. J Appl Psychol. 1982 Feb;67(1):53–59. doi: 10.1037/0021-9010.67.1.53

17. Koopman C, Pelletier KR, Murray JF, Sharda CE, Berger ML, Turpin RS, et al. Stanford Presenteeism Scale: health status and employee productivity. J Occup Environ Med. 2002 Jan;44(1):14–20. doi: 10.1097/00043764-200201000-00004
18. McGonagle AK, Schmidt S, Speights SL. Work–health management interference for workers with chronic health conditions: construct development and scale validation. Occup Health Sci. 2020 Dec;4(4):445–70. doi: 10.1007/s41542-020-00073-2
19. Stanton JM, Balzer WK, Smith PC, Parra LF, Ironson G. A general measure of work stress: the stress in general scale. Educ Psychol Meas. 2001 Oct;61(5):866–88. doi: 10.1177/00131640121971455
20. Chen G, Gully SM, Eden D. Validation of a new general self-efficacy scale. Organ Res Methods. 2001 Jan;4(1):62–83. doi: 10.1177/109442810141004
21. Spector PE, Fox S. Reducing subjectivity in the assessment of the job environment: development of the Factual Autonomy Scale (FAS). J Organiz Behav. 2003 Jun;24(4):417–32. doi: 10.1002/job.199
22. Morgeson FP, Humphrey SE. The Work Design Questionnaire (WDQ): developing and validating a comprehensive measure for assessing job design and the nature of work. J Appl Psychol. 2006;91(6):1321–39. doi: 10.1037/0021-9010.91.6.1321
23. Matthews RA, Barnes-Farrell JL. Development and initial evaluation of an enhanced measure of boundary flexibility for the work and family domains. J Occup Health Psychol. 2010 Jul;15(3):330–46. doi: 10.1037/a0019302
24. French KA, Agars MD, Arvan ML. The shift flextime scale: a measure of flextime availability, use, and consequences for shift workers. J Bus Psychol [internet]. 2023 Mar 25 [cited 2023 May 28]; Available from: https://link.springer.com/10.1007/s10869-023-09879-7
25. Spector PE, Jex SM. Development of four self-report measures of job stressors and strain: interpersonal conflict at work scale, organizational constraints scale, quantitative workload inventory, and physical symptoms inventory. J Occup Health Psychol. 1998 Oct;3(4):356–67. doi: 10.1037//1076-8998.3.4.356
26. Eisenberger R, Stinglhamber F, Vandenberghe C, Sucharski IL, Rhoades L. Perceived supervisor support: contributions to perceived organizational support and employee retention. J Appl Psychol. 2002;87(3):565–73. doi: 10.1037/0021-9010.87.3.565
27. McGonagle A, Roebuck A, Diebel H, Aqwa J, Fragoso Z, Stoddart S. Anticipated work discrimination scale: a chronic illness application. J Manag Psychol. 2016 Feb 8;31(1):61–78. doi: 10.1108/JMP-01-2014-0009
28. Shanock LR, Eisenberger R, Heggestad ED, Malone G, Clark L, Dunn AM, et al. Treating employees well: the value of organizational support theory in human resource management. Psychol-Manag J. 2019 Aug;22(3–4):168–91. doi: 10.1037/mgr0000088
29. Patterson MG, West MA, Shackleton VJ, Dawson JF, Lawthom R, Maitlis S, et al. Validating the organizational climate measure: links to managerial practices, productivity and innovation. J Organiz Behav. 2005 Jun;26(4):379–408. doi: 10.1002/job.312
30. Sakr N, Son Hing LS, González-Morales MG. Development and validation of the marginalized-group-focused diversity climate scale: group differences and outcomes. J Bus Psychol. 2023 Jun;38(3):689–722. doi: 10.1007/s10869-022-09859-3
31. Zweber ZM, Henning RA, Magley VJ. A practical scale for multi-faceted organizational health climate assessment. J Occup Health Psychol. 2016;21(2):250–59. doi: 10.1037/a0039895
32. Matthews RA, Pineault L, Hong YH. Normalizing the use of single-item measures: validation of the single-item compendium for organizational psychology. J Bus Psychol. 2022 Aug;37(4):639–73. doi: 10.1007/s10869-022-09813-3
33. Attridge M. Employee Assistance Programs: Evidence and Current Trends. In: Gatchel RJ, Schultz IZ, editors. Handbook of occupational health and wellness [internet]. Boston:

Springer US; 2012 [cited 2023 May 8]. p. 441–67. Available from: https://link.springer.com/10.1007/978-1-4614-4839-6_21

34. Bevan S, Bajorek Z. Designing and testing a return on investment tool for EAPs [internet]. Brighton, UK: Institute for Employment Studies; 2019 Jan [cited 2023 Jun 11]. Report No.: 515. Available from: https://www.eapa.org.uk/wp-content/uploads/2019/02/IES-Designing-and-testing-a-Return-on-Investment-tool-for-EAPs-Stephen-Bevan-Zofia-Bajorek_FINAL.pdf

35. Health Enhancement Research Organization and Population Health Alliance. Program measurement and evaluation guide: core metrics for employee health management [Internet]. 2015 [cited 2023 Jun 13]. Available from: https://hero-health.org/wp-content/uploads/2015/02/HERO-PHA-Metrics-Guide-FINAL.pdf

Index

For the benefit of digital users, indexed terms that span two pages (e.g., 52–53) may, on occasion, appear on only one of those pages.

Tables, figures, and boxes are indicated by *t*, *f*, and *b* following the page number

A

ableism. *See also* discrimination; stigma
   accommodations and, 68
   acknowledging existence of, 68
   allyship to combat, 69
   automatic reactions informing, 68
   avoiding of, 68
   awareness of, 68, 114
   definition of, 68
   inspiration porn as form of, 23
   language informing, 68, 129
   manager recommendations for, 68
   organizational culture and, 114
   supervisor support and, 129
   work-health challenges and, 68–69
absenteeism, 8, 16, 45–46, 60–61, 73, 82, 106, 122–123, 173–174
accessibility. *See* diversity, equity, inclusion, and accessibility (DEIA)
accommodations
   ableism and, 68
   ADA as legally requiring reasonable forms of, 21, 30–34, 32t, 48
   costs associated with, 33, 88
   DEIA and, 137–138
   disclosure of CHCs and, 48, 74, 138
   discrimination and, 70–71, 138
   examples of, 32t
   failures of, 70–71
   formal and informal forms of, 48
   HR recommendations for, 32–33, 92–93
   importance for workers with CHCs of, 10, 26, 67, 137–138
   individual worker-focused strategies and, 148
   integrated approach to CHCs and, 165–166
   intervention framework for CHCs and, 47–48
   interviewee quotes on, 27, 91, 137
   invisible nature of CHCs and, 138
   Job Demands and Accommodation Planning Tool (JDAPT) and, 155
   manager recommendations for, 68, 71, 92–93
   medical "proof" required for, 138
   as most common secondary preventive strategy, 48, 55–56
   myths surrounding, 33, 88, 138
   organizational challenges and, 84, 86, 88, 92–93
   organization-focused strategies and, 107–109
   overpromising on possibilities of, 133
   overview of, 137–138
   plateauing and, 77
   public accommodations, 28
   remote work and, 34–35
   RTW programs and, 52, 54–55
   self-accommodations, 120–121
   skepticism about necessity of, 71, 84, 86, 138
   supervisor support and, 126–127, 133
   universal design and, 107–108
   work-health challenges and, 67
ADA. *See* Americans with Disabilities Act (1990)
ADAA. *See* Americans with Disability Amendments Act (ADAA) (2008)
Affordable Care Act (2010) (US), 17, 100–101
Allaire, Saralynn, 153
allyship, 69
Americans with Disabilities Act (ADA) (1990)
   categories of discrimination in, 29–30
   CHCs qualifying as disabilities in, 29–33
   COVID-19 pandemic and, 34–35

Americans with Disabilities Act (ADA) (1990) (*Continued*)
  disabilities defined by, 24, 28–30
  discrimination prevented through, 28–30
  essential job function determination in, 30–33
  harassment discrimination in, 29–30
  other provisions of, 30–35
  overview of, 24, 28–30
  passage of, 28
  pre-employment questions prohibited by, 30
  reasonable accommodations required in, 21, 30–34, 32*t*, 48
  resistance to compliance with, 88
  return-to-office policies and, 34–35
  RTW programs and, 50
  Title I of, 28
  undue hardships and, 33–35, 34*t*
  unfair treatment discrimination in, 29–30
Americans with Disabilities Amendments Act (2008)
  CHCs qualifying as disabilities in, 28–29
  disabilities redefined in, 24, 28–30
  discrimination prevented through, 28–30
  goals of, 28
  limitations to qualifying disabilities in, 29
  long COVID and, 29
  major bodily function provision added in, 28
  overview of, 24, 28–30
  passage of, 28
  'substantially limits' redefined in, 28–29
anxiety disorders, 18–19, 45, 78, 89, 92, 128, 137
autonomy
  chronic pain and, 120–121
  definition of, 120
  discrepancy between workers with disabilities and those without on, 121–122
  flexible work arrangements as, 119–120, 122–126
  as fundamental psychological need, 120
  importance for workers with CHCs of, 66–67, 120–122
  individual worker-focused strategies and, 143
  integrated approach to CHCs and, 165–166, 169
  intervention framework for CHCs and, 43–45, 51, 54–55
  interviewee quotes on, 120–122
  job control as, 120–122
  job demands-resources model and, 60, 120
  manager recommendations for, 51
  motivational benefits of, 120
  overview of, 119–122
  reflection exercise on job control and, 122
  self-accommodation and, 120–121
  STAR intervention's prioritization of, 134
  supervisor support and, 126–127
  work-health challenges and, 66–67

B

Baicker, Katherine, 45–46
Beatty, Joy, 48–49, 77, 145
best practices. *See* human resources (HR) recommendations; individual worker-focused strategies; integrated approach to CHCs; intervention framework for CHCs; manager recommendations; organization-focused strategies; supervisor support; work- and management-focused strategies
BJ's Wholesale Club wellness program research, 45–46
Blake, Holly, 154–155
blue-collar/manual labor positions, 83
Bosma, A., 84, 88
bridge employment, 17–18
burnout, 59–60, 65–66, 74, 82–83, 134, 145–146, 158
Bush, George H. W., 28
Bush, George W., 28

C

career and work identity
  categories of, 77–78
  coaching and, 146–147
  disclosure of CHCs and, 74, 75*t*
  identity management strategies for, 74
  impact of CHCs on, 77–78
  manager recommendations for, 77–78
  misconceptions about CHCs and, 77
  organizational culture and, 108–109
  strategies for management of, 74, 75*t*, 146–147

work-health challenges and, 77–78
challenges for workers with CHCs. *See* ableism; discrimination; organizational challenges for CHCs; stigma; worker well-being; work-health challenges of CHCs
chronic fatigue, 7–8, 47, 63–66, 71, 87, 107–108, 125, 140
chronic health conditions (CHCs). *See also* costs associated with CHCs; disclosure of CHCs; integrated approach to CHCs; intervention framework for CHCs; organizational challenges for CHCs; prevalence of CHCs; work-health challenges of CHCs
  aims of current volume on, 3, 8–9
  bridge employment and, 17–18
  causes of, 8
  common characteristics of, 10
  cultural norms surrounding, 1
  definition of, 7–9
  as disabilities, 8, 28–29, 30–33
  disabilities outside of, 3, 9–10
  distinctness of, 9–10
  diversity category of, 3
  examples of, 7–8, 11
  growing interest in, 1–3
  health promotion and wellness programs and, 9
  hesitancy to engage with, 1
  inclusion for workers with, 3
  increases in workers with, 8
  interviewee quotes on, 7, 14, 16*b*, 18–19
  invisible nature of, 66–67, 71, 73–74, 138
  legal concerns surrounding, 1, 3–4
  multiple cooccurring forms of, 13–14
  overview of, 1–4, 7–9
  prevention and management as not focus of current volume on, 9
  proactive strategies required to address, 8–9
  quality of life impact of, 18
  scope of current volume on, 9
  stigma surrounding, 9–10, 19, 26, 165
  structure of current volume on, 3–4
  survey on perceived challenge of, 8
  takeaways on, 20
  work-health challenges associated with, 8–10
chronic pain
  autonomy and, 120–121
  costs associated with, 16
  detrimental cycle involving, 66
  interviewee quotes on, 14, 66, 94, 120–121
  maintaining work ability despite symptoms of, 66
  organizational challenges and, 84, 94
  overview of, 14
  Pain at Work Toolkit (PAW) for, 154–155
  as precursor to disability and unemployment, 14
  prevalence of, 14
  productivity losses and, 16
  social issues associated with, 14
  stress and, 66
  work- and management-focused strategies and, 120
  work-health challenges of CHCs and, 66
climate of authenticity, 74
Clinton, Bill, 35–36
coaching
  career and work identity management and, 146–147
  contracting with coaches with experience with work-health issues in, 149
  costs associated with, 149
  EAPs and, 149–150
  effectiveness of, 145–146, 149
  external, contracted coach use recommended in, 149
  HR recommendations for, 148–150
  interviewee quotes on, 146–147
  job demands-resources model and, 145–146
  lack of providers for, 149–150
  manager recommendations for, 148–150
  mentoring programs as less costly than, 151
  overview of, 145–150
  psychotherapy distinguished from, 150
  success drivers for, 149–150
  themes in, 148
  tips for coaching workers with CHCs, 150*b*
  trainings for, 149–150
  vocational counseling programs distinguished from, 153–154
  work disengagement and job satisfaction not benefitted by, 146

cognitive-behavioral therapy (CBT), 159–160
cognitive fog, 107–108, 123
corporate social responsibility (CSR), 9, 110, 174
cost effectiveness analysis (CEA), 175
costs associated with CHCs
  absenteeism and, 16
  accommodations and, 33, 88
  anxiety disorders and, 18–19
  bridge employment and, 17–18
  chronic pain and, 16
  coaching and, 149
  constant adjustment and, 19
  financial burdens to individuals, 17–18
  healthcare coverage and, 100–101
  health insurance costs, 17
  indirect financial costs, 16
  interviewee quotes on, 16b, 18–19
  long COVID and, 16–18
  mentoring programs and, 151
  overview of, 15–19
  presenteeism and, 16, 16b
  productivity losses, 16
  psychosocial costs, 18–19
  resilience and, 19
  vocational counseling programs and, 154
  work-health challenges and, 8
COVID-19 pandemic. *See also* long COVID
  ADA and, 34–35
  allyship during, 69
  flexible work arrangements spurred by, 122, 124–126
  remote work spurred by, 34–35
  telemedicine made popular during, 103
  vaccine disclosure during, 125–126
CSR (corporate social responsibility), 9, 110, 174
culture of organizations. *See* organizational culture

D

DEIA. *See* diversity, equity, inclusion, and accessibility (DEIA)
Deloitte, 113
depression, 11–12, 17–18, 36, 67, 71, 78, 123, 132, 137
diabetes, 7–8, 11–13, 16–17, 19, 29, 65, 112, 120–121, 166–167
Dimoff, Jennifer, 136

disabilities. *See also* ableism; Americans with Disabilities Act (ADA) (1990); Americans with Disabilities Amendments Act (ADAA) (2008); disclosure of CHCs
  additional resources on, 41
  CHCs as, 24, 26–27, 28–29
  definitions of, 24–27, 25t, 28
  discrimination prevention on the basis of, 28–30
  distinctness of CHCs compared to other, 9–10, 67
  diversity statements that include, 110
  EEOC definition of, 24
  episodic disabilities, 67
  ICF classification of, 24
  identity-first language for persons with, 22
  inspiration porn and, 23
  legal status in US of, 27–37
  medical model of, 22–23
  models of, 21–24
  person-first language for persons with, 22
  prevalence of, 21–22, 26–27
  recommendations for, 37–38
  Rehabilitation Act of 1973 definition of, 24, 26–27
  research definitions of, 24–25
  self-identification as persons with, 22, 26–27
  social model of, 23–24
  stigma surrounding, 25–26
  takeaways on, 37–38
  terminology for persons with, 22
  underrecognition of, 21–22
  universal design for, 23
  WHO classification of, 24
  workplace definitions of, 25–26
disability benefits, 49–50, 52, 105
Disability Employment Policy Office (US DoL), 49
disclosure of CHCs
  accommodations and, 48, 74, 138
  benefits of, 73, 86, 131
  building trust to facilitate, 87
  career and work identity and, 74, 75t
  challenges, fear, and stress surrounding, 73–74, 85, 87, 131
  creating feelings of safety to mitigate concerns about, 74
  decisions to, 73

Index 209

definition of, 26–27
HR recommendations for, 132–133
identity management strategies and, 74, 75t
intervention framework for CHCs and, 47
interviewee quotes on, 87
invisible nature of CHCs and, 73–74
manager recommendations for, 74, 87–88
non-disclosing contrasted with, 86–88
organizational challenges and, 85–88
organizational culture and, 87, 90–94
pitfalls to avoid in, 133
prevalence of, 73
responding in supportive manner to, 131–134
stigma and, 73–74, 85, 87, 131
supervisor support for, 131–133
trainings for supervisors lacking for, 131–132
women as reporting fewer positive outcomes of, 73
work-health challenges of CHCs and, 67–68, 72–74
discrimination. *See also* ableism; Americans with Disabilities Act (ADA) (1990); Americans with Disabilities Amendments Act (ADAA) (2008); Equal Employment Opportunity Commission (EEOC); Rehabilitation Act of 1973; stigma
accommodations and, 70–71, 138
categories of, 29–30
disclosure of CHCs and, 72
examples of, 70
examples of legal cases based on, 31t
fear of unintentional forms of, 72
fewer opportunities for development as form of, 70
harassment discrimination, 29–30, 72
HR recommendations for, 69–71, 84–86, 88–90
intersectionality and, 72
interviewee quotes on, 70–72
invisible nature of CHCs and, 66–67, 71
lowered assumptions of capability as form of, 70
organizational challenges and, 84–86
ostracism and disrespectful treatment as form of, 70
overt forms of, 69–71

prevalence of, 69
prevention of, 28–30
subtle forms of, 69–70
threats to job security, termination, and scrutiny as form of, 71
unfair treatment discrimination, 29–30
work-health challenges of CHCs and, 69–72
disengagement, 59–60, 146
diversity, equity, inclusion, and accessibility (DEIA)
accessibility as explicitly included in, 109–110
accommodations and, 137–138
CHCs as category of, 3
disability as underrepresented aspect of, 109
diversity statements including disability, 110
investing resources into, 110
manager recommendations for, 110
organizational culture as supporting, 108–110
organization-focused strategies and, 109–110
overview of, 109–110
terminology of, 109–110
trainings for, 116–117
worker well-being and, 109–114

E
EAPs. *See* employee assistance programs (EAPs)
EEOC. *See* Equal Employment Opportunity Commission (EEOC)
emotional labor, 74
employee assistance programs (EAPs)
coaching and, 149–150
definition of, 106
goals of, 106
lack of utilization of, 106
overview of, 106
ROI assessment of, 106, 173
employee engagement surveys, 27, 109–110, 112–113, 166
employee resource groups (ERGs). *See also* THRIVE Ability Network
activities of, 115

employee resource groups (ERGs) (*Continued*)
  individual worker-focused strategies and, 151–153, 161
  mentoring programs and, 151–153
  organizational culture and, 115–116, 161
  overview of, 108, 110, 115–116
  supervisor support and, 132
empowerment training programs, 159
engagement, 59–60, 120, 124, 146, 152, 156–158, 166, 175
epilepsy, 28–29, 77, 116
Equal Employment Opportunity Commission (EEOC)
  disabilities defined by, 24
  essential job functions and, 34–35
  harassment complaints as most common to, 29–30
  reasonable accommodation failures and, 34–35
  work-from-home policies and, 34–35
ERGs. *See* employee resource groups (ERGs)
essential job functions, 30–33, 34–35, 138

F
Family and Medical Leave Act (FMLA) (1993)
  coverage of CHCs by, 36
  employee eligibility for, 35–36
  HR recommendations and, 36
  implementation of, 36
  intermittent leave and, 36
  overview of, 35–36
  passage of, 35–36
  reduced schedules and, 36
  rheumatoid arthritis and, 36
  RTW programs and, 50
fatigue-related issues, 7–8, 30, 47, 63–66, 71, 87, 107–108, 125, 140
flexible spending account (FSA), 102
flexible work arrangements
  absenteeism reductions linked to, 122–123
  autonomy and, 119–120, 122–126
  best practices for, 124–126
  COVID-19 pandemic as spurring, 122, 124–126
  definition of, 120
  distinct benefit to workers with CHCs of, 122–124
  fair workweek legislation and, 124
  integrated approach to CHCs and, 165–166
  intervention framework for CHCs and, 43–45
  interviewee quotes on, 123
  manager recommendations for, 124
  organizational culture to support, 124–125
  overview of, 119–120, 122–126
  predictability of shift schedules and, 124
  reduced-load work, 139–140
  remote work and, 123–125
  shift flexibility, 124
  shift swaps without managerial approval and, 124
  supervisor support and, 128–129
  time and place dimensions of, 122
  work-health challenges of CHCs and, 65–67
Fragoso, Zachary, 66

G
Gray, Cheryl, 130
group programs, 155–160

H
healthcare coverage. *See also* life and long-term care insurance
  coding errors and, 103
  costs associated with, 100–101
  flexible spending accounts (FSAs) and, 102
  gaps in, 100–101
  HR recommendations for, 103
  importance of, 100–101
  organizational recommendations for, 102
  outcomes in healthcare and, 101
  overview of, 100–103
  plan choice in, 101–102
  prevalence of employee-tied forms of, 100–101
  requirement to "fail" drugs for CHCs and, 102–103
  surprise insurance exclusions and, 103
  telemedicine and, 103
  US Affordable Care Act (2010) and, 100–101
Health Insurance Portability and Accountability Act (HIPAA) (1996), 37
health promotion programs, 9, 167

human resources (HR) recommendations
  accommodations and, 32–33, 92–93
  coaching and, 148–150
  disclosure of CHCs and, 132–133
  discrimination and, 69–71, 84–86, 88–90
  FMLA and, 36
  healthcare coverage and, 103
  individual worker-focused strategies and, 148, 149–150, 154–155
  intervention framework for CHCs and, 51
  organizational challenges and, 82–83, 84–86, 88–90, 92–93
  organizational culture and, 111
  organization-focused strategies and, 105, 111
  reduced-load work and, 140
  RTW programs and, 55
  time off benefits and policies and, 105
  trainings and, 131–132
  work-health challenges of CHCs and, 69–71

I

identity at work and identity management. *See* career and work identity
implementing and evaluating an integrated approach. *See* integrated approach to CHCs
individual worker-focused strategies
  accommodations and, 148
  additional resources on, 163
  autonomy and, 143
  Chronic Disease Self-Management Program (CDSMP), 157–159
  coaching, 145–150
  empowerment training programs, 159
  ERGs and, 151–153, 161
  flexibility and customizability approach in, 144–145
  group programs, 155–160
  HR recommendations for, 148, 149–150, 154–155
  individualized programs, 144–154
  Job Demands and Accommodation Planning Tool (JDAPT), 155
  job demands-resources model and, 144
  Manage at Work program, 156–157
  mentoring programs, 151–153
  online programs, 154–155
  organizational culture and, 143, 153, 155–156, 158–159
  other group programs, 159–160
  overview of, 143–144
  Pain at Work Toolkit (PAW), 154–155
  personal resources built on in, 144
  recommendations for, 160–161
  reflection exercise for, 162*b*
  scope of, 144
  stigma and, 152–154
  summary of, 160–161
  takeaways on, 162–163
  targeted nature of, 143–145
  themes of, 144
  trainings and, 156–157
  vocational counseling programs, 153–154
  worker well-being and, 149, 161
inspiration porn, 23, 68, 114, 129
insurance. *See* healthcare coverage; life and long-term care insurance
integrated approach to CHCs
  accommodations and, 165–166
  additional resources for, 177
  autonomy and, 165–166, 169
  examples of, 169
  flexible work arrangements and, 165–166
  framework for, 167–169, 168*f*
  hierarchy of support strategies and, 168*f*
  importance of, 166, 169
  long COVID and, 164–165
  making a business case for, 164–167
  organizational culture and, 165–166, 169
  overview of, 164, 176
  reactive programs and, 166
  recommendations for, 176–177
  ROI assessment of, 167, 173–175
  steps for, 169, 172*b*, 173*b*
  supervisor support and, 165–166
  takeaways on, 176–177
  Total Worker Health as example of, 169
  VOI assessment and, 175
  wellness programs and, 166–167, 173
  worker well-being and, 165–167, 169
intersectionality, 13–14, 72, 113
intervention framework for CHCs
  accommodations and, 47–48
  anxiety and, 45
  autonomy and, 43–45, 51, 54–55
  categories of, 42–50
  disclosure of CHCs and, 47

intervention framework for CHCs (*Continued*)
  fears of backlash and, 47
  flexible work arrangements and, 43–45
  interviewee quotes on, 45, 47
  limitations of typical approaches and, 42–43
  organizational culture and, 43
  overview of, 42
  primary prevention strategies in, 43–46, 44*f*
  proactive approach required for, 55–56
  public health model of, 42–43
  recommendations for, 56
  rehabilitation and, 49
  relations between categories of prevention in, 43–45
  remote work and, 45
  RETAIN initiative and, 49
  RTW programs as tertiary prevention in, 50–55
  secondary prevention strategies in, 47–49
  stay-at-work programs and, 49–50
  takeaways on, 56
  tertiary prevention strategies in, 49–50
  wellness programs and, 45–46
  worker well-being and, 43–45

J
Job Accommodation Network, 33
job accommodations. *See* accommodations
job control, 65–67, 120–122
job demands-resources model
  application of, 60–62, 62*f*
  autonomy and, 60, 120
  boosting resources in, 62
  burnout in, 59–60
  categories in, 59–60
  coaching and, 145–146
  definition of, 59–60
  individual worker-focused strategies and, 144
  job demands defined in, 60
  job resources defined in, 60
  manager recommendations and, 62
  organizational challenges and, 82
  overview of, 59–62
  perceptions of work ability and, 60–61
  personal resources included in, 60, 144
  prevention and mitigation of excessive demands and, 62
  reflection exercise for managers on, 62*b*
  visualization of, 61*f*
  work ability and, 60–62, 62*f*
  work engagement in, 59–60
  work-health challenges of CHCs and, 59–62, 65–66
job modifications, 137–138
Joffe, Rosalind, 145

K
Kaye, H., 88
Kelloway, Kevin, 136

L
legal considerations. *See also* Americans with Disabilities Act (ADA) (1990); Americans with Disabilities Amendments Act (ADAA) (2008); discrimination; Equal Employment Opportunity Commission (EEOC); Rehabilitation Act of 1973
  additional resources on, 41
  answers to quiz on, 41
  company attorneys and, 27
  definition of disability and, 24–26
  examples of disability discrimination cases and, 31*t*
  interviewee quotes on, 27
  overview of, 27
  preventing disability discrimination through, 28–30
  quiz on, 38–41
  recommendations for, 37–38
  takeaways on, 37–38
  zero-tolerance approach to harassment and, 29–30
LGBTQIA+ workers, 21, 113, 126
life and long-term care insurance. *See also* healthcare coverage
  denials of claims frequent with CHCs in, 103
  economic barriers to, 103–104
  Medicaid and, 103–104
  organizational offering to all workers of, 103
  racial and ethnic dimensions of denial of, 103
Linton, Steven, 159–160

Live Healthy, Work Healthy program, 157–159, 161
long COVID. *See also* COVID-19 pandemic
  ADAA and, 29
  common symptoms of, 15, 29, 63
  costs associated with, 16–18
  integrated approach to CHCs and, 164–165
  overview of, 1, 7–8, 15
  prevalence of, 1, 7–8, 11, 15, 15b, 164–165
  productivity impact of, 17–18
  work-health challenges of CHCs and, 63
Lorig, Kate, 157

M
Manage at Work program, 156–157
manager recommendations. *See also* supervisor support; work- and management-focused strategies
  ableism and, 68
  accommodations and, 68, 71, 92–93
  autonomy and, 51
  career and work identity and, 77–78
  climate of authenticity and, 74
  coaching and, 148–150
  DEIA and, 110
  disclosure of CHCs and, 74, 87–88
  emotional labor and, 74
  flexible work arrangements and, 124
  job demands-resources model and, 62
  managers with CHCs, 51
  organizational challenges and, 82, 84, 85–86, 87–90, 92–94
  organizational culture and, 110–111, 115–116
  organization-focused strategies and, 105, 110–111
  reduced-load work and, 140
  reflection exercise for job demands-resources model and, 62b
  remote work and, 124–126
  RTW programs and, 51–52
  time off benefits and policies and, 105
  work-health challenges of CHCs and, 60, 62, 65–68, 71, 74, 77–78
Medicaid, 100–101, 103–104
medical model of disability. *See* disabilities
Medicare, 100–101
Mental Health Awareness Training (MHAT), 136–137

mental health support interventions, 136–137
mentoring programs
  costs lower than coaching for, 151
  effectiveness of, 152
  emotional support through, 151
  ERGs and, 151–153
  facilitating opportunities for interactions in, 152–153
  forms of, 151
  informal forms of, 152–153
  matching mentor-protégé dyads in, 151–152
  socialization through, 151
  success conditions for, 152
  THRIVE Ability Network and, 152
meta-analysis, 116
MHAT (Mental Health Awareness Training), 136–137
Milken Institute report, 16
Miserandino, Christine, 63
models for workers with CHCs. *See* integrated approach to CHCs; intervention framework for CHCs; job demands-resources model
multiple sclerosis (MS), 64–65, 77

N
Nelson, Candace, 127
Nestlé USA, 115
Nixon, Richard, 35

O
O'Connell, Meg, 27
organizational challenges for CHCs
  accommodations and, 84, 86, 88, 92–93
  accountability for, 91
  barriers to support and, 84
  blue-collar/manual labor positions and, 83
  building collaborative relationships to mitigate, 84
  chronic fatigue and, 87
  chronic pain and, 84, 94
  complexity of, 82
  disclosure of CHCs and, 85–88
  discrimination, 84–86
  ensuring work gets completed, 82
  hourly workers and, 83
  HR recommendations for, 82–83, 84–86, 88–90, 92–93

organizational challenges for CHCs (*Continued*)
  informal supports required for, 93
  insufficient communication and support, 92–94
  insufficient research on, 81
  interviewee quotes on, 81–83, 85–86, 88–94
  job demands-resources model and, 82
  knowledge and skills insufficient, 88–90
  manager recommendations for, 82, 84, 85–86, 87–90, 92–94
  non-disclosing of CHCs by employees and, 86–88
  operational forms of, 82–84
  organizational culture and, 90–91
  overview of, 81
  paid time off insufficient, 83
  practical management forms of, 82–84
  providing flexibility and support to meet, 82
  recommendations for, 94–95
  shared accountability for problem-solving to mitigate, 84
  smaller organizations as particularly impacted by, 82–83
  stigma, 84–86, 90
  system-level support for, 90
  takeaways on, 94–95
  team cultures of support to mitigate, 84
  trainings to mitigate, 86, 93–94
  understanding and compassion insufficient, 84–86
  unsupportive organizational culture, 90–91
organizational culture
  ableism awareness and, 114
  career and work identity and, 108–109
  definition of, 108
  DEIA and, 108–110
  diabetes and, 112
  disclosure of CHCs and, 87, 90–94
  diversity statements that include disabilities and, 110
  employee engagement surveys including disability and, 112–113
  ERGs and, 115–116, 161
  examples of strategies for changing, 114–117
  flexible work arrangements supported by, 124–125
  food accessibility and, 112
  HR recommendations for, 111
  importance of, 108–109
  individual worker-focused strategies and, 143, 153, 155–156, 158–159
  integrated approach to CHCs and, 165–166, 169
  intervention framework for CHCs and, 43
  interviewee quotes on, 90–94
  language use and, 113–114
  manager recommendations for, 110–111, 115–116
  organizational challenges and, 90–91
  overview of, 105, 108–117
  PTO and, 110
  reflection exercise for strategies on, 114*b*
  strategies for changing, 110–114
  summary of recommendations for, 117
  THRIVE Ability Network (Nestlé USA), 115–117
  trainings for, 116–117
  unsupportive forms of, 90–94
  value alignment and, 111
  worker well-being and, 106–107, 109–114
organization-focused strategies
  accommodations and, 107–109
  additional resources for, 117–118
  Affordable Care Act and, 100–101
  benefits offered by organizations and, 100–107
  cognitive fog and, 107–108
  culture strategies, 110–114
  definition of, 99
  DEIA, 109–110
  diabetes and, 112
  disability benefits, 105
  diversity statements that include disabilities, 110
  EAPs, 106
  ERGs, 108, 110, 115–116
  examples of culture-related strategies, 114–117
  fatigue-related issues and, 107–108
  healthcare coverage, 100–103
  hierarchy of support strategies in, 99, 100*f*
  HR recommendations for, 105, 111
  interviewee quotes on, 100, 104
  life insurance, 103–104

long-term care insurance, 103–104
manager recommendations for, 105, 110–111
organizational culture, 105, 108–117
overview of, 99
reflection exercise on culture strategies, 114*b*
remote work and, 115
stigma and, 111, 115–116
summary of recommendations on benefits and policies, 107*b*
summary of recommendations on culture for, 117
time off benefits and policies, 104–105
trainings, 116–117
universal design, 107–108
valuing of worker well-being, 109–110
wellness programs, 106–107
overt discrimination. *See* discrimination

P

paid time off (PTO), 83, 104–105, 110
pain (chronic). *See* chronic health conditions (CHCs); chronic pain; worker well-being
participatory approach, 169
Patient Advocate Foundation, 103
practical tips for HR professionals. *See* human resources (HR) recommendations
practical tips for managers. *See* manager recommendations; supervisor support
presenteeism, 16, 16*b*, 104, 106, 124, 167, 173–174
Presley, Steve, 115–116
prevalence of CHCs
 age as factor in, 11–14
 chronic pain and, 14
 disabilities outside of CHCs and, 21–22, 26–27
 gender-based stereotypes and, 12–13
 generational factors in, 11–12
 intersectionality and, 13–14
 long COVID and, 1, 7–8, 11, 15, 15*b*, 164–165
 multiple cooccurring forms in, 13–14
 overview of, 11–15
 race and ethnicity as factors in, 13–14
 sex and gender as factors in, 12–13
 socioeconomic status as factor in, 13

primary prevention. *See* intervention framework for CHCs
proactive strategies, 8–9, 51, 55–56, 166–167

Q

quality of life, 11–12, 18, 50

R

reasonable accommodations. *See* accommodations
recommendations. *See* human resources (HR) recommendations; individual worker-focused strategies; integrated approach to CHCs; intervention framework for CHCs; manager recommendations; organization-focused strategies; supervisor support; work- and management-focused strategies
reduced-load work, 139–140
Rehabilitation Act of 1973
 affirmative action required in, 35
 amendments to, 35
 contractor discrimination outlawed in, 35
 disabilities defined in, 24, 26–27
 discrimination in federally funded agencies outlawed in, 35
 federal workforce discrimination outlawed in, 35
 minimum employee numbers not contained in, 35
 overview of, 35
 passage of, 35
 section 501 of, 35
 section 503 of, 35
 section 504 of, 35
 section 508 of, 35
remote work
 accommodations and, 34–35
 adjustments to, 124–125
 best practices for, 124–125
 COVID-19 pandemic spurring, 34–35
 equipment needed for, 124–125
 flexible work arrangements and, 123–125
 intersectionality and, 126
 intervention framework for CHCs and, 45
 interviewee quotes on, 125
 LGBTQ workers and, 126

remote work (*Continued*)
   manager recommendations for, 124–126
   marginalized identities and, 126
   organization-focused strategies and, 115
   return-to-office policies and, 125–126
   social isolation resulting from, 124–125
   transparent, equitable, and consistent policies required for, 125–126
   work-health challenges of CHCs and, 65–66
RETAIN initiative, 49
return on investment (ROI) assessment
   EAPs and, 106, 173
   integrated approach to CHCs and, 167, 173–175
   wellness programs and, 45–46
return-to-office policies, 125–126
return to work (RTW) programs
   accommodations and, 52, 54–55
   ADA and, 50
   aims of, 50
   benefits of, 50
   challenges of, 51
   components of, 52
   definitional challenges for, 53
   effectiveness of, 53–54
   FMLA and, 50
   HR recommendations for, 55
   intervention framework for CHCs and, 50–55
   manager recommendations for, 51–52
   overview of, 50–52
   proactive support for, 51
   recommendations for, 56
   reviews of, 52–54
   success conditions of, 51, 53–55
   takeaways on, 56
   as tertiary prevention, 50–55
   work-health challenges of CHCs and, 8–9
rheumatoid arthritis, 12, 36, 66–67, 74, 128
ROI. *See* return on investment (ROI) assessment
RTW programs. *See* return-to-work (RTW) programs
Ruggs, Enrica, 116
Rutigliano, Peter, 27, 112–113

S
Schoo, Brian, 115
secondary preventions. *See* intervention framework for CHCs
Shaw, William, 156
Shockley, Kristen, 124–125
Smith, Matthew, 157–158
social model of disability. *See* disabilities
socioeconomic status, 7, 11, 13, 15*b*
Song, Zirui, 45–46
spoon theory, 63–65
STAR intervention
   assessment of, 134
   costs associated with, 134–135
   family-to-work conflict workers benefitted by, 135
   implementation of, 134
   organizational culture change through, 135
   phases of, 134–135
   sludge eradication and, 134–135
   tailored nature of, 134–135
stay-at-work programs, 49–50
stigma. *See also* ableism; discrimination
   CHCs as subject to, 9–10, 19, 26, 165
   disabilities and, 25–26
   disclosure of CHCs and, 73–74, 85, 87, 131
   individual worker-focused strategies and, 152–154
   intersectionality and, 72
   mental illness and nonapparent illnesses as carrying more, 85–86
   organization-focused strategies and, 111, 115–116
   overview of, 84–86, 90
   reduction of, 3, 111, 152
   vocational counseling programs and, 153–154
   work-health challenges of CHCs and, 67–69, 77
strategies. *See* human resources (HR) recommendations; individual worker-focused strategies; integrated approach to CHCs; intervention framework for CHCs; manager recommendations; organization-focused strategies; supervisor support; work- and management-focused strategies
subtle discrimination. *See* discrimination
supervisor support

ableism and, 129
accommodations and, 126–127, 133
appraisal forms of, 127
autonomy and, 126–127
challenges to, 129–130
coworker support building and, 129
cross-training workers and, 129
definition of, 126–127
disclosure of CHCs and, 131–133
emotional forms of, 127
encouraging teamwork through, 129
ERGs and, 132
flexible work arrangements and, 128–129
gatekeeping role of supervisors and, 126–127
informal forms of, 128–129
informational forms of, 127
instrumental forms of, 127
interviewee quotes on, 128
mental health interventions and, 136–137
overview of, 126–134
pitfalls of, 129–130, 133
reflection exercise on, 129b
STAR intervention and, 134–136
supportive responses to disclosure in, 131–134
tips for responding to disclosures of CHCs for, 132
trainings and, 134, 136
trust building and, 127
types of, 127–129
work ability maintenance through, 128

T

tertiary prevention. *See* intervention framework for CHCs
THRIVE Ability Network (Nestlé USA), 110, 115–116, 152
time off benefits and policies
  donation of personal leave to support CHCs and, 104–105
  full-day requirements for medical appointments and, 104
  HR recommendations for, 105
  interviewee quotes on, 104
  manager recommendations for, 105
  overview of, 104–105
  paid time off (PTO), 104–105
  "regular" sickness of workers with CHCs and, 104
  unlimited PTO offers, 105
Total Worker Health (NIOSH), 169
trainings
  coaching and, 149–150
  DEIA and, 116–117
  disclosure of CHCs trainings lacking, 131–132
  empowerment training programs, 159
  HR recommendations for, 131–132
  individual worker-focused strategies and, 156–157
  manager recommendations for, 86
  Mental Health Awareness Training (MHAT), 136–137
  organizational challenges mitigated by, 86, 93–94
  overview of, 116–117
  supervisor support and, 129, 134, 136

U

universal design, 23, 107–108
US Affordable Care Act (2010), 17, 100–101

V

value of investment (VOI) assessments, 164, 169, 175–176
Varekamp, Inge, 159
vocational counseling programs, 153–154

W

wellness programs
  challenges to properly evaluating, 46
  effectiveness of, 45–46
  integrated approach to CHCs and, 166–167, 173
  intervention framework for CHCs and, 45–46
  limitations of, 46
  overview of, 9, 106–107
  prevalence of, 45
  ROI assessment of, 45–46
Work, Family, and Health Network, 134
work ability. *See* job demands-resources model; work-health challenges of CHCs
work- and management-focused strategies
  accommodations, 137–138
  additional resources on, 141–142
  autonomy and, 119–122
  chronic pain and, 120

work- and management-focused strategies
    (*Continued*)
  definition of, 119–120
  design strategies, 119–126
  examples of, 134–137
  flexible work arrangements, 119–120,
    122–126
  importance of, 119
  job control, 120–122
  job modifications, 137–138
  mental health support interventions,
    136–137
  overview of, 119
  reduced-load work, 139–140
  reflection exercise on job control, 122*b*
  secondary strategies, 137–140
  STAR intervention as example of, 134–136
  summary of recommendations, 141
  supervisor support, 126–134
work arrangements. *See* flexible work
    arrangements
work design recommendations. *See* work-
    and management-focused strategies
worker well-being
  individual worker-focused strategies and,
    149, 161
  integrated approach to CHCs and,
    165–167, 169
  intervention framework for CHCs and,
    43–45
  organizational culture and, 106–107,
    109–114
  overview of, 109–110
  valuing of, 109–110
  work-health challenges of CHCs and,
    59–60, 74
work from home. *See* remote work
work-health challenges of CHCs
  ableism and, 68–69
  accommodations and, 67
  allyship and, 69
  autonomy and, 66–67
  burnout and, 59–60, 65–66, 74, 82–83
  career and work identity implications of,
    77–78
  characteristics of CHCs that result in,
    9–10, 67
  chronic pain and, 66
  climate of authenticity and, 74
  costs associated with, 8
  creating feelings of safety to mitigate, 74
  definition of, 8

depression and, 67
detrimental cycle of, 66
disclosure of CHCs, 67–68, 72–74
discrimination, 69–72
emotional labor required for, 74
epilepsy and, 77
episodic disabilities and, 67
fatigue-related issues, 63–64, 65–66
final points on, 78
flexible work arrangements and, 65–67
HR recommendations for, 69–71
identity management strategies and, 74,
    75*t*
intermittent issues and, 67
intersectionality and, 72
interviewee quotes on, 63, 65–66, 70–72,
    74, 77–78
invisible nature of CHCs and, 66–67, 71,
    73–74
job demands-resources model and, 59–62,
    65–66
long COVID and, 63
maintaining work ability despite
    symptoms, 66–67
manager recommendations for, 60, 62,
    65–68, 71, 74, 77–78
MS and, 64–65, 77
as not proactively addressed, 8–9
open and effective communication to
    mitigate, 67
organizing frameworks for understanding,
    59–64
overview of, 8–10
performance expectations and, 64–65
prevalence of, 65
recommendations for, 79–80
remote work and, 65–66
rheumatoid arthritis and, 66–67
RTW programs and, 8–9
spoon theory and, 63–65
stigma and, 67–69, 77
surface acting in fact of, 74
takeaways on, 79–80
time-related issues, 65
as underrecognized, 8–9
worker well-being and, 59–60, 74
work-health management interference,
    64–66

Y
Young, Stella, 23